The Dow Jones–Irwin Guide to
Buying and Selling Treasury Securities

The Dow Jones–Irwin Guide to
Buying and Selling Treasury Securities

Howard M. Berlin

DOW JONES-IRWIN
Homewood, Illinois 60430

© DOW JONES-IRWIN, 1984

ISBN 0-87094-464-9
Library of Congress Catalog Card No. 83–72199
Printed in the United States of America

1 2 3 4 5 6 7 8 9 0 B 10 9 8 7 6 5 4

Preface

Depending on the financing needs of the U.S. Treasury, Uncle Sam typically borrows approximately $12 billion each week in debt management. Up until approximately 1978, very few average investors, outside of the large institutional investors and banks, knew about lending money to the U.S. government in return for T bills, notes, and bonds. Many people who make their living in the financial and investment world have long held the position that these Treasury securities are the closest thing to the ideal investment instrument. Since they are fully backed by the full faith, authority, and taxing power of the U.S. government, they are virtually risk free, although it should be emphasized that no investment is guaranteed to be foolproof.

This book tells you what Treasury bills, notes, and bonds are, how to buy them, and how to sell them. It uncovers the mystique about and explains the various methods of dealing with faceless, monolithic government agencies such as the Federal Reserve system and the Bureau of the Public Debt. In nine chapters, this book discusses virtually every aspect of analyzing, buying, and selling various Treasury securities, either as outright conservative purchases with minimal risks, or by indirect methods such as futures and options trading, which involve higher risks.

Chapter 1 is a collection of the most common questions and answers I have been asked concerning Treasury securities. Although the answers are brief, a full discussion of each question is covered in the appropriate chapter of this book.

Chapter 2 gives a broad overview and history of Uncle Sam's debt management using Treasury securities and compares their relative merits against other popular money market instruments. Chapter 3 discusses how to buy and sell T bills, either directly from the Federal Reserve banks or indirectly through commercial banks or brokerage houses. Since T notes and bonds are treated differently than T bills, they are similarly discussed in Chapter 4.

Besides the traditional and conservative methods, alternative schemes such as coupon stripping, mutual funds, futures contracts, interest rate options, and futures options are covered in Chapter 5. Although substantially more risky, these methods are appealing in that they generally require less money. Chapter 6 discusses how to determine whether or not Treasury securities are a worthwhile investment, taking into account one's federal, state, and local tax brackets.

As information concerning Treasury securities is available in most major daily newspapers, as well as in *Barrons* and *The Wall Street Journal*, Chapter 7 tells you how to interpret the quotations given for those T bills, notes, and bonds traded on the open market, as well as those quotations used by various exchanges that trade Treasury futures and options. In addition, this chapter discusses how to determine the yield to maturity of a T note or bond and how to amortize a security bought at a premium, as well as the effect of reinvesting your proceeds on the security's overall yield.

For those of you who have a personal computer, Chapter 8 presents a number of financial programs written in both BASIC and the VisiCalc "electronic spreadsheet" analysis program format. For each program, the source code and a numerical example with its result are presented.

As with any investment, we ultimately have to deal with the IRS. Chapter 9 discusses the tax treatments of buying and selling Treasury securities, zero coupon bonds, futures, and options in accordance with the Tax Act of 1982. This chapter also explains what possible deductions you are allowed.

A series of eight useful appendixes conclude this book; they present information about the Federal Reserve banks, the Bureau of the Public Debt, and regulations concerning Treasury securities, as well as copies of the most commonly used forms used by the Bureau of the Public Debt.

As with any major undertaking, there are those who, behind the scenes, have provided, the needed encouragement and assistance so that this book could be completed. In expression of my appreciation, I would like to acknowledge the assistance of the following individuals, organizations, and agencies:

Individuals:
    Joseph L. Amos, E. F. Hutton.
    Nancy Beckman, Source Telecomputing Corporation.
    Kathleen V. Boyle, Dow Jones News/Retrieval.

U.S. Government Agencies:
    Bureau of the Public Debt.
    Federal Reserve Bank of New York.
    Federal Reserve Bank of Richmond.
    Federal Reserve Bank of St. Louis.
    Internal Revenue Service.

Security Exchanges and Banks:
    American Board of Trade.
    Bank of Delaware.
    Chicago Board of Options Exchange.
    Chicago Board of Trade.

Chicago Mercantile Exchange.
International Money Market.
Mid-America Exchange.

In addition, a special note of thanks is extended to Joel M. Klein, CPA, who provided many helpful suggestions and clarifications concerning the tax treatments discussed in this book.

Howard M. Berlin

Contents

Knowing how to make money, and also how to keep it; either one of these gifts might make a rich man.

Seneca, *Epistulae ad Lucilium*

Commonly Asked Questions and Answers about Treasury Securities

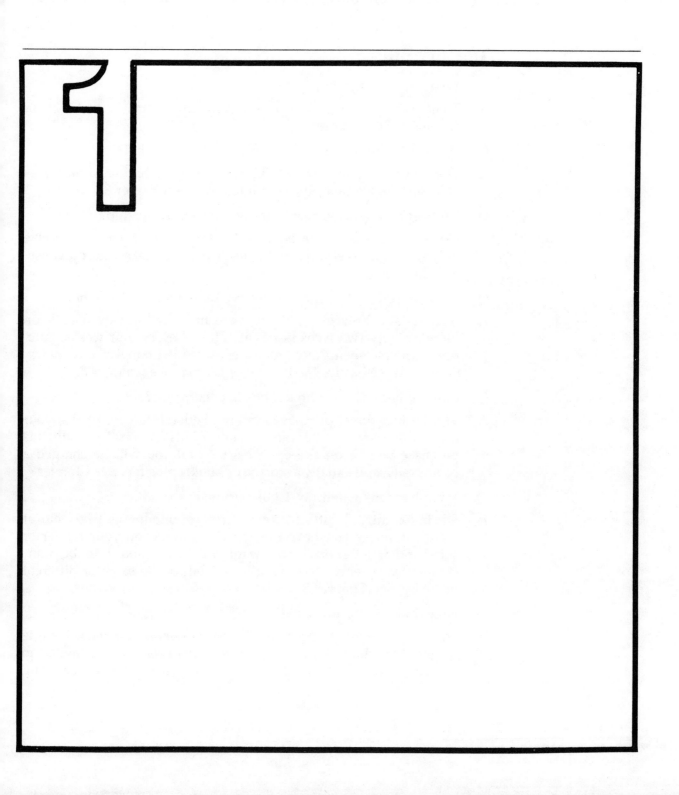

The following is a collection of the most commonly asked questions about the purchase, use, and sale of Treasury bills, notes, and bonds as direct obligations of the U.S. government, or indirectly as zero coupon issues, mutual funds, commodity futures, or options. Since the answers presented here are brief, you are strongly recommended to read the indicated chapter reference for a more comprehensive discussion.

Treasury Bills

Q. What are Treasury bills?

A. T bills are short-term debt securities having maturities of 13, 26, or 52 weeks. See Chapter 3.

Q. What is the minimum purchase amount for a T bill?

A. The minimum purchase is $10,000, but may be higher in multiples of $5,000, above this $10,000 minimum. See Chapter 3.

Q. Do I get an engraved certificate as proof of ownership?

A. No. T bills are issued in book-entry form, so that you will receive only an official receipt (Form PD 4949) as evidence of your purchase. See Chapter 3.

Q. How often does the Federal Reserve hold auctions for T bills?

A. New 13- and 26-week T bill issues are auctioned weekly, usually on Monday. Fifty-two-week issues are offered every four weeks. Auction announcements are published weekly in major city newspapers, as well as in *The Wall Street Journal*. See Chapter 3.

Q. Can my bank or stockbroker buy T bills for me?

A. Yes. Besides direct purchase from the Federal Reserve banks, your own bank or stockbroker can purchase T bills for you. Normally this purchase will be on the open market and you will be charged a commission and usually a storage or safekeeping fee. See Chapter 3.

Q. What happens when my T bill matures?

A. For book entry T bill accounts, the face amount will be paid at maturity unless you have previously indicated on your tender or subscription letter that you want the face amount to be non-competitively reinvested into a new T bill of the same or different maturity. See Chapter 3.

Q. How do I pay for my T bill?

A. For direct purchases from the Federal Reserve, you must include payment for the full face value. The form of payment is limited to cash, a certified personal check, a bank cashier's check, or maturing

Treasury securities. The Treasury will not accept personal checks unless they are certified. Money orders are also not accepted. See Chapter 3.

Q. Can I submit a tender without using an official form?

A. Yes. T bills may be purchased by mail using a simple handwritten or typed subscription letter instead of using Form PD 4632. See Chapter 3.

Q. Can I sell my T bill before it matures?

A. Yes. If you have a book-entry T bill account, you cannot sell your T bill within 20 business days of the purchase date or within 20 business days of the maturity date—you must use Form PD 4633. If you bought your T bill on the open market through a bank or securities dealer, then they will be able to sell it for you. See Chapter 3.

Q. Although I indicated that I did not want to roll over my T bill at maturity, can I change my mind?

A. Yes. Use form PD 4633. See Chapter 3.

Q. Can I use T bills as collateral?

A. No. The Treasury will not recognize a pledge of your book-entry T bills for collateral. However, if a commercial bank purchased the T bill for you on the open market and is presently holding it for you, then they may allow you to use it as collateral. See Chapter 3.

Q. What are cash management bills?

A. Cash management bills are short-term debt securities having shorter maturities than T bills. See Chapter 3.

Q. What is the minimum purchase of a cash management bill?

A. The minimum purchase is usually $1 million and is only on a competitive (bid) basis. See Chapter 3.

Treasury Notes and Bonds

Q. What is the difference between T notes and bonds?

A. T notes are medium-term debt securities that have fixed maturities greater than 1 year and up to 10 years from the date of issue. On the other hand, T bonds are long-term debt securities having fixed maturities longer than 10 years, usually with a maximum of 30 years. See Chapter 4.

Q. What is the minimum face value denomination for a T note or bond?

A. For T notes having maturities less than four years, the minimum denomination is $5,000 with increments of $1,000; otherwise the minimum denomination and increment is $1,000. For T bonds, the minimum denomination is usually $1,000. Engraved certificates for notes and bonds are issued in denominations of $1,000, $5,000, $10,000, $100,000, and $1,000,000. See Chapter 4.

Q. How often does the Federal Reserve hold auctions for T notes and bonds?

A. In general, at least one T note is offered each month, which may consist of 2-, 4-, 5-, 7-, or 10-year maturities. T bonds are issued less often than notes. You can find out the date of the next scheduled offering by telephoning the Federal Reserve bank or branch nearest you. Auction announcements are also published in major city newspapers, as well as in *The Wall Street Journal*. See Chapter 4.

Q. Can my bank or stockbroker buy T notes and bonds for me?

A. Yes. Normally this purchase will be on the open market and you will be charged a commission and, if you want to take physical possession, a delivery fee. See Chapter 4.

Q. How are T notes and bonds issued?

A. Prior to 1983, T notes and T bonds were issued either in bearer or registered form when purchased directly from the Treasury. Now T notes and bonds are issued only in registered form by the Treasury. However, bearer issues can still be bought on the open market. See Chapter 4.

Q. How is the interest paid?

A. For bearer issues, interest is paid by cashing a semiannual coupon at a commercial bank or one of the Federal Reserve banks, or its branches. For registered issues, a Treasury check for the interest is mailed to the registered owner twice a year. See Chapter 4.

Q. What is an exchange offering?

A. An exchange offering is when specific T notes or bonds may be issued in exchange for other outstanding notes or bonds. Only those issues specifically listed in the public announcement are eligible for such an exchange. See Chapter 4.

Q. Are T notes and bonds subject to call?

A. The Treasury periodically issues only T bonds with a call provision, and the call date is usually not more than five years earlier than the original maturity date. Depending on the economic conditions, the Treasury may call in those bonds which have the call provision. See Chapter 4.

Q. Can I submit a tender without using an official form?

A. Yes. T notes and bonds may be purchased by mail using a simple handwritten or typed subscription letter instead of using a specially printed form. See Chapter 4.

Q. Can I break up a T note or bond certificate into smaller denominations?

A. Yes. Bearer and registered T notes and bonds are eligible for denominational exchange into smaller denominations for bearer certificates of the same issue (maturity). See Chapter 4.

Zero Coupon Securities

Q. What are the key features of zero coupon Treasury securities?

A. Zero coupon Treasury securities combine the safety of a U.S. government security with the advantages of a zero coupon bond. Investors can choose from a wide range of maturities from as little as 3 months up to about 10 years, locking in a guaranteed rate of return with virtually no risk. See Chapter 5.

Q. Are zero coupon Treasury securities a good investment?

A. Zero coupon securities offer a guaranteed rate of return with the full security of a U.S. government obligation. See Chapter 5.

Q. What is the minimum investment?

A. This minimum varies with the length of maturity and is set by the activity of the open market. Generally, a $1,000 security will sell for less than $500 for maturities in the 5–10 year range. See Chapter 5.

Q. When will interest on zero coupon Treasury securities be paid?

A. Since these securities are bought at a discount from their face value, the amount of discount (i.e., accrued interest) is paid at maturity in addition to repayment of the original investment amount. See Chapter 5.

Q. Is the quoted yield on a zero coupon Treasury security guaranteed?

A. Yes. The yield that is quoted at the time of purchase is locked in for the life of the security. Because these securities have no redeemable coupons, the quoted yields are considered to be *yields to maturity* and are not subject to market fluctuations or reinvestment risks. See Chapter 5.

Q. Are zero coupon Treasury securities "marginable"?

A. No. See Chapter 5.

Q. Do zero coupon Treasury securities have any advantages over a money market fund?

A. Unlike zero coupon Treasury securities, money market funds are generally not obligations of the U.S. government. In addition, money market fund rates change daily, whereas the yield of the zero coupon Treasury security is fixed. See Chapter 5.

Q. Who has custody of my zero coupon bond?

A. Generally, the brokerage house or its bank acts as the custodian. For example, if you bought a zero coupon bond through E. F. Hutton Group, Inc., the custodian bank is Manufacturers Hanover Corporation. See Chapter 5.

Q. Is there a secondary or open market for zero coupon Treasury securities?

A. Yes. Several brokerage houses, such as E. F. Hutton Group, Inc., Merrill Lynch Pierce, Fenner, & Smith, Inc., Salomon Brothers Inc., and Lehman Bros. Corp. maintain an active secondary market for those investors who wish to sell their zero coupon Treasury securities before they mature. The future market price is based on the current market yields. See Chapter 5.

Q. Can zero coupon Treasury securities be "called"?

A. No. See Chapter 5.

Q. Can zero coupon Treasury securities be issued in bearer form?

A. No. These are issued in registered form only. See Chapter 5.

Q. Can zero coupon Treasury securities be made part of a pension plan?

A. Yes. These can be used for IRA accounts, Keogh plans, IRA rollovers, pension plans, self-directed deferred compensation plans, as well as other investments not subject to federal income taxes. A single IRA purchaser, for example, can now invest the maximum $2,000 ($2,250 for a "spousal" account) annual amount to provide a maturity value of up to as much as several times the original investment. See Chapter 5.

Treasury Mutual Funds

Q. Are "Treasury" mutual funds the same as money market funds?

A. Both funds are basically the same. However, the Treasury mutual fund restricts its portfolio to U.S. Treasury issues, such as T bills. Money market funds, although they invest in T bills, primarily invest in a variety of other short-term obligations, such as bank certificates of deposit. See Chapter 5.

Q. Are these funds insured?

A. No. Although Treasury mutual funds invest in securities backed by the direct guarantee of the U.S. government, they nevertheless are not insured. See Chapter 5.

Q. How do yields offered by Treasury mutual funds compare with money market funds?

A. In general, money market funds have higher yields, as the majority of their portfolio is tied up in securities that have a higher risk than Treasury securities. See Chapter 5.

Q. What services do Treasury mutual funds provide?

A. Most Treasury mutual funds provide the same services as money market funds. These may include systematic investing, automatic withdrawals, and redemption of shares by telephone, check, or telegram. See Chapter 5.

Treasury Options

Q. What are Treasury options?

A. An option on a Treasury security is the right to control a large face-valued security for a set period of time with a relatively small amount of money. Options on Treasury securities are frequently called *Interest rate options*. See Chapter 5.

Q. What options are available?

A. The American Stock Exchange trades $200,000 T bills and $20,000 T notes, while the Chicago Board of Options Exchange trades only T bonds in contract sizes of either $20,000 or $200,000. See Chapter 5.

Tax Treatment and Liability

Q. How are T bills treated for tax purposes?

A. If held to maturity, the interest earned, (i.e., the discount) is treated as ordinary income, subject only to federal income taxes. If sold before maturity, any profit is ordinary income, while any loss is a short-term capital loss. See Chapter 9.

Q. If I buy either a T note or bond and let it mature, what is my tax liability?

A. The interest paid on the security, whether in bearer or registered form, must be reported annually, but only on your federal tax return. See Chapter 9.

Q. Are T notes and bonds subject to capital gains?

A. If T notes and bonds are bought and then sold before maturity, you must report the gain or loss as a capital gain or loss on Schedule D of your tax return. See Chapter 9.

Q. Can I amortize Treasury securities?

A. Only those securities bought at a premium can be amortized. See Chapters 7 and 9.

Q. What are the tax liabilities of zero coupon Treasury securities?

A. Holders of zero coupon Treasury securities are required to annually report interest that is accrued, although not actually received. See Chapters 5 and 9.

Treasury Securities: A Virtual Risk-Free Loan to Uncle Sam

Introduction

Many people who make their living in the financial and investment world have long held the position that Treasury securities are the closest thing to the ideal investment instrument. Since Treasury securities are fully backed by the full faith, authority, and taxing power of the U.S. government, they are virtually risk free, although it should be emphasized that no investment is guaranteed to be foolproof.

When a Treasury security is purchased, the buyer is basically lending Uncle Sam, who happens to be a better-than-average credit risk, a specified amount of money for a specified time. Consequently, if the U.S government stays afloat, then the purchaser will receive periodic interest and, at maturity, the principal. To my knowledge, Uncle Sam has never defaulted on any loan obligation in over 200 years. On the other hand, corporations, banks, and other government bodies (state, local, and foreign) can and do default on their obligations. In the final run, as long as the Federal Reserve Bank, in conjunction with the Treasury Department, has the authority to print and distribute money, Uncle Sam will always be able to meet his obligations to investors.

Debt Management Using Treasury Securities

One of the primary responsibilities of the U.S. Treasury Department is to provide for the financial needs of the federal government. This responsibility includes the function of *debt management*, which involves the raising of funds, or "fresh cash", to cover the difference between revenues (taxes collected by the IRS, for example) and outlays and providing for the refunding of or repaying of maturing debt. Depending on the financing needs of the U.S. Treasury, Uncle Sam typically borrows upwards to approximately $12 billion each week in debt management.

Other than collecting taxes through the IRS, the Treasury raises much of its funds by publicly selling marketable securities. These securities, which are obligations of debt of the United States, may be purchased directly from the Federal Reserve Bank and the Bureau of the Public Debt or through commercial banks and stockbrokers.

What Types of Treasury Securities Are Available?

Marketable Treasury securities fall into three major categories—bills, notes, and bonds—and span the loan period from as little as 13 weeks on up to as much as 30 years.

Treasury Bills

Treasury bills, or *T bills* as they are most commonly called, are short-term obligations of either 13-week (91 days or 3 months), 26-week (182 days or 6 months), or 52-week (365 days or 1 year) maturities. In recent years, T bills have been very popular with a large class of people who desire a safe investment with relatively high comparable yields, that won't tie up their money for extended periods of time. In addition, money managers of pension funds, banks, money market funds, credit unions, and even foreign governments such as Saudi Arabia have loaned Uncle Sam money in return for T bills.

Although T bills have been around for a long time, they never enjoyed a widespread popularity with the small, or individual, investor up until the later part of the 1960s. This was because the rate of return on T bills was really not too competitive with other available, but more risky investments. Prior to February 1970, the minimum T bill purchase amount was a mere $1,000, a bargain by today's standards. Then, probably because of the U.S. government's increasing need to finance the war effort in Vietnam, inflation rose to a point where investors found T bills provided up to a 2 percent better return than most other instruments.

Then, in February 1970, the Treasury raised the minimum T bill denomination from $1,000 to $10,000. The Secretary of Housing and Urban Development, George Romney, was quoted in a February 26, 1970, Treasury Department press release as its reasons for the increase:

> The outflow of savings from Savings and Loan Associations, Mutual Savings Banks, and other thrift institutions has aggravated the shortage of mortgage funds and contributed to a serious decline in housing production. To avoid a serious, growing housing shortage, it is essential that we discourage the outflow of funds from mortgage lending institutions. This Treasury action should substantially improve our housing outlook.

In addition, the increased costs in the handling of the large volume of T bill transactions was cited, in the same press release, as another reason for the increase—there are no fees imposed by the Treasury when newly issued T bills are purchased, redeemed, or transferred.

During President Carter's term, inflation further rose to a point where money-wise investors, pensioners, housewives, doctors, and virtually anyone else who "had $10,000 to spare" picked up on buying T bills. Prior to 1978, purchasers of T bills received an engraved certificate. However, in an effort to reduce costs, the Treasury stopped issuing these certificates and began issuing T bills in book-entry form.

Treasury Notes

T notes, considered medium-term obligations, are issued with fixed maturities greater than 1 year up to 10 years. Unlike T bills which are issued in book-entry form, T notes are in the form of engraved certificates. Prior to 1983, these certificates, at the option of the buyer, could have been issued in either bearer or registered form. At the present time, T notes are only issued in registered form. Unlike T bills, T notes bear a specific rate of interest which is paid every six months to the owner.

Treasury Bonds

T bonds, not to be confused with savings bonds, are the Treasury's long-term obligations. Like T notes, they are now issued as registered engraved certificates (since September 23, 1982) with fixed maturities greater than 10 years, although many are issued for 20 to 30 years. Like some corporate and tax-free municipal bonds, many T bonds are callable at par value no more than five years from maturity. Obviously, T bonds are for those who want a locked-in guaranteed rate of return for an extended period of time.

At the present time, President Reagan's administration is studying a number of changes in the way T bills, notes, and bonds could be sold to further cut government costs and reduce competition with private industry. The options being discussed by the Treasury include:

- Charging a fee, possibly $25, to purchasers of a new Treasury security at auction.

- Raising the minimum denomination securities available from the Treasury and Federal Reserve banks, possibly to $50,000 or $100,000. Lesser denominations would likely continue to be available through commercial banks and brokerage houses.

- Eliminating the Treasury and the Federal Reserve banks as buying outlets, thus leaving the job to private-sector financial institutions.

I personally feel that all the above options, with the exception of a buyer's fee, will be rejected. Just as the stock market was built on the participation of the "little guy," not the institutional investors, so will the federal government realize that the potential money supply of individuals for investments cannot be overlooked when the government wants to periodically raise fresh cash.

Performance Record of Treasury Securities

Historically, Treasury securities generally parallel the patterns set by various money rate indicators. Among these money barometers are the prime rate, the M1 index, federal funds rate, discount rate, commercial paper, and negotiable certificates of deposit.

Unlike the stock market, the interest rates of Treasury securities are not, on a daily basis, severely affected by whether the President of the United States or some other major world leader sneezes the wrong way or has a headache on a given day. Furthermore, interest rates of Treasury securities are not subject to internal or external "manipulation" which goes on in the stock, commodities, and futures markets.

The chart of Figure 2–1 shows how the interest rates of Treasury securities compared with the average prime rate from 1960 to 1981. Appendix D gives a more detailed weekly breakdown of Treasury rates, along with

Figure 2–1   **Yields of Treasury Securities and Average Prime Rate from 1960 to 1981**

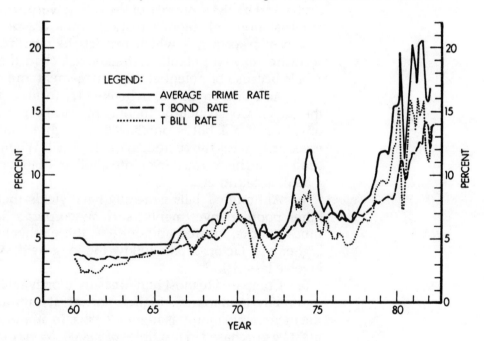

Source: U.S. Department of Commerce, Bureau of Economic Analysis.

the average prime rate and the average yield of municipal tax-free bonds for the 1977–1982 period.

Advantages and Disadvantages

Treasury securities, like any other investment or financial institution, have their pros and cons. Since some of these points vary among the three major types of Treasury securities, the more obvious and important points that follow are treated separately.

T Bills

1.   T bills, by their nature, are short-term securities so your money is not tied up for an unreasonable amount of time, especially if interest rates are expected to rise. On the other hand, T bills do not enjoy the virtual instant liquidity often touted by various savings institutions and money market funds.

2.   Although funds deposited with savings institutions are insured by either the FDIC or FSLIC up to $100,000, T bills are as safe, since they are backed by the authority of the U.S. government. It should be pointed out that nonbank money market funds are not insured. Even those money market funds which restrict their entire portfolio to Treasury securities have a potentially higher risk than the outright purchase of T bills because of potential mismanagement and overhead costs.

3.   As T bills are issued in book-entry form, only a receipt is issued to the buyer. Consequently, there is physically nothing for you to lose or misplace. If a T bill is purchased through a bank or stockbroker, they essentially act as the custodian for the T bill. When it matures, they either send you a check, roll it over into another T bill, or deposit the funds into a bank account, etc.

4.   Although T bills generally have yields that are often lower than other popular investments, such as corporate bonds, money market funds, stocks, futures, and options, these others nevertheless assume a higher risk factor. T bills follow the long-held axiom that lower yields involve less risk.

5.   Compared to most non-Treasury money rate instruments, the minimum buy-in amount is higher, starting at a minimum of $10,000. Also, the increment amount is higher. T bills, in amounts higher than $10,000, must be purchased in multiples of $5,000. Money market funds and those serviced by banks generally require only a $100 minimum increase.

6.   Unlike money market funds and all bank-issued instruments, T bills are only subject to federal income taxes. Only municipal tax-free bonds enjoy a more favorable tax treatment when conservative investing

is considered. However, in order to decide which type of investment is the best, one must consider the federal, state, and local tax brackets that apply, reducing all yields to a truly tax-free common denominator. This is discussed in Chapter 6.

7.   This last item is purely subjective. Some people don't like to deal with the federal government, since they feel that it is a faceless, monolithic, and bureaucratic monster that cannot give the individual the attention and counseling banks and brokerage houses are willing to provide. In a variety of cases, this is so. However, if you know the rules of the game, this apprehension can be minimized or eliminated altogether, and this book discusses each step in detail.

T Notes and Bonds

The above points 2, 4, 6, and 7 also apply to both Treasury notes and bonds. However, the following additional items should be considered when thinking about investing in T notes or bonds.

1.   Notes and bonds are now issued in registered form. Although they can be difficult to sell if stolen, they nevertheless can be replaced. However, for those issued prior to 1983, *bearer* notes and bonds can still be bought on the secondary, or open market. Consequently, they must be safeguarded against theft or loss.

2.   Notes and bonds have much lower minimum purchase requirements than T bills. For notes having maturities of four years or less, the minimum purchase price is $5,000 and can be increased in multiples of $1,000. For notes of over four years, the minimum purchase is $1,000 with multiples of $1,000. All bonds, on the other hand, have a minimum purchase price of $1,000 with increments of $1,000.

Treasury bills, or *T bills* as they are often referred to, are short-term securities issued with maturities of 13, 26, or 52 weeks. These are also referred to as 3-month, 6-month, or 1-year T bills respectively. All three types are sold in minimum amounts of $10,000 and may be higher in multiples of $5,000 above this minimum (i.e., $15,000, $20,000, etc.).

Book-Entry Issues

T bills are issued in what is called *book-entry* form, which means that you, the purchaser, will receive only a receipt rather than an engraved certificate as evidence of your purchase, as is the case with Treasury notes and bonds. Once purchased, ownership is recorded in a book-entry account and assigned an account number by the Treasury. Purchasers will receive notification of a book-entry account number for each T bill issued.

Offering Schedule

The three types of T bills are offered on a frequent and regularly predictable schedule. The 13- and 26-week (3- and 6-month) bills are offered every week as follows:

- The offering is publicly announced every Tuesday.
- The bills are auctioned the following Monday.
- The bills are issued on Thursday, three days after the auction.

The above schedule is modified slightly when national holidays fall on Mondays and Thursdays, or when other special situations occur. When a holiday falls on a Monday, the Treasury usually auctions the bills on the next day. However, the bills are still issued on the following Thursday as before.

Fifty-two-week (or 1-year) T bills are regularly issued every four weeks as follows:

- The offering is publicly announced every fourth Friday.
- The 52-week bills are auctioned the following Thursday.
- The bills are then issued the following Thursday, one week later.

Again, this schedule is modified (usually one day later) when either the auction, issue, or maturity date falls on a holiday or other special occasion.

The Treasury publishes its T bill auction schedule weekly in major city newspapers throughout the country, such as *The New York Times* or *The Wall Street Journal* (see Figure 3–1).

Figure 3–1   Weekly Auction Notice for the Public Sale of
                                  13-Week and 26-Week Treasury Bills

Treasury Sale Friday
To Raise $225 Million

By a WALL STREET JOURNAL *Staff Reporter*
WASHINGTON—The Treasury plans to
raise about $225 million in fresh cash Friday
with the sale of $9.8 billion in short-term
bills to redeem about $9.57 billion in matur-
ing bills.

The offering will be divided evenly between 13-week and 26-week bills. The bills
will be dated June 3 and mature on Sept. 2
and Dec. 2.

Tenders for the bills, available in minimum $10,000 denominations, must be re-
ceived by 1:30 p.m. EDT Friday at the
Treasury or at Federal Reserve banks or
branches.

The weekly bill auctions generally are
held on Mondays. This auction is being held
Friday because of federal observance of the
Memorial Day holiday next Monday.

Courtesy The Wall Street Journal, *May 26, 1982*

How to Purchase T Bills

T bills may be purchased in several ways: directly from the U.S. Treasury
through any Federal Reserve bank or the Bureau of the Public Debt (a
division of the Department of the Treasury); from a commercial bank; or
from a stockbroker. In addition, speculation in T bills as a commodity is
also possible, as is described in Chapter 5.

Purchasing from the Government—
Submitting a Tender

Direct purchase from the U.S. Treasury is done by submitting what is
known as a *tender*, either by mail or in person at one of the 12 Federal
Reserve banks or any of its 25 branches. As with virtually all aspects of
the federal government, a tender is nothing more than a special form

Figure   3–2

Form PD 4632 Used for Buying Treasury Bills at Auction from a Federal Reserve Bank (26-Week Treasury bill version shown)

FORM PD 4632-2
Dept. of the Treasury
Bur. of the Public Debt

TENDER FOR TREASURY BILLS
IN BOOK-ENTRY FORM AT THE
DEPARTMENT OF THE TREASURY
26-WEEK BILLS ONLY

FOR OFFICIAL USE ONLY

FRB Request No. _____

Issue Date _____

Due Date _____

Cusip No. 912793

ACCOUNT NO.

MAIL TO:
☐ Bureau of the Public Debt, Securities Transactions Branch
Room 2134, Main Treasury, Washington, D C 20226
☐ Federal Reserve Bank or Branch
of your District at: _____

BEFORE COMPLETING THIS FORM READ THE
ACCOMPANYING INSTRUCTIONS CAREFULLY

Pursuant to the provisions of Department of the Treasury Circular, Public Debt Series No. 27-76, the public announcement issued by the Department of the Treasury, and the regulations set forth in Department Circular, Public Debt Series No 26-76, I hereby submit this tender, in accordance with the terms as marked, for currently offered U.S. Treasury bills for my account. (Competitive tenders must be expressed on the basis of 100, with three decimals. Fractions may not be used.) I understand that noncompetitive tenders will be accepted in full at the average price of accepted competitive bids and that a noncompetitive tender by any one bidder may not exceed $500,000.

TYPE OF BID
NONCOMPETITIVE ☐   or   COMPETITIVE ☐   at: Price _____

AMOUNT OF TENDER $ _____
(Minimum of $10,000. Over $10,000 must be in multiples of $5,000.)

ACCOUNT IDENTIFICATION: (Please type or print clearly using a **ball-point pen** because this information will be used as a mailing label.)

Depositor(s) _____

Address _____

PRIVACY ACT NOTICE
The individually identifiable information required on this form is necessary to permit the tender to be processed and the bills to be issued, in accordance with the general regulations governing United States book-entry Treasury bills (Department Circular PD Series No. 26-76) The transaction will not be completed unless all required data is furnished.

DEPOSITOR(S) IDENTIFICATION NUMBER

	SOCIAL SECURITY NUMBER		EMPLOYER IDENTIFICATION NO.
FIRST NAMED	☐☐☐ – ☐☐ – ☐☐☐☐	OR	☐☐ – ☐☐☐☐☐☐☐
SECOND NAMED	☐☐☐ – ☐☐ – ☐☐☐☐		

DISPOSITION OF PROCEEDS

The par amount of the account will be paid at maturity unless you elect to have Treasury reinvest (roll-over) the proceeds of the maturing bills. (See below)

☐ I hereby request noncompetitive reinvestment of the proceeds in book-entry Treasury bills.

METHOD OF PAYMENT
TOTAL SUBMITTED $ _____   Cash $ _____   Check $ _____   Maturing Treasury Securities $ _____

DEPOSITOR'S AUTHORIZATION

Signature _____   Date _____   Telephone Number During Business Hours (____) _____   Area Code

FOR OFFICIAL USE ONLY

ALPHA-CROSS-REF.

required by the Treasury for you to make an application to purchase a T bill. Shown in Figure 3–2, is the Department of the Treasury Form PD 4632, which has four noncarbon type copies and is normally used for tender applications. The four copies are labeled so that:

- Copy A: Department of the Treasury Copy.
- Copy B: Department of the Treasury Copy.
- Copy C: Federal Reserve Bank Copy.
- Copy D: Depositor's Copy.

A different numbered and colored form is used for 13-, 26-, and 52-week T bills:

- 52-week bills: PD 4632-1 (blue).
- 26-week bills: PD 4632-2 (yellow).
- 13-week bills: PD 4632-3 (pink).

These are easily obtained from any Federal Reserve bank, its branches, or from the Bureau of the Public Debt. The following steps, used in completing this form, are summarized below:

1. Mail to.   On Form PD 4632, first check off whether you will be mailing your tender offer to (1) the Bureau of the Public Debt, Securities Transaction Branch, Room 2134, Main Treasury, Washington, DC 20226, or (2) submitting it either in person or by mail to the Federal Reserve bank in your district, or one of its branch offices. A list of the Federal Reserve banks and their branch offices is given in Appendix A. As the United States is subdivided into 12 Federal Reserve districts, *it is important that you send or present your tender offer to the correct Federal Reserve bank office, as it may not be processed.* More about this will be explained later. If you are presenting the tender in person or sending it to a Federal Reserve bank or branch office, its location should be filled in, for example: St. Louis, MO; Baltimore, MD, etc.

2. Type of Bid.   You now must check off if you are submitting a competitive or noncompetitive bid. For a *competitive* bid, you must state the price, expressed on the basis of 100 with three decimal places (e.g., 99.235), at which you are willing to accept. Fractions may not be used. Competitive bidding is a highly skilled art routinely practiced by institutional buyers such as banks, brokerage houses, pension fund managers, etc., and should not be attempted by inexperienced investors.

For a *noncompetitive* bid, you do not specifiy a given price or yield but instead agree to pay the average of the competitive bids accepted by the Treasury at its periodic auctions for one of the three T bill issues. The Treasury first accepts, or satisfies, all noncompetitive bids and then fills the remainder of the offering from the competitive bids for each issue, proceeding from the highest to the lowest price until the issue is fully subscribed (as indicated in the public announcement, see Figure 3–1). Those bids submitted below the accepted price, called the *stop-out price*, are not filled. Noncompetitive bids are then awarded at the average price of the accepted competitive bids (see Figure 3–3). Therefore, by submitting a noncompetitive bid, you are assured of receiving a T bill issued to you in the requested amount up to a $500,000 maximum. For competitive bids, there is no maximum amount. If you are fortunate to have more than $500,000 and want to submit a noncompetitive bid, you should break up this amount into two or more separate noncompetitive bids, requiring a separate tender offer for each.

For both competitive and noncompetitive bids, all tenders submitted in person must be received by the Treasury or a Federal Reserve bank no later than 1:30 P.M. eastern time (standard time or daylight savings time, whichever is in effect) on the auction date. For those tenders submitted by mail, they may arrive after the auction date but must be postmarked no later than midnight of the previous day to be eligible.

Figure 3–3

**Auction Results from the Public Sale
of 52-Week Treasury Bills**

Treasury Sells Bills
Totaling $5.5 Billion

By a WALL STREET JOURNAL *Staff Reporter*

WASHINGTON—The Treasury sold $5.5 billion of 52-week bills at an average annual return of 12.173%.

The return was down from 12.194% at the previous auction on May 13 and was the lowest since 10.506% last Nov. 25.

The Treasury said it received $12.26 billion in bids for the bills. It accepted those ranging from 12.13% to 12.199%, including $293.1 million in noncompetitive bids at the average return. The Treasury accepted 61% of the bids at the highest return. The average price was 87.692.

The coupon-equivalent rate was 13.61%, compared with 13.64% in May. The bills will be dated June 17 and mature June 16, 1983.

Courtesy The Wall Street Journal, *June 11, 1982*

3. Amount of Tender.   You fill in the amount requested. A $10,000 minimum is required, and higher amounts must be in multiples of $5,000.

4. Account Identification.   This section requires the name, address, and social security number (or employee identification number if applicable) of the depositor(s). This identifies the name or title of the depositor for whom the book-entry account is to be maintained.

Accounts may be maintained in the name(s) of individuals, executors, trustees, partners, officers of corporations or unincorporated associations, natural or voluntary guardians, etc. In general, book-entry accounts for private individuals will be either in one or two forms:

A single name, for example:

John A. Doe (123-45-6789)

Or two names with the connective "or":

John A. Doe (123-45-6789) or
Jane C. Doe (987-65-4321)

Other proper forms that are authorized for registration of Treasury securities are fully described in Appendix B.

The taxpayer identifying number (either a social security number or employer identification number) is required on the tender; otherwise book-entry accounts will not be established for you. If two individuals are named, as in the example above, then *both* social security numbers must be entered. However, taxpayer identifying numbers are not required for foreign governments, nonresident aliens not engaged in trade or business within the United States, international organizations and foreign corporations not engaged in trade or business and not having an office, place of business, or financial or paying agent within the United States, and other persons or organizations as may be exempt according to IRS regulations.

5. Disposition of Proceeds.   When the T bill you purchased matures, you have two options as to what happens to the proceeds. You can choose either to reinvest, or roll over the face value of the T bill into another bill of the same or different length of maturity, or you may elect to be paid the amount of your account in the form of a Treasury check.

As an example, suppose you have purchased a 26-week T bill in the amount of $15,000. Depending on your instructions to the Treasury, this T bill can be rolled over into another $15,000 T bill (with a noncompetitive bid) having either a 13- or 26-week maturity. As there is no provision on the Form PD 4632 for you to indicate which maturity you desire for a reinvestment, the Treasury will send you a form to indicate your choice, as will be explained in the section on "After You Submit Your Tender." If you do not elect reinvestment, you will receive a green Treasury check for $15,000 when the T bill matures.

6.   Method of Payment.   You must include payment for the full face value of the T bill with each tender. Regulations permit payment to be made in one of the following three forms:

- In U.S. currency (cash). This should only be done when purchasing T bills in person at one of the Federal Reserve banks or its branches. *Never send cash through the mail!*

- By check. The Treasury will not accept personal checks. However, you may submit payment with a certified personal check or a cashier's check. These checks must then be drawn in U.S. dollars from a commercial bank, savings or thrift institution, savings and loan association, or credit union. They must be made payable as appropriate either to (1) the Bureau of the Public Debt or (2) the specific Federal Reserve bank where the tender is being submitted, for example, the Federal Reserve Bank of Philadelphia. You should be careful to send either the certified or cashier's check to the Federal Reserve bank in the district to which the bank belongs; otherwise your tender may not be accepted. More about Federal Reserve districts is explained later in this chapter and in Appendix A.

- By maturing Treasury securities. The Treasury will accept maturing securities, such as T notes and bonds, as payment for the purchase of new T bills. If the Treasury securities are in bearer form, then it is not a good idea to send them through the mail, even if they are insured. You should instead present these certificates in person at a Federal Reserve bank or any of its branches when purchasing new T bills.

7.   Depositor's Authorization.   Here you sign your name as given in the "Account Identification" section of the form. If two names are given, then the first named individual signs. Also include the date of application and a telephone number (including area code) where you can normally be reached during business hours in case the Treasury or Fed has to contact you regarding your tender.

Submitting a Tender Without Using Form PD 4632

You may purchase T bills by mail using a simple subscription letter instead of using Form PD 4632. This letter should basically contain the same information as Form PD 4632:

- The face amount of the T bill requested.

- The desired maturity (13, 26, or 52 weeks).

- Whether you are submitting a competitive or noncompetitive bid, and if competitive, the price.

- Whether the face amount will be reinvested at maturity.

- Your name(s) and address.

- Taxpayer identifying number(s).

- Your telephone number during business hours.

- Your signature and the date of application.

A sample subscription letter illustrating the required information is shown in Figure 3–4. When your letter is received, the information is transferred to the appropriate version of Form PD 4632 and Copy D is sent back to you as a receipt. Your signature along with the original subscription letter is kept on file for future reference.

Mailing Your Tender

If you are mailing a tender for purchasing T bills, either using Form PD 4632 or a subscription letter similar to that shown in Figure 3–4, both the tender/letter and payment should be mailed either to the

> Bureau of the Public Debt
> Securities Transactions Branch
> Room 2134, Main Treasury
> Washington, DC 20226

or to the Fiscal Agency Department of the Federal Reserve bank or branch of the district in your area. For example:

> Federal Reserve Bank of Richmond
> Baltimore Branch
> Fiscal Agency Department
> P.O. Box 1378
> Baltimore, MD 21203

To minimize delay once your envelope reaches the Fed, you should include the words *TENDER FOR TREASURY BILLS* at the lower left corner of the envelope.

Although payment will be in a check made payable to either the Treasury or the Federal Reserve Bank, and maturing security checks will be endorsed to the Federal Reserve Bank, you should nevertheless make it a habit to send your tender/letter by certified mail with a return receipt so you are notified that the tender was received.

Figure   3−4   **Informal Subscription Letter Which Can Be Used for the Purchase**
of Treasury Bills from a Federal Reserve Bank

P. O. Box 9876
Wilmington, DE   19801

April 29, 1982

Fiscal Agency Department
Federal Reserve Bank of Philadelphia
P.O. Box 66
Philadelphia, PA   19105

Dear Sir/Madam:

Please accept in lieu of an official tender Form PD 4632,
this subscription letter for the noncompetitive purchase of
13-week (91-day) Treasury bills from the May 6, 1982, sale
as follows:

1. Noncompetitive bid.
2. Amount: $15,000 13-week T bills.
3. Account Identification:
        John C. Doe   (123-45-6789) or
        Jane B. Doe   (987-65-4321)
        P. O. Box 9876
        Wilmington, DE   19801

4. Request noncompetitive reinvestment of proceeds.
5. Payment enclosed: $15,000 cashier's check.
6. I may be reached during business hours at
   (302) - 555-1234.

Sincerely,

John C. Doe

John C. Doe

After You Submit Your Tender

The Discount Check

Once you have submitted your tender, either in person or by mail, and it was accepted by the Treasury, you will receive a green-colored Treasury check in the mail approximately three to five days after the auction date. Since the day of auction is usually a Monday, you should receive a check on Thursday up to Saturday. Since T bills are always sold at a discount, or less than their value at maturity, this check represents the amount of difference between the purchase price and the value of the T bill at maturity, which is called the *discount*.

As illustrated by the announcement in Figure 3–5, the 13-week T bills auctioned on April 30, 1982, had an average purchase price of 97.088, which, for a $10,000 T bill, means its purchase price was $9,708.80 and the discount is then $10,000 − $9,708.80, or $291.20. This $291.20 is the interest that will be earned on a $10,000 T bill for 13 weeks (91 days). The *discount rate* in the announcement is 11.52 percent which can be easily found from:

$$DR = (MV - PP) \times 360/(MV \times DM)$$
$$= (10,000 - 9,708.80) \times 360/(10,000 \times 91)$$
$$= 291.20 \times 360/910,000$$
$$= 0.1152 \text{ or } 11.52\%$$

where:

DR = Discount rate
MV = Value at maturity
PP = Purchase price
DM = Days to maturity

If 26- or 52-week T bills are purchased, then use 182 or 365 days respectively for DM.

If, on the other hand, we know the discount rate, for example, 11.589 percent for the 26-week T bill shown in Figure 3–5, we can go in the opposite direction and determine the discount for a $15,000 T bill, so that:

$$D = (DR \times FV \times DM)/360$$
$$= (0.11589 \times 15,000 \times 182)/360$$
$$= 316,379/360$$
$$= \$878.83$$

where:

D = Amount of discount
MV = Value at maturity
DR = Discount rate (as a decimal)
DM = Days to maturity

Figure 3—5

**Auction Results from the Public Sale of
13-Week and 26-Week Treasury Bills**

Six-Month Certificate Rate to Fall to 12.172%

A WALL STREET JOURNAL *News Roundup*

The top rate banks and savings institutions can pay on six-month money-market certificates will drop to 12.172%, beginning today, from 12.47% previously.

The reduction reflects recent declines in interest rates on 26-week Treasury bills auctioned by the government. Last Friday, the average rate on the bills declined to 11.589% from 11.677% at the previous auction May 24. The average rate on the latest 13-week bill, however, increased slightly to 11.52% from 11.48%.

Bill auctions normally are conducted on Monday, but the latest sale was held Friday because of the long Memorial Day weekend.

The maximum rate on the popular six-month money-market certificates is determined by adding a quarter percentage point to the average rate on 26-week bills at the latest auction or the average rate at the latest four auctions, whichever is higher.

Here are the results of Friday's bill auction:

Rates are determined by the difference between the purchase price and face value. Thus, higher bidding narrows the investor's return while lower bidding widens it. The percentage rates are calculated on a 360-day year, while the coupon equivalent yield is based on a 365-day yield.

	13-Week	26-Week
Applications	$13,222,450,000	$13,324,750,000
Accepted bids	$4,080,950,000	$4,901,000,000
Accepted at low price	48%	70%
Accepted noncompetitively	$897,230,000	$582,485,000
Average price (Rate)	97.088 (11.520%)	94.141 (11.589%)
High price (Rate)	97.101 (11.469%)	94.147 (11.577%)
Low price (Rate)	97.076 (11.567%)	94.131 (11.609%)
Coupon equivalent	12.03%	12.46%

Both issues are dated June 3. The 13-week bills mature Sept. 2 and the 26-week bills mature Dec. 2.

Courtesy The Wall Street Journal, *June 1, 1982*

The purchase price is $15,000 − $878.83, or $14,121.17. It should be remembered that the purchase price quoted in Figure 3–5 is based on 100 points, which is really equivalent to a face value of $10,000 or $100 per point. In order to relate the $14,121.17 purchase price for the $15,000, 26-week T bill to a 100-point basis, we then *divide* $14,121.17 by 150 (since the face value is 15,000/100 or 150 times larger than the basic $10,000, 100-point bill), which gives a purchase basis of 94.141.

From this last example, it can now be seen that the discount check represents the interest you would have received for 182 days. It should be pointed out that the *discount rate is based on a 360-day year*. To determine the annual percentage rate, or coupon equivalent, we must make our calculation based on a *365-day year* as follows:

$$APR = (D \times 365)/(PP \times DM)$$

So that for the 13-week T bill we have:

$$APR = (\$291.20 \times 365)/(\$9708.80 \times 91)$$
$$= 0.1203 \text{ or } 12.03\%$$

While for the 26-week T bill:

$$APR = (\$878.83 \times 365)/(\$14121.17 \times 182)$$
$$= 0.1248 \text{ or } 12.48\%$$

Consequently, the $291.20 is the interest you will earn by lending the U.S. government $10,000 for 91 days at an annual percentage rate of 12.03 percent, while $878.83 is the interest earned by $15,000 for 182 days at 12.48 percent. In contrast to the discount rate the coupon equivalent, or annual percentage rate, is based on the actual purchase price of the T bill and thus reflects the actual yield on your investment. This rate can be directly compared with the stated annual rates of interest of other investment instruments which are not quoted at a discount. In this way, we are comparing apples with apples.

You should notice that in both examples, the coupon equivalent yield is greater than the discount rate. This is always the case because the equivalent yield is computed on the basis of the purchase price of the T bill, while the discount rate is computed on the value at maturity. Furthermore, since the T bill purchase price is always lower than the value at maturity, it follows that the coupon equivalent yield will always be greater than the discount rate.

The Statement of Account—Form PD 4949

Approximately two weeks after the auction date, the Treasury sends out a blue and white computerized Treasury Form PD 4949, "Statement of Account for Treasury Bills" (see Figure 3–6). This nonnegotiable statement, containing an original and a duplicate carbon copy, is mailed to you when a T bill book-entry account is initially established. Form PD 4949 confirms most of the information that was entered on the tender/letter.

Your book-entry account number that was established for your T bill consists of four parts. Taking the account number AU8-2-123 45 6789-01 as an example, the four parts are broken down as:

Figure 3—6   **Form PD 4949, Statement of Account for Treasury Bills**

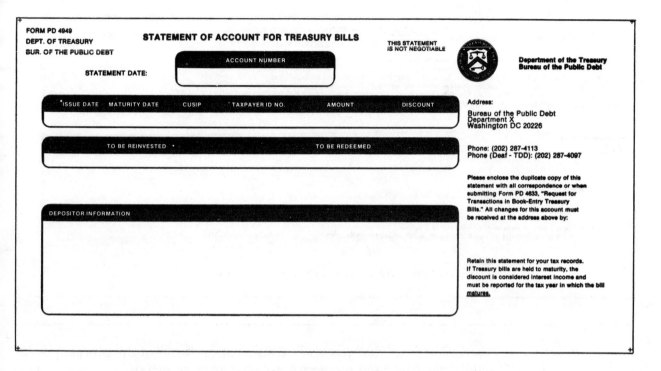

1. **"AU8."**   The last three digits of the Committee of Uniform Securities Identification Procedures, or CUSIP number (e.g., 912794AU8), is different for each issue and changes each time a T bill is reinvested.

2. **"2."**   The hyphen code: 1—entities; 2—individuals.

3. **"123-45-6789."**   The taxpayer identifying number.

4. **"01."**   A two-digit suffix—a different one for each account due the same week.

It is very important that you keep this statement because if you have any questions about your account, or want to sell, transfer, or change the disposition of the proceeds of your T bill, you will have to furnish this number.

The IBM-Style Card—Form PD 4633-2

The face amount of a book-entry account T bill will be paid at maturity by a Treasury check unless (1) you indicated on your tender or sub-

Figure 3–7 **Form PD 4633-2, Request for Reinvestment of Book-Entry Treasury Bills (IBM card)**

This is NOT a check **REQUEST FOR REINVESTMENT OF BOOK ENTRY TREASURY BILLS** **This is NOT a check**

This card should be used to request the reinvestment of a book-entry bill account maintained by the Treasury. If you desire reinvestment, check the appropriate block, sign the card and return it to BUREAU OF THE PUBLIC DEBT, DEPT X, WASHINGTON, D.C 20226. Requests for reinvestment must be received on or before the cut-off date indicated below which is twenty (20) business days prior to maturity. A request for continuous reinvestment will not be accepted. BEFORE YOU CHECK ONE OF THE BOXES BELOW, READ THE BACK OF THIS FORM

CUT-OFF DATE
AMOUNT
TITLE OF SECURITIES AND DUE DATE

TREASURY ACCOUNT NO:

I hereby request that the proceeds of the above Treasury bill be reinvested at maturity on a noncompetitive basis for the number of weeks indicated.

CHECK ONE BOX ONLY
☐ 52 week bill
26 week bill ☐
☐ 13 week bill

Signature and Date

PLEASE DO NOT FOLD, STAPLE OR MUTILATE

FORM PD 4633-2 · Dept. of Treas.- Bur. Public Debt

scription letter that you wished automatic rollover of the proceeds or (2) the T bill had been previously rolled over once before.

If your account is scheduled to be redeemed, which will be pointed out on Form PD 4949, you will receive an IBM-style card, Form PD 4633-2 (see Figure 3–7), approximately two months before maturity. This form is preprinted and prepunched with your account information. It also indicates the cutoff date by which the Bureau of the Public Debt must receive your request if you decide to change your mind and want to reinvest the face value noncompetitively. In addition, you must indicate whether you want reinvestment in a 13-, 26-, or 52-week T bill. Fifty-two-week T bills can only be reinvested into other 52-week T bills, but 13- or 26-week bills cannot be rolled over into 52-week bills. However, a 13-week bill can be rolled over to a 26-week bill, and vice versa.

After signing your request, then mail this form in an envelope to:

Bureau of the Public Debt
Department X
Washington, DC 20226

Buying T Bills through a Bank or Broker

Many persons find it more convenient to have their commercial bank or stockbroker submit their tender bids instead of dealing directly with the

Federal Reserve Bank or any of its branches. Unlike dealing directly with the Fed where there are no charges or commissions, the bank or broker will charge a fee.

In most cases, the bank or broker will purchase T bills for you on the open or secondary market. In this case, you not only pay the market price, which may be higher or lower than the price at which the particular bill was originally issued at, but you also pay a commission and usually a safekeeping fee. One particular Maryland bank charged me $25 for purchasing the T bill plus a $5 safekeeping fee. Some other banks I have dealt with have a flat $35 charge. As T bills are actually issued in book-entry accounts, the bank is really doing nothing but keeping a record of the purchase on file. For this privilege they charged me $5. As will be pointed out later, having the broker or bank hold the T bill for you does have its advantages, especially when you want to sell the T bill before it matures.

Another advantage of dealing through a bank or broker is that you do not have to do any paperwork, such as filling out and mailing a tender form or purchasing either a certified or cashier's check. But then, that's why they charge you a fee or commission. They don't like to tell you that you can buy a T bill yourself and save approximately $25 to $35, because that's why they are in business—to get that money. Nobody does anything for nothing, especially banks and brokers!

At Maturity—Cashing In or Rolling Over

For T bills held in a book-entry account, the face amount will be paid at maturity by a Treasury check unless you previously indicated on either (1) the original tender or (2) the Form PD 4633-2 IBM card that the proceeds be noncompetitively reinvested or rolled over automatically. It should be strongly emphasized that automatic reinvestment of T bills will be done only on a noncompetitive basis, even if the original purchase was an accepted competitive bid.

If your T bill is automatically rolled over, you will then receive a Treasury check for the discount of the new T bill. The same account number will again be used on the newly issued T bill. Although it is not specifically stated on the tender form, you are allowed only a single rollover. Once you have rolled over the proceeds from the original T bill purchase, the "Statement of Account" form (PD 4949) will then indicate that the amount of the book-entry account is scheduled for redemption at maturity. Since the bill is now scheduled for redemption, you will have a chance to request that the proceeds again be reinvested at maturity if desired.

If you purchased a T bill through the services of a commercial bank or broker, you will probably have (1) the bank deposit the face value into your savings or checking account or (2) the broker issue you a check for the face value at maturity. Unlike buying and selling the same stock issue through a broker (a "round-turn"), you should not again be charged a commission or fee when the T bill matures.

Transferring or Selling Your T Bill before It Matures

Perhaps the single-most advantage that can be gained by buying a T bill through a bank or broker is the ease in which you can sell or transfer the T bill weeks or months before it matures. You simply tell the bank or broker from whom you have purchased the T bill that you want to sell it. For this they will probably charge you a commission or fee, since they now have to go to the open market and sell it.

On the other hand, suppose you've decided to manage your own destiny and had originally purchased a T bill directly from the Treasury at auction, thereby saving yourself the charges imposed by banks and brokers. Consequently, you have now established a book-entry account and will need to do some paperwork to have either the T bill transferred to a bank's account, sold, or both.

A friend of mine had $60,000 tied up in a single 13-week T bill. A few weeks after rolling over the proceeds into a new 26-week bill, he and his wife wanted to buy a new house. Although they had enough on hand to make an offer deposit, they nevertheless needed most of the 26-week T bill they had just rolled over for the mortage downpayment due within three months.

In order to transfer a T bill maintained in a book-entry account, you must use Form PD 4633, "Request for Transactions in Book-Entry Treasury Bills Maintained by the Bureau of the Public Debt." This is a two-sided form, as shown in Figure 3–8. Unlike the informality you may have enjoyed by using a written letter in lieu of a printed tender to purchase a T bill, you may not use this same method when transferring book-entry account T bills before their maturity. Rigid bureaucratic procedure prevails and Form PD 4633 *must be used. No substitutes or written letters will be accepted.*

In addition to the mandatory use of Form PD 4633, book-entry T bills may not be transferred or sold either within 20 business days of issue or within 20 days of maturity. In counting the number of business days, be sure not to include Saturdays, Sundays, or any national holidays that may occur during this period.

The following steps briefly illustrate how Form PD 4633 is filled out for the transfer of book-entry T bills.

Figure 3–8

Form PD 4633, Request for Transactions in Book-Entry Treasury Bills Maintained by the Bureau of the Public Debt

FORM PD 4633
Dept of the Treasury
Bur of the Public Debt
(Rev Mar 1980)

(For Official Use Only)

REQUEST FOR TRANSACTIONS IN
BOOK ENTRY TREASURY BILLS MAINTAINED
BY THE BUREAU OF THE PUBLIC DEBT

REQUESTS FOR TRANSACTIONS CONCERNING TREASURY BILLS ISSUED PRIOR TO JANUARY 15, 1980 MUST BE RECEIVED BY THE BUREAU OF THE PUBLIC DEBT NOT LATER THAN TEN (10) BUSINESS DAYS PRIOR TO MATURITY REQUESTS FOR BILLS ISSUED AFTER JANUARY 15, 1980, MUST BE RECEIVED NOT LATER THAN TWENTY (20) BUSINESS DAYS PRIOR TO MATURITY' (NOTE: DO NOT COUNT SATURDAYS, SUNDAYS OR FEDERAL HOLIDAYS.)

BUREAU OF THE PUBLIC DEBT
DEPT X
WASHINGTON, D. C. 20226

TELEPHONE   (202) 287-4113
(TTY) TELEPHONE FOR THE DEAF   (202) 287-4097

The undersigned hereby requests that the action indicated below be taken on the following described book-entry Treasury bills maintained at the Bureau of the Public Debt

1. **CURRENT ACCOUNT IDENTIFICATION (as shown on Statement of Account):**   Amount _____

   a.   Description of bills.
        Account No.

        Issue Date _____

        Due Date _____

   b.   Depositor(s) _____

   c.   Address _____

   d.   Depositor's Taxpayer Identifying Number

   FIRST NAMED   SOCIAL SECURITY NUMBER ☐☐☐ – ☐☐ – ☐☐☐☐   OR   EMPLOYER IDENTIFICATION NUMBER ☐☐ – ☐☐☐☐☐☐☐

2. **ACTION REQUESTED [Check appropriate block(s)]**

   a. ☐ Wire Transfer (see footnote 1) $ _____ of the above described bills through the

      Federal Reserve Bank or Branch at _____

      to ☐☐☐☐☐☐☐☐☐ _____
         (Wire Routing No)   (Member bank name and address, including branch or office)

      If account is not to be maintained at member bank shown above, furnish name and address of financial institution or securities dealer which will act as custodian   Please include branch or office and to whose attention the transfer should be directed.

   b. ☐ Reinvestment of the redemption proceeds at maturity into bills then being issued for the term checked; this request will constitute a noncompetitive tender for such new bills which are offered concurrently. Only one type of bill may be selected when requesting reinvestment. Please note that 26 week and 13 week bills are interchangeable. Fifty-two week bills maturing on or before October 14, 1980 may be reinvested in 52 week bills only. Fifty-two week bills maturing on or after November 6, 1980 may be reinvested in 52 week, 26 week or 13 week bills.

      Check one type only   (2) ☐ 52 week bill   (6) ☐ 26 week bill   (3) ☐ 13 week bill

   c. ☐ Payment of the redemption proceeds at maturity instead of reinvestment as previously requested. (See footnote 2)

   d. ☐ Change of address. (See footnote 2 and complete item 3.b. on reverse)

   e. ☐ Recognition of fiduciary or other change in status of the Depositor(s) (evidence required) (See footnote 2 and complete item 3 on reverse)

   f. ☐ Change of name (evidence may be required) (See footnote 2 and complete item 3.a. on reverse)

   g. ☐ Other (See footnote 2 and complete item 3 as appropriate) _____
        (specify)

1/   Signature must be certified. Certification by a notary public WILL NOT be accepted. See instruction 5

2/   Signature must be certified Certification by a notary public will be accepted.

Figure 3–8 *(concluded)*

3. REVISED ACCOUNT IDENTIFICATION [Complete applicable portion(s) if item
2.d., 2.e., or 2.f. is checked]

a. Depositor(s) _____

b. Address for mailing Statement of Account

| Address for mailing checks (If different from address for mailing Statement of Account) |

c. Depositor's Taxpayer Identifying Number

FIRST NAMED   SOCIAL SECURITY NUMBER   OR   EMPLOYER IDENTIFICATION NUMBER

(Please include account number if this is a financial institution)

PRIVACY ACT NOTICE

The individually identifiable information required on this form is necessary to permit the request to be processed in accordance with the general regulations governing United States book-entry Treasury bills (Department Circular PD Series No. 26-76, as amended). The transaction will not be completed unless all required data is furnished.

4. _____
    (signature)

    _____
    (fiduciary capacity, if any)

Telephone Number and Area Code
during the hours of 8:30 am and 5:00 pm
Eastern time.

5. I CERTIFY that the above-named person as described, whose identity is well known or proved to me, personally appeared before me this_____ day of_____ at _____
    and signed this request.   (month and year)   (city and state)

    _____
    (signature and title of certifying officer)

(OFFICIAL SEAL
OR STAMP)

    _____
    (address)

FOR NOTARY USE ONLY
My Commission Expires _____

1. **Current Account Information—Block 2.**   This information can be taken from either the tender copy returned to you (Form 4633-1, -2, or -3, Copy D), or the "Statement of Account for Treasury Bills" (Form PD 4949). Required information is:

- Amount of the T bill.
- CUSIP number.

- Issue date.
- Due (maturity) date.
- Depositor(s) name(s) and address.
- Applicable taxpayer identifying number.

2.   Action Requested—Block 2.

A.   Check Block a (Blocks 2b through 2g are explained in the section on "Other Uses for Form PD 4633"). Fill in the amount that you want to "wire transfer" (a book-entry account T bill must be first wired to a Federal Reserve bank before it can be sold). The amount can be less than the amount of the account, but the remainder must be at least $10,000. In addition, the amount to be transferred must be at least $10,000 and must be a multiple of $5,000 above the $10,000 minimum.

For example, the friend mentioned earlier had a book-entry account for a $60,000, 26-week T bill. He needed only $45,000 but could have transferred anywhere from $10,000 to $50,000 without completely wiping out the account or could have transferred the entire $60,000, thereby canceling the account.

B.   The name of the Federal Reserve bank or branch of the district that services your commercial bank or that of the broker's fiscal agent who will actually sell the T bill on the open market. This is usually the same office where you submitted your original tender. In my friend's case, although he lived in Delaware and had sent his tender to the Federal Reserve Bank of Philadelphia in whose district he lived, he nevertheless had a bank account with a Maryland bank and was required to have the T bill transferred to the Federal Reserve Bank of Richmond (Baltimore branch) in whose district the Maryland bank belonged to.

In the case of using a broker instead of a commercial bank, the Federal Reserve bank of the district where the broker's fiscal agent belongs must be used. For example, my friend had an account with a Delaware office of a nationally known brokerage house, whose fiscal agent is Irving Trust Co. located in New York. In this case, the transfer would have to be done through the Federal Reserve Bank of New York. See how easy it is to deal with the Federal Reserve?

C.   The next piece of information required for this section is known as the *wire routing number* of the bank. Each commercial bank has a unique nine-digit wire routing number. You will have to ask the bank for their number. Until I finally learned a very easy method for determining a particular bank's wire routing number, I went to the vice presidents and financial officers of almost a half dozen banks before one knew what I was talking about.

The wire routing number is easily obtained by examining a bank check used by that particular bank. Figure 3–9 shows a typical check from

Figure 3–9   **Bank Check Showing a Bank's Wire Routing Number**

Bank wire routing number
Federal Reserve district code

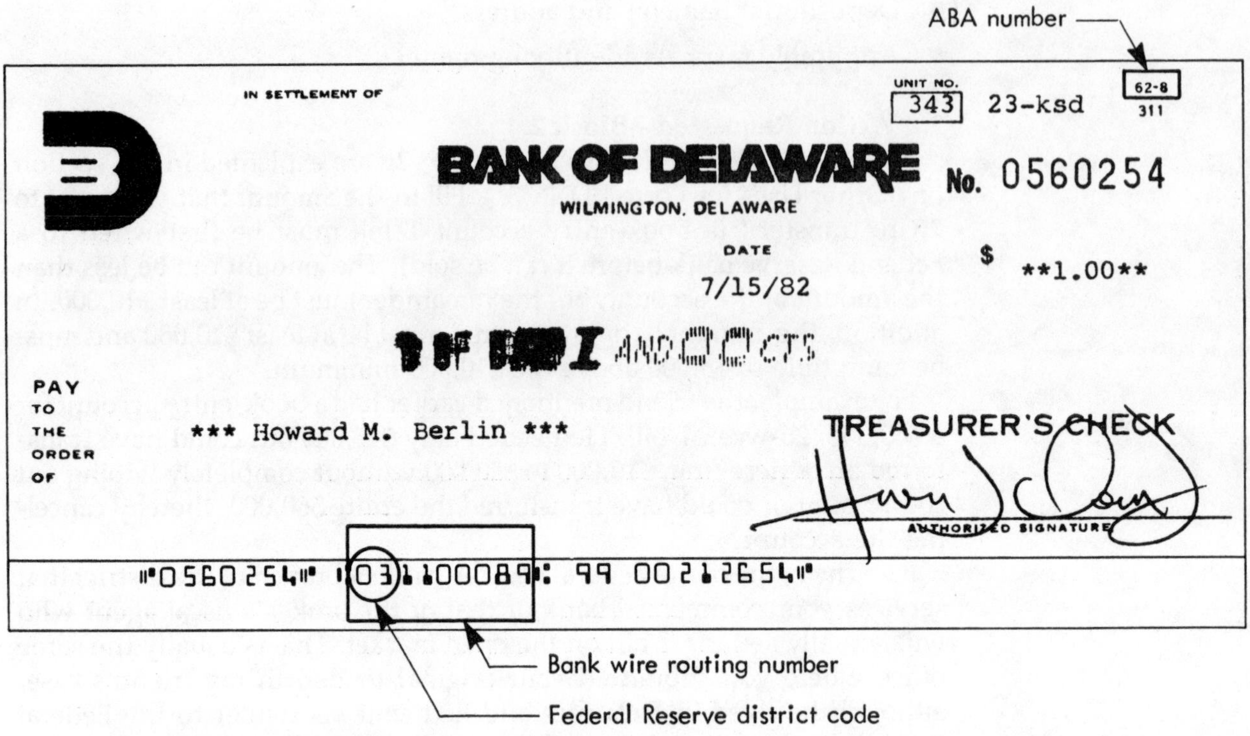

the Bank of Delaware. At the upper right-hand corner are two numbers separated by a horizontal line: 62–8 and 311. The numerator, or top number after the hyphen (i.e., 8), and the entire denominator, or bottom number (i.e., 311), in part make up a bank's wire routing number. The actual wire routing number is located at the bottom of the check in the form of odd-looking numbers known as *magnetic ink recognition characters.*

The wire routing number begins with the number that was the bottom of the two given in the upper right-hand corner of the check, which in this case is 311. We then see the number that matches this is 031100089. The first two digits identify the Federal Reserve district to which the bank belongs. Consequently, the Bank of Delaware belongs to the 3d (i.e., district number 03) Federal Reserve district. In this case Philadelphia is number 3 (see Appendix A for the listing of the Federal Reserve banks by district and their branches). The 3d digit designates the bank or branch serving the territory in which the bank is located; the head office is 1; the 4th digit is used to facilitate the cashing of checks; the 8th digit represents the "8" of the number 62–8, which is the American Bankers Association number assigned to the Bank of Delaware.

You really don't have to know all this information about the wire routing number. I have included it so you will be able to impress the bank officer when you ask him (or her) for the bank's wire routing number and you receive back a blank stare. Just ask for a bank check and point it out. You now know it's the nine-digit number at the bottom of the check! Dealing with ignorant bank officials, like credit card companies, can be frustrating—and I've made my share of enemies.

D. Finally, you must indicate name and address (including the branch or office) of the member bank where the wire transfer will wind up. Banks usually will have specific departments set up to handle wire transfers from other banks and the Fed. For example, the 1st National Bank of Maryland uses the form:

> 1st National Bank of Maryland
> P.O. Box 1596
> Attn: Investment Department
> Baltimore, MD 21203

3. Signatures—Block 4. You must sign your name exactly as it appeared on your original tender/letter along with a telephone number where you can be reached during business hours (8:30 A.M. to 5:00 P.M. eastern time) in case there are questions about your request.

4. Certification—Block 5. Since you will be transferring all or part of the book-entry account to a commercial bank, you must have your signature certified by an officer or employee of either:

A. A bank or trust company chartered by or incorporated under the laws of the United States.

B. A federal savings and loan association or other organization which is a member of the Federal Home Loan Bank System.

Generally, it is best to have your signature certified by the bank to whom your book-entry account will be transferred.

The bank, unless they know you as a regular customer, will require proof of your identity and signature. Usually this can be done by showing a driver's license which has your photograph or by a passport. Finally, the bank will affix their bank seal or stamp with the date of certification.

It has always amused me that to lend money to the U.S. government in the form of T bills, one does not need to have one's signature certified, but signature certification is required to have a book-entry T bill account transferred.

The completed Form PD 4633 must then be mailed to:

Bureau of the Public Debt
Department X
Washington, DC 20226

As with mailing your tender/letter, it is best to have this letter sent by certified mail with a return receipt to make sure that the bureau received your request in a timely manner.

Once your request for wire transfer is received by the bureau and is either 20 days after issue or more than 20 days from maturity, the wire transfer process from the Treasury through the Federal Reserve Bank to the member bank's account takes place in matter of seconds. When you are at the bank getting your signature certified, it is a good idea to inform them they will be receiving a wire transfer from the Fed for a given amount. From that point, you can request them to either hold the T bill account to maturity or immediately sell the T bill on the open market. I have found that the wire transfer process, including the immediate sale on the open market, takes an average of 15 minutes. Once sold, the funds may be either cashed or deposited in your checking or savings account.

Other Uses for Form PD 4633

Besides requesting the transfer of all or part of your T bill book-entry account, Form PD 4633 must be used for any of the following:

1. Reinvestment—Block 2b. Use to authorize noncompetitive reinvestment of T bills, rather than their cash redemption, at maturity. This action then constitutes the submission of a noncompetitive tender for the issue of a new T bill of the term indicated.

2. Cancellation of Reinvestment—Block 2c. Use to cancel a previous reinvestment authorization and request that the face value of the T bill be paid to the depositor at maturity.

3. Change of Address—Block 2d. Use for a change of address. Also complete Block 3b, and indicate SAME for Block 3a and 3c if there are no other changes.

4. Change of Name—Block 2. Use when the depositor's name has been changed by court order or marriage. If changed by court order, then the depositor must attach a certified copy of the court order. If changed by marriage, then no certification is necessary, but the signature in Block 4 must show both names. For example:

Jane C. Doe, changed by marriage
from Jane C. Smith

Block 3 should then be completed as appropriate.

5.   Other Changes—Block 2g.   Use for making changes or corrections such as a misspelled name, incorrect taxpayer identifying number, etc. Block 3 should then be completed as appropriate and identified on a separate sheet of paper attached to the form.

A single Form PD 4633 may be used to request a combination of changes of name, address, or status of the depositor(s), as well as wire transfer, reinvestment, or cancellation of a previous reinvestment request. For the above changes only, the depositor's signature need only be certified by a notary public. *Only for a wire transfer of a book-entry T bill account must the signature be certified by a bank official.*

Pledging T Bills as Collateral

The U.S. Treasury will not recognize a pledge by you of your book-entry T bill(s) for collateral, nor will it transfer securities among book-entry accounts that the Treasury maintains for you. However, a commercial

---

Figure   3–10

**Auction Notice for the Public Sale of
14-Day Cash Management Bills**

Treasury Bills Sale
To Raise $6 Billion

By a WALL STREET JOURNAL *Staff Reporter*

WASHINGTON—The Treasury plans to raise fresh cash today with the sale of $6 billion of 14-day cash management bills.

The bills, which represent an addition to one-year bills issued June 18, 1981, will be dated June 3 and mature June 17.

Tenders for the bills, available in minimum $1 million denominations, must be received by 1:30 p.m. EDT today at Federal Reserve banks or branches. Noncompetitive tenders from the public won't be accepted, and tenders won't be received at the Treasury.

Courtesy The Wall Street Journal, *June 1, 1982*

bank that purchased a T bill for you and is presently holding it may allow you to use it as colateral, provided the T bill will be allowed to mature. You should check with your particular bank about its policies regarding the ability to pledge T bills which they are holding for you as collateral.

Cash Management Bills

Several times a year as the need arises, the Treasury needs to raise fresh cash by selling what is termed *cash managment bills*. These bills are similar to T bills except they are issued for shorter periods of time, typically from 10 to 20 days, and are issued in minimum denominations of $1 million. Needless to say, these are not for the average investor!

As shown in the public announcement in Figure 3–10, tenders for cash management bills are bid only on a competitive basis. Depending on the particular issue, tenders may be received at all Federal Reserve banks and their branches, or may be limited to a single Federal Reserve district, usually the Federal Reserve Bank of New York. Furthermore, the public notice of such an issue is usually less than a day. The announcement notice of Figure 3–10 was published in *The Wall Street Journal* the same day of the deadline for the bids. Institutional investors are generally aware when cash management bills are being offered.

Treasury notes and bonds have longer maturities than T bills. By regulation, T notes have fixed maturities greater than 1 year but not greater than 10 years from their date of issue. On the other hand, T bonds, not to be confused with U.S. savings bonds, have a fixed maturity greater than 10 years from their date of issue. As T notes and bonds are treated in exactly the same way, differing only in their lengths of maturity, and have many similarities with municipal or public authority bonds, they will be discussed in this chapter as if they were the same unless stated otherwise. Specific regulations governing T notes and bonds are presented in Appendix G.

Bearer and Registered Issues

Unlike T bills, which are issued only in book-entry form, T notes and bonds, like commercial stocks and bonds, are printed on an engraved certificate having denominations of $1,000, $5,000, $10,000, $100,000, and $1,000,000. T notes having maturities of less than four years are not usually issued in denominations of less than $5,000.

Prior to 1983, T notes and bonds were issued both in bearer and registered forms. As bearer instruments, T notes and bonds have no name typed on the certificate. Therefore, they are treated as cash and are payable to anyone who has possession of them. Just like most tax-free bonds, bearer type T notes and bonds carry a series of interest coupons that must be clipped and redeemed for cash every six months. Consequently, they should be treated and safeguarded as you would other security instruments, cash, or jewelry.

On the other hand, registered T notes and bonds are registered as to principal and interest, and in addition, bear the owner's (or owners') name on the face of the certificate. In most cases, registration can be in one of the following forms:

- One name.

> John A. Doe (123-45-6789)

- Two names.

> John A. Doe (123-45-6789) and/or
> Jane C. Doe (987-65-4321)

- Joint tenancy.

> either   John A. Doe (123-45-6789) or
>   Jane C. Doe
>
> or   John A. Doe or
>   Jane C. Doe (987-65-4321)

where either party's taxpayer identifying number is acceptable.

- Minors.

either   John A. Doe as natural guardian for
Jack B. Jones, a minor (123-45-6789)

or   John A. Doe, a custodian for Jack B. Jones,
a minor (123-45-6789) under the Delaware
Uniform Gifts to Minors Act.

Other acceptable forms of registration are described in Appendix B.

In addition, the ownership of registered T notes and bonds is also recorded in the records of the Treasury Department. In this manner, the record provides a degree of protection to the owner if the note or bond is lost, stolen, or destroyed.

As of 1983, however, T notes and bonds are only issued in registered form, although bearer issues may still be purchased on the secondary market.

Offering Schedule

Forthcoming sales of T notes and bonds are announced publicly in most major daily and financial newspapers as shown in Figure 4–1, in addition to newsletters sent by the Treasury to individuals and financial institutions (see Figure 4–2). In general, at least one T note is offered each month which may consist of either 2-, 4-, 5-, 7-, or 10-year maturities. T bonds are also issued on a periodic schedule but not nearly as often as T notes. If you are interested in purchasing T notes or bonds, you can find out the date of the next scheduled offering by telephoning the Federal Reserve bank or branch nearest you.

Exchange Offerings

On occasion, the Treasury issues what is termed an *exchange offering* in which specific T notes and bonds may be issued in exchange for other outstanding T notes or bonds. Only those issues specifically listed in the public announcement by the Treasury are eligible for such an exchange. Depending on the specific terms of the offering, either an additional payment may be required from, or a refund may be due to the purchaser.

Call Provisions for T Bonds

Like some municipal bonds, the Treasury periodically issues T bonds with a call provision. The call date is usually not more than ten years from the maturity date.

Figure   4-1   Auction Notice for the Public Sale of
                                    5-Year, 2-Month Treasury Notes

Treasury Will Raise
$2.53 Billion New Cash

By a WALL STREET JOURNAL *Staff Reporter*
WASHINGTON—The Treasury plans to
raise $2.53 billion in fresh cash by selling
$5.5 billion of two-year notes next Wednes-
day and $4 billion of four-year notes on June
23, and redeeming $6.97 billion of notes ma-
turing June 30.

Tenders for the two-year notes, available
in minimum denominations of $5,000, must
be received by 1:30 p.m. EDT Wednesday at
the Treasury or at Fedeal Reserve banks or
branches.

Tenders for the four-year notes, available
in minimum denominations of $1,000, must
be received by 1:30 p.m. EDT June 23 at the
same places.

Both issues will be dated June 30. The
two-year notes will mature June 30, 1984,
while the four-year notes will mature June
30, 1986.

The Treasury will postpone the four-year
note auction unless it is assured that
Congress will act on legislation to raise the
$1.08 trillion debt ceiling before the sched-
uled auction date.

Courtesy The Wall Street Journal, *June 10, 1982*

How to Purchase T Notes and Bonds

T notes and bonds may be purchased in the same manner as T bills:
directly from the U.S. Treasury through any Federal Reserve bank, from
the Bureau of the Public Debt, from a commercial bank, or from a stockbroker. Also like T bills, speculation in T notes and bonds as a commodity
is possible, as is described in Chapter 5.

Purchasing from the Government—
Submitting a Tender

Direct purchase from the U.S. Treasury is done by submitting a tender
either by mail or in person at one of the 12 Federal Reserve banks, any of

Figure 4–2   **Federal Reserve Bank of Richmond Newsletter
Announcing the Sale of Treasury Notes**

FEDERAL RESERVE BANK OF RICHMOND

FISCAL AGENT OF THE UNITED STATES

RICHMOND, VIRGINIA   23261

June 10, 1982

To All Banking Institutions and Others Concerned
in the Fifth Federal Reserve District:

There is printed below for your information, a press statement
issued by the Treasury Department on June 9:

TREASURY TO AUCTION 2-YEAR AND 4-YEAR NOTES

TOTALING $9,500 MILLION

The Department of the Treasury will auction $5,500 million of
2-year and $4,000 million of 4-year notes to refund $6,971 million of
notes maturing June 30, 1982, and to raise $2,529 million new cash.
The $6,971 million of maturing notes are those held by the public,
including $1,615 million of maturing 2-year notes and $355 million of
maturing 4-year 1-month notes currently held by Federal Reserve Banks
as agents for foreign and international monetary authorities.

In addition to the public holdings, Government accounts and
Federal Reserve Banks, for their own accounts, hold $838 million of the
maturing notes that may be refunded by issuing additional amounts of
the new notes at the average prices of accepted competitive tenders.
Additional amounts of the new securities may also be issued at the
average prices to Federal Reserve Banks, as agents for foreign and
international monetary authorities, to the extent that their aggregate
tenders for each of the new notes exceed their aggregate holdings of
each of the maturing notes.

The Treasury will postpone the 4-year note auction unless it has
assurance of Congressional action on legislation to raise the temporary
debt ceiling before the scheduled auction date of June 23, 1982.

Details about each of the new securities are given in the highlights
of the offering printed on the reverse side of this announcement and in
the official offering circulars which are available upon request.

FEDERAL RESERVE BANK OF RICHMOND
Fiscal Agent of the United States

Figure 4-2 *(concluded)*

HIGHLIGHTS OF TREASURY OFFERINGS TO THE PUBLIC
OF 2-YEAR AND 4-YEAR NOTES TO BE ISSUED JUNE 30, 1982

June 9, 1982

Amount Offered:

To the public	$5,500 million	$4,000 million

Description of Security:

Term and type of security	2-year notes	4-year notes
Series and CUSIP designation	Series T-1984 (CUSIP No. 912827 NH 1)	Series H-1986 (CUSIP No. 912827 NJ 7)
Maturity date	June 30, 1984	June 30, 1986
Call date	No provision	No provision
Interest coupon rate	To be determined based on the average of accepted bids	To be determined based on the average of accepted bids
Investment yield	To be determined at auction	To be determined at auction
Premium or discount	To be determined after auction	To be determined after auction
Interest payment dates	December 31 and June 30	December 31 and June 30
Minimum denomination available	$5,000	$1,000

Terms of Sale:

Method of Sale	Yield Auction	Yield Auction
Accrued interest payable by investor	None	None
Preferred allotment	Noncompetitive bid for $1,000,000 or less	Noncompetitive bid for $1,000,000 or less
Payment by non-institutional investors	Full payment to be submitted with tender	Full payment to be submitted with tender
Deposit guarantee by designated institutions	Acceptable	Acceptable

Key Dates:

Deadline for receipt of tenders	Wednesday, June 16, 1982, by 1:30 p.m., EDST	Wednesday, June 23, 1982, by 1:30 p.m., EDST
Settlement date (final payment due from institutions)		
a) cash or Federal funds	Wednesday, June 30, 1982	Wednesday, June 30, 1982
b) readily collectible check	Monday, June 28, 1982	Monday, June 28, 1982
Delivery date for coupon securities	Thursday, July 8, 1982	Thursday, July 15, 1982

its 26 branches, or the Bureau of the Public Debt. As established by the Treasury's public announcement, competitive tenders must be received by 1:30 P.M. eastern time, while noncompetitive tenders may be received after this deadline provided they are postmarked no later than the day prior to the auction date.

The official printed tender for T notes and bonds usually varies in size and format among the 12 Fed banks. Figure 4–3 shows the tender issued by the Federal Reserve Bank of Richmond, while Figure 4–4 shows the tender furnished by the St. Louis Fed for the same 2-year note. Both basically require the same information.

As these tenders are specially printed up for a specific T note or bond issue, they may not arrive by mail in time for submission when you request a tender form by telephone after its public announcement. However, Fed banks and their branches usually will have these on hand, as well as personnel to assist you in completing the tender if you appear in person to submit it.

Since T notes and bonds are sold at auction, you may buy these securities either by competitive or noncompetitive bidding. By submitting a noncompetitive bid, you agree to pay an unspecified price determined by the average price set by the competitive bidders. Although the eventual average price may be either below, at, or above par, you are guaranteed acceptance of your bid. Like T bills, the Treasury first accepts or satisfies all noncompetitive bids, and the remainder of the offering is filled from the competitive bids, starting from the highest bid price on down.

Competitive bidders must specify the price on the basis of 100 with two decimal places, for example, 99.37, 101.64, etc.

Submitting a Bid without Using a Printed Form

You may purchase T notes or bonds by mail using a simple subscription letter instead of using a specially printed form from the Fed. This letter should basically contain the following information:

- Your home address with zip code.
- Your telephone number during business hours.
- The amount of the T notes or bonds.
- Whether you are submitting a competitive or noncompetitive bid and, if competitive, the price on the basis of 100 to two decimal places.
- The name(s) and taxpayer identifying number(s) of the owner(s).
- Whether you intend to take delivery of the securities in person at the Fed bank or branch or want them mailed to you.

Figure   4–3

Printed Tender for Treasury Notes Used by the Federal Reserve Bank of Richmond

Tender for Treasury Notes of Series T-1984

Dated and bearing interest from June 30, 1982   Due June 30, 1984

TO _____
(Insert—Head Office, Baltimore Branch or Charlotte Branch)

Federal Reserve Bank of Richmond,   Date
Fiscal Agent of the United States:

Pursuant to the provisions of the Treasury Department Offering Circular the undersigned offers to purchase the Treasury Notes as indicated below and on the reverse.

			FOR USE OF FEDERAL RESERVE BANK

NONCOMPETITIVE TENDER* $ $ $

*Tenders for $1,000,000 or less without stated yield from any one bidder may be accepted in full at the average price of accepted competitive bids. This price will be at or more or less than 100.000.

COMPETITIVE TENDERS { $.   @   % $ $
                              @   %
                              @   %
                              @   %

Certification by competitive bidders: The Bidder's ( ) Customer's ( ) net long position in these securities (including those acquired through "when issued" trading, and futures and forward transactions) as of 12:30 p.m. Eastern time on the day of this auction was ( ) not in excess of $200 million; ( ) in excess of $200 million, amounting to $_____ million.

Payment for notes allotted hereunder to financial institutions must be made or completed on or before Wednesday, June 30, 1982 in cash or other funds immediately available by that date as indicated below. Payment in full must accompany tenders from individuals and non-financial institutions.

METHOD OF PAYMENT	DELIVERY INSTRUCTIONS
(Payment cannot be made by credit to Treasury Tax and Loan Account)	☐ Hold in safekeeping for our account $_____
☐ Charge our reserve account $_____	☐ Hold in our General Account $_____
☐ Draft or check on _____ (A. B. A. Number) $_____	☐ Hold in our Trust Account $_____
☐ Payment to be made by _____	☐ Hold in our Dealer Account $_____
(Name of Bank)	☐ Hold as collateral for Treasury Tax and Loan Account $_____
☐ Maturing securities $_____	☐ Deliver to _____

COUPON SECURITIES TO BE ISSUED

Serial Numbers	No. Pieces	Denom.	Amount
		$ 5.000	$
		10.000	
		100.000	
		1.000.000	

Total coupon securities . . . . . . $_____
Total registered securities . . . . . . $_____
(listed on reverse)
Total coupon and registered securities . . $_____

THIS TENDER MUST BE MANUALLY SIGNED BY SUBSCRIBER

TO BE COMPLETED BY INDIVIDUALS AND OTHERS	TO BE COMPLETED BY COMMERCIAL BANKS ONLY
	Certifications
(Name of Individual or Other Subscriber)	WE HEREBY CERTIFY that we have received tenders from customers in the amounts set opposite their names on the reverse which is made a part of this tender. and that we have received and are holding for the Treasury, or that we guarantee payment to the Treasury, of the deposits stipulated in the official offering circular.
(Street and Number)	
(City or Town) (State) (Zip Code)	WE FURTHER CERTIFY that tenders received by us. if any, from other commercial banks or primary dealers for their own account, and for the account of their customers, have been entered with us under the same conditions, agreements, and certifications set forth in this form.
SIGN HERE _____	
(Signature)	
	(Name of Bank)
☐ This is an original tender	(City or Town) (State) (Zip Code)
☐ This is a confirmation	BY _____ (Official Signature) (Title)

IMPORTANT: In order that tenders may be received promptly they should be sent under separate cover and not included with other mail to the Federal Reserve Bank Tenders may be addressed to the Head Office or nearest Branch of this Bank, and the envelope should be marked "Tender for Treasury Notes Series T-1984".

PRIVACY ACT STATEMENT—The individually identifiable information required on this form is necessary to permit the tender to be processed and the securities to be issued. If registered securities are requested, the regulations governing United States securities (Department Circular No. 300) and the offering circular require submission of social security numbers; the numbers and other information are used in inscribing the securities and establishing and servicing the ownership and interest records. The transaction will not be completed unless all required data is furnished.

(left margin, vertical) IMPORTANT — Tenders are invited and will be received up to one-thirty p.m., Eastern Daylight Saving time, Wednesday, June 16, 1982. Noncompetitive tenders mailed will be considered timely if they are postmarked no later than Tuesday, June 15.

Figure 4–4

**Printed Tender for Treasury Notes Used by
the Federal Reserve Bank of St. Louis**

CASH TENDER

TREASURY NOTES OF SERIES T-1984 (CUSIP 912827NH1)

Closing Hour for Receipt of Tenders 12:30 P.M., Central Daylight Saving Time, WEDNESDAY, JUNE 16, 1982
Noncompetitive tenders will be considered timely received if postmarked no later than midnight, TUESDAY, JUNE 15, 1982

To the Federal Reserve Bank of St. Louis   or–
Fiscal Agent of the United States

The _____ Branch   Date _____
(Little Rock)   (Louisville)   (Memphis)

F.R.B.	0 - ST.L.
08	1 - L.R.
	2 - LV.
	3 - MPS.
Cols. 1-3	

① Pursuant to the provisions of Treasury Department Circular dated   June 10, 1982   the undersigned hereby enters tender for
Treasury Notes of Series T-1984, dated and bearing interest from   June 30, 1982   due   June 30, 1984   and will tender payment
therefor as indicated below.

② (LIST YOUR OWN AND CUSTOMERS' TENDERS ON THE REVERSE SIDE)

TO BE A VALID TENDER THIS SECTION MUST BE COMPLETED

		PRICE	SALE PRICE	DIS./PREM.
* NONCOMPETITIVE TENDER $ _____		$	$ _____	$ _____

④

[2] ▲ COL 22 ▼ [1]

*Bidders submitting noncompetitive Tenders should realize that it is possible
that the average price may be above par, in which case they would have to
pay more than the face value for the Notes.
Noncompetitive Tenders for $1,000,000 or less from any one bidder will be
accepted in full at the average price of accepted competitive bids.

Or

COMPETITIVE TENDERS (must be expressed in terms of annual yield with two decimal places, e.g., 7.11. Tenders at a yield that will produce a price less than 99.501 will not be accepted)

$ _____ at the yield of |__|__|__|·|__|__| $ _____ $ _____
$ _____ at the yield of |__|__|__|·|__|__| $ _____ $ _____
$ _____ at the yield of |__|__|__|·|__|__| $ _____ $ _____
$ _____ at the yield of |__|__|__|·|__|__| $ _____ $ _____

⑤ Cols. 23–28   TOTAL $ _____ $ _____

TYPE of SECURITY	Number of Pieces	Denomination (Maturity Value)	Total Amount (Maturity Value)
	(Bearer Securities)		
		$ 5,000	$ __ __ , __ __ __
		10,000	__ __ , __ __ __
		100,000	__ __ , __ __ __
		$1,000,000	__ __ , __ __ __
			__ __ , __ __ __
1	Total (Bearer Securities)		__ __ , __ __ __
2	Registered Securities (See Schedule on reverse side)		__ __ , __ __ __
3	Book Entry Total		__ __ , __ __ __
⑦	Grand Total		__ __ , __ __ __
Col. 46	⑥	(Cols. 29–34)	

DELIVERY INSTRUCTIONS (notes in
bearer form may not be available until after
Thursday, July 8, 1982)

Definitive Securities
☐ Will Call (on or about July 8, 1982)
☐ Forwarded to us by registered mail
☐ Delivery to ....
☐ Please deliver interim certificates for
bearer securities on June 30, 1982
which will be exchangeable for the notes
when available but must be returned at
the expense and risk of the holder.
Hold under book entry procedure at
Federal Reserve Bank as indicated.

☐ For General Acct.
☐ For Investment Acct.
☐ Trust Acct.
☐ Pledged as Treasury Tax and Loan
collateral
☐ Other ....

F.R.B. ONLY

RECEIVED FOR EXCHANGE

$ _____
$ _____
BY

Tender
Checked by _____
Audited by _____
Application
Number _____

③ FINANCIAL INSTITUTIONS ONLY

	Route Symb.	Bank No.	CD
	Cols. 14–17	18–21	

We HEREBY CERTIFY that we have received tenders from customers in the amounts set forth opposite their names on the list which is made a part of this
tender, and that we have received and are holding for the Treasury, or that we guarantee payment of the Treasury, of the deposits stipulated in the official offering
circular.
We FURTHER CERTIFY that tenders received by us, if any, from other commercial banks or primary dealers for their own account, and for the account
of their customers, have been entered with us under the same conditions, agreements, and certifications set forth in this form.

METHOD OF PAYMENT (Please indicate)

Note: Individuals must enclose full payment of Notes
applied for.
☐ Charge our Reserve Account
☐ By Draft in Immediately Available Funds
☐ By Personal Check, Cashiers Check or Bank Money Order
(Checks payable to individual subscriber, and endorsed to
Federal Reserve Bank will not be accepted).

Check No. _____
Drawn on _____
Drawn by _____
Amount $ _____

☐ 8-5/8% Notes T-1982
☐ 8-1/4% Notes H-1982
☐ OTHER _____

Name of Financial Institution or Other Subscriber (Please Print)

Street or Post Office Box

City   State   Zip Code

By _____
Signature   Official Title   Individual's Phone No.

"The Bidder's ( ) customer's ( ) net long position in these
securities (including those acquired through "when issued" trading, and
futures and forward transactions,) as of 12:30 p.m. Eastern time on the
day of this auction, was — ( ) not in excess of $200 million
( ) in excess of $200 million, amounting to
$ _____ million."

- Your address for delivery of the securities and interest checks.
- Your signature and the date.

A sample letter for a noncompetitive bid for a 5-year, 2-month T note illustrating the above required information is shown in Figure 4–5. Your signature along with your original letter is kept on file for future reference.

Mailing Your Tender

If you are mailing a tender for purchasing T notes or bonds using either a printed tender or a subscription letter similar to that shown in Figure 4–5, both the tender/letter and payment for the full face amount should be mailed either to

> Bureau of the Public Debt
> Securities Transactions Branch
> Room 2134, Main Treasury
> Washington, DC 20226

or to the Fiscal Agency Department of the Federal Reserve bank or branch of the district in your area. To minimize delay once your envelope reaches the Federal Reserve, you should include the words *TENDER FOR TREASURY NOTES* (or *BONDS*) at the lower-left corner of the envelope.

Although payment will be in a check made payable to either the Treasury or a specific Federal Reserve bank, and maturing security checks will be endorsed to that Federal Reserve bank, you should nevertheless make it a habit to send your tender/letter by certified mail with a return receipt so you are notified that the tender was received.

After You Submit Your Tender

Once the average competitive bid price has been determined, a noncompetitive bid will be determined as to whether it was below, at, or above par. A below par price means that, for example, a $5,000 face value T note or bond's purchase price was set at an amount below $5,000. In this case, you will receive a refund check for the difference provided you submitted your initial payment covering the face value of the note. If the average price is above par, then you will receive a letter requesting additional funds. Once the engraved security certificates are printed for a particular issue, they will be sent to you by registered mail at the Treasury Department's expense.

Figure 4-5   **Informal Subscription Letter Which Can Be Used for the Purchase
of Registered Treasury Notes from a Federal Reserve Bank**

P. O. Box 9876
Wilmington, DE   19801

November 28, 1980

Fiscal Agency Department
Federal Reserve Bank of Philadelphia
P. O. Box 66
Philadelphia, PA   19105

Dear Sir/Madam:

Please accept in lieu of an official tender, this
subscription letter for the noncompetitive purchase of
5-year, 2-month Treasury notes from the December 3, 1980,
sale as follows:

1. 5-year, 2-month Treasury notes - $9,000.
2. Mailing address: P. O. Box 9876
                      Wilmington, DE   19801
3. Treasury note should be registered as follows:
                      John C. Doe (123-45-6789).

I may be reached during business hours at (302)-555-1234.

Sincerely,

John C. Doe

John C. Doe

Buying T Notes and Bonds through a Bank or Broker

As with T bills, some persons find it more convenient to have their commercial bank or stockbroker submit their tender bid instead of dealing directly with the Federal Reserve Bank or any of its branches. Unlike dealing directly with the Fed where there are no charges or commissions, the bank or broker will charge a fee.

In most cases, the bank or broker will purchase T notes or bonds of a particular series for you on the open market or will sell you issues they themselves have purchased. In this case, you not only pay the "asked" market price, which may be higher or lower than the price at which the particular note or bond was originally issued, but you also pay any accrued interest.

In actuality, prices quoted in newspapers such as *The Wall Street Journal* for T notes and bonds are for lots of $100,000. Consequently, for a certificate of an amount less than $100,000, you will pay a slight premium above this price. Furthermore, you will be charged a commission, which is typically $25 to $35 *for each certificate*. Fro example, you want to buy $8,000 of T bonds. You therefore have four certificates—one $5,000 and three $1,000 certificates. At a rate of $25, you will then be charged $100 as a commission for acting as a broker.

Unlike purchasing tax-free municipal bonds from a broker, virtually all brokers hold the T notes and bonds for you in their vaults. For instance, issues purchased through the firm of Dean Witter Reynolds, Inc., are physically held by Irving Trust Co. in New York. Checks for the coupon interest are then mailed to you when due. However, a lot of people prefer to have the certificate(s) instead of having them held by the broker. If this is the case, brokers may charge you fees up to approximately $75 for each certificate to deliver the securities to you. I personally feel that this handling and paperwork fee is a rip-off as they are already receiving a commission for the transaction.

As for banks, I have generally found them more competitive, but their practices do vary. One Maryland bank charged $25 per certificate for purchasing a security but no fee for its delivery. However, a particular Delaware bank charges $35 for a similar purchase and a $50 fee for the delivery of each certificate; otherwise, they hold them in the vault of their main office.

Although T notes and bonds may, in certain cases, be issued in denominations as low as $1,000, some brokers will not accept purchase orders for amounts less than $10,000 as it may not appear to be worth their trouble. Banks, on the other hand, will generally accept smaller orders. All of this can then be summed up as: *it will pay for you to shop around, comparing prices of banks and brokers and, when possible, minimizing the number of certificates that you buy at one time.*

Rate of Return

Both T notes and bonds carry a fixed coupon interest rate. Consequently, you are able to quickly determine the annual interest. On the other hand, suppose you purchased the security at a price other than at par, which is generally the case. Your interest earnings may be an effective investment yield that may be less or greater than the stated coupon interest rate.

If you purchase a T note or bond below par, i.e., below its face value or less than 100 basis points, then this amounts to purchasing at a discount, and the effective investment yield will be *greater* than the coupon interest rate. On the other hand, if you purchase the security above par or greater than 100 basis points, then the purchase is at a premium and the effective investment yield will be *less* than the coupon interest rate. When the Treasury posts the public announcement of the results of a T note or bond auction, the effective investment yield as well as the coupon interest rate is stated as illustrated by the auction results shown by Figure 4–6.

The determination of the effective investment yield is done through a rather complicated formula. A discussion of an easy-to-use short-cut method for determining the investment yield for notes and bonds is presented in Chapter 7, while BASIC and VisiCalc computer program solutions that can be used on most any of the personal type computers are discussed in Chapter 8.

Payment of Interest

For both T notes and bonds, interest is paid twice a year, or every six months. With registered securities, you receive a Treasury check by mail for each interest payment. For bearer securities, you clip or carefully detach the appropriate coupon from the certificate (like tax-free municipal bonds), which then can be cashed on demand at any commercial bank, or Fed bank and its branches.

Since interest payment for registered T notes and bonds is mailed to the address furnished with the tender or subscription letter, Form PD 345 must be completed if the mailing address changes. This form must be signed by the owner(s) or an authorized representative, show the owner's taxpayer identifying number and old and new addresses, and

Figure 4–6 **Auction Results from the Public Sale of Treasury Notes**

Treasury Notes Draw Average 13.71% Yield In $3.76 Billion Sale

By a WALL STREET JOURNAL *Staff Reporter*

WASHINGTON—The Treasury sold $3.76 billion of five-year, two-month notes at an average annual yield of 13.71%.

The return was down from the 14.01% average at the previous auction of these notes Feb. 24 and the lowest since the 12.83% average on Nov. 24, 1981.

The department received $9.64 billion in bids for the notes and accepted those in a range of 13.67% to 13.73%, including $689 million of noncompetitive bids at the average return. The Treasury accepted 41% of the bids at the highest return. The average price was 99.970.

The Treasury sold an additional $280 million of the notes at the average return to Federal Reserve banks, acting as agents for foreign monetary authorities, to raise fresh cash.

The coupon interest rate was 13¾%, down from 14% in the February action.

The notes will be dated June 2 and mature Aug. 15, 1987.

Courtesy The Wall Street Journal, *May 27, 1982*

include the serial number, title, and denomination of each certificate. As an example:

13½% Treasury Note Series C-1986, dated December 8, 1980, $5,000 S/N 12345

If you do not receive an interest payment check within a reasonable period after a scheduled interest payment date, you should write to:

Bureau of the Public Debt
Division of Securities and Operations
Washington, DC 20226.

On the other hand, if an interest check is lost, stolen, or destroyed after you receive it, then you should write to:

> Treasurer of the United States
> Check Claims Division
> Washington, DC 20227

In either situation, the letter must state:

- The name and address of the owner(s).
- Taxpayer identifying number(s).
- Serial number, denomination, and title of the certificate(s) for which the interest was to be paid.
- The circumstances for this notification.

Obviously, if the check is subsequently received in the mail or found, *you must then notify the Treasurer of the United States, Check Claims Division!*

In certain cases, the first interest payment may be more or less than six months from the issue date. Such is the case, for example, when a 5-year, 2-month T note is issued. The first interest payment is eight months from the issue date and every six months thereafter. This is done so the final interest payment will coincide with the note's maturity date. Consequently, the first interest will be an amount that is larger (actually ⅓ larger) than the remaining regular, 6-month payments. Using a 5-year, 2-month T note having a face value of $1,000 and a 13.5 percent coupon as an example, the first payment, eight months after the issue date, is $90 (i.e., 8/12 × $1,000 × 0.135), while the remaining nine 6-month payments are in equal amounts of $67.50 (½ × $1,000 × 0.135).

At Maturity

When a particular T note or bond reaches maturity, two things happen. First, the last interest payment is made to you, either as a check directly from the Treasury in the case of registered securities, or by cashing the last coupon from bearer type certificates.

The second, and most important event, is that you are now due the payment of the principal or face amount of the security certificate. You may redeem matured certificates, whether they be bearer or registered, at a commercial bank or any of the Fed banks. Since these certificates are basically negotiable, payable on demand, and "possession is 9/10ths of the law," no questions will be asked.

Once matured, T notes and bonds do not continue to earn interest, unlike savings bonds which can usually continue to earn interest for a specified time. However, if for some reason you delay redemption of T notes having maturities of less than seven years by more than three months, or those T notes and bonds having maturities greater than seven years by more than six months, then the Treasury will generally require proof of ownership, requiring the completion of Form PD 1071.

Exchanging, Transferring, or Selling before Maturity

Since you will, in most cases, physically have possession of the T note or bond certificate(s), exchanging, transferring ownership, or selling these securities before they mature is somewhat easier than it is with T bills.

Registered T notes and bonds are eligible for denominational exchange as well as exchange for bearer certificates of the same issue. For example, you might want to break up a $10,000 T note into smaller denominations, such as 2 $5,000 notes, 1 $5,000 and 5 $1,000 notes, or 10 $1,000 notes. In this manner, you are able to sell or transfer any part of your original $10,000 T note.

Bearer issues are also eligible for denominational exchange. However, they may not be exchanged for registered certificates of the same issue unless stated in the original offering announcement. Specific instructions for the issuance and delivery of new certificates must be signed by the owner or his/her authorized representative, and must accompany the certificates that are to be exchanged. Either Form PD 1827 or PD 3905 may be used for this purpose.

For bearer T notes and bonds, the transfer or sale before maturity is the easiest. One way is to let a broker sell them on the open market, for which you will be charged a fee, typically $25. As I know of no reason to the contrary, you can cut out the broker and sell the securities yourself to another person at a mutually agreed price and save the commission costs. As a matter of fact, you can even give away the certificates as a gift to an individual such as a minor or as a donation to a charity without problems, as the Treasury does not have records as to who actually holds claim to its various outstanding bearer T notes and bonds.

Getting Fancy: Zero Coupon Securities and Treasury Mutual Funds, Futures, and Options

Introduction

The conventional and conservative buying and selling of Treasury bills, notes, and bonds, as discussed in Chapters 3 and 4, may be dull to some investors. This chapter is intended for the investor who wants a little more excitement and is looking for alternative methods of buying and selling Treasury securities. Such schemes involve coupon stripping, mutual funds, Treasury futures, and options. Of these, Treasury futures and options involve the highest degree of speculation. The associated risks, then, are substantially higher than the methods discussed in Chapters 3 and 4 and are not recommended for the purely conservative and cautious investor. For those of you who are still interested, you should first carefully read the prospectus outlining the particular investment. Remember, "A fool and his money are soon parted," and ignorance will cost you money.

Coupon Stripping—Zero Coupon Treasury Securities

In the summer of 1982, several major national investment firms kicked off a novel open market method for purchasing and selling obligations of the U.S. government, namely Treasury notes and bonds. This investment method is referred to as *coupon stripping* and has resulted in a class of marketable Treasury notes and bonds called *zero coupon securities*.

The basic idea is that the original purchaser separates, or "strips away" all of the interest bearing coupons of Treasury notes and bonds from the principal certificate. The purchaser then sells either the coupons or the principal certificate as separate investment instruments, usually at different times. Because the interest bearing coupons are stripped away, the note or bond principal is generally sold at a price below the face value of the certificate. On the other hand, dealers also sell the coupons which entitles the holder to a series of semiannual payments. The buyer who buys the stripped, or zero coupon certificate, receives a lump-sum payment when the security matures. When coupon-stripped Treasury issues became available in 1982, European investors were particularly attracted to them because they locked in relatively high interest rates and represented U.S. government obligations that are considered risk free.

Although the U.S. Treasury itself does not issue any notes or bonds in zero coupon form, there are five major brokerage firms that actively buy and sell zero coupon Treasury securites. Like any other new idea, novel acronyms or abbreviations have been used to identify these programs, which are:

- Dean Witter Reynolds, Inc.—Easy-growth Treasury Receipts (ETR).
- E. F. Hutton Group Inc.—Treasury Bond Receipts (TBR).
- Lehman Bros. Corp.—Lehman Investment Opportunity Notes (LION).
- Merrill Lynch, Pierce, Fenner, & Smith Inc.—Treasury Investment Growth Receipts (TIGR).
- Salomon Brothers Inc./Bache Halsey Stuart Shields Incorporated—Multiplier Treasury Receipts, or Certificates of Accrual on Treasury Securities (CATS).

Lehman's lions, Merrill Lynch's tigers, and Bache's cats have been collectively referred to as the "animals." Figure 5–1 shows the October 7, 1982, advertisement in *The Wall Street Journal* describing the CATS zero coupon series offered jointly by Salomon Brothers and Bache. Figure 5–2 shows E. F. Hutton's TBR offering of February 7, 1983.

There is one catch to stripped securities. You will be taxed each year for the income you would theoretically have earned, even though no interest was actually paid. However, these stripped bonds are ideal for approved retirement accounts as they are not subject to any tax until an annuity is paid. Furthermore, stripped bonds are ideal for children if their total income is small enough that no tax liability is incurred.

The Treasury Mutual Fund

How They Work

Rather than the direct purchase of a book-entry T bill, as was discussed in Chapter 3, an alternate approach is to buy shares in a mutual fund whose investments are limited to U.S. Treasury securities that carry the direct guarantee of the U.S. government. This would include T bills, notes, and bonds, as well as those debt securities issued by other governmental agencies, like the Government National Mortgage Association and the Farmers Home Administration. Once in a fund, your investment is spread out over a wide range of Treasury issues with varying maturities and rates which will give you the best yield, especially when interest rates fluctuate up and down on a daily basis. Consequently, you are not locked-in to a specific rate paid by one or several T bills. Furthermore, the initial share investment is substantially less than the $10,000 minimum required for T bills, which makes it attractive for small investors as well as IRA, Keogh, or other tax-sheltered and retirement plans.

Figure 5–1 Advertisement for the Sale of Zero Coupon Treasury
Securities—Salomon Brothers/Bache

This advertisement does not constitute an offer to sell or the solicitation of an offer to buy.
Offers to sell are made only by the Offering Memorandum.

New Issue / October 7, 1982

$50,000,000

MONEY MULTIPLIER TREASURY RECEIPTS*
(**CATS** — Certificates of Accrual on Treasury Securities, Series A)

Price to the Public per Receipt	Amount Payable at Maturity per Receipt	Maturity	Yield to Maturity
$250.00	$1,000	May 15, 1995	11.33%
200.00	1,000	May 15, 1997	11.35

Money Multiplier Treasury Receipts evidence interests in direct
obligations of **The United States of America.**

In lieu of interest, a purchaser of Money Multiplier Treasury Receipts will receive
four or five times the original investment if held to maturity.

Application will be made to list the Receipts on the New York Stock Exchange.

This new issue is designed primarily for purchase by IRA's, Keogh Plans, IRA Rollovers,
Pension Plans and certain other investors not subject to federal income taxes.

Copies of the Offering Memorandum may be obtained from the undersigned.

Salomon Brothers Inc   **Bache Halsey Stuart Shields**
                                   Incorporated

*Trademark of Salomon Brothers Inc

Courtesy The Wall Street Journal, *October 7, 1982*

Figure 5–2   **E. F. Hutton Information Memorandum Concerning Zero Coupon Bonds**

 **Information Memorandum**

Corporate Finance Department   February 7, 1983

$115,312,500
ZERO COUPON
TREASURY BOND RECEIPTS
SERIES 3

Issues:	$65,312,500 Serial TBR's, consisting of 237,500 Units, each with a Face Amount of $275.
	$50,000,000 Principal TBR's, consisting of 50,000 Units, each with a Face Amount of $1,000.
Maturities:	*Serial TBR's:* Semi-annually May 15 and November 15, May 15,1983 to May 15, 1992.
	Principal TBR's: May 15, 1992.
Obligor:	The United States of America is the obligor on all TBR's.
Serial TBR's:	Serial TBR's represent separate claims to interest payments on United States Treasury Notes. The maturity date of each Serial TBR is the coupon payment date of the related Treasury Note. There will be no payments on Serial TBR's prior to their maturity.
Principal TBR's:	Principal TBR's represent claims to principal payments on United States Treasury Notes. The maturity date of each Principal TBR is the principal payment date of the related Treasury Note. No payments will be made on Principal TBR's prior to their maturity.
Discounts:	Both Serial TBR's and Principal TBR's will be sold at deep discounts from face amounts.
Underlying Treasury Securities:	$50,000,000 Principal Amount United States Treasury 13 3/4% Notes due May 15, 1992.
Custodian Bank:	Manufacturers Hanover Trust Company will hold the Treasury Notes for the benefit of TBR owners.
Face Amount and Denominations of Units:	*Serial TBR's—* ● May 15, 1983 – May 15, 1992: Each Unit has a Face Amount of $275. The minimum purchase is 5 Units, and this can be increased by integral multiples of one Unit. *Principal TBR's—* ● May 15, 1992: Each Unit has a Face Amount of $1,000. The minimum purchase is 1 Unit.
Offering Price:	The TBR's will be sold at prices to be determined by E.F. Hutton based upon market conditions at the time of sale. Please check your INF system for current price and yield indications for all maturities. (INF, New Line, TBR 1-6)
Production Credit:	Production credit is expressed as a percentage of dollars invested. See column 8 of page 2.
AE Payout:	Regular corporate syndicate payout of 33%, subject to escalation.
Expected Offering Date:	Monday, February 7, 1983.
Expected Settlement Date:	Tuesday, February 22, 1983.
Call Protection:	Neither the TBR's nor the Treasury Notes can be called for redemption prior to maturity.
Secondary Market:	E.F. Hutton intends to make a secondary market in TBR's.
Form of TBR's:	TBR's will be issued in registered form.
Blue Sky:	This offering is exempt from registration under "Blue Sky" or state securities laws.
Order Procedure:	Orders for TBR's must be entered by face amount (see Column 4 on p. 2) and maturity, *not* by dollars invested. An Operations Wire containing order format and corrections procedures will be sent to each branch.

This special kind of mutual fund, in addition to directly purchasing T bills and similar short-term securities of the U.S. government, usually will also invest in *repurchase agreements* involving these securities. Repurchase agreements are short-term (generally less than one week) instruments through which the mutual fund purchases a security, called the *underlying security*, from a well-established securities dealer or a bank which is a member of the Federal Reserve System. At that time, the bank or securities dealer agrees to repurchase the underlying security at the same price plus a specified interest. Although these repurchase agreements involve risks not associated with the direct purchase of Treasury securities with payments protected by the government, these types of mutual funds nevertheless generally strive to acquire only those purchase agreements that are fully collateralized.

Although most mutual funds specializing in Treasury issues may have the objective of maintaining a constant share value of $1, the price of the fund is not guaranteed or insured. Furthermore, the fund's yield is not fixed, since a rise in market interest rates would probably reduce the value of its portfolio of investments. On the other hand, a drop in market interest rates would increase the portfolio value. The yields of Treasury mutual funds, because of their added safety, are usually slightly lower than money market funds, although it should be emphasized that no mutual fund is directly insured by any federal insurance corporation as are banks (FDIC) and savings and loan association (FSLIC).

Treasury mutual funds, whether called a money market fund or some specific name by an investment company are generally able to provide specific services to shareholders. As an example, the T. Rowe Price U.S. Treasury Money Fund, which is a no-load fund (i.e., no sales commissions), provides the following services in the buying, transferring, and selling of its shares:

- Systematic investing—The shareholder arranges to have regular investments automatically deducted from the bank checking account.

- Automatic withdrawals—The shareholder arranges to make systematic cash withdrawals, either in fixed or variable amounts, from his account.

- Transfer shares—The shareholder can transfer shares in the fund to another owner.

- Redemption of shares—The shareholder can redeem shares by a written check, by telephone, or by telegram.

Advantages and Disadvantages

Unlike buying T bills directly with a minimum purchase price of $10,000 (not including the discount), you can open an account in a Treasury mutual fund for as little as $1,000 to $2,000, while subsequent share purchases can typically be made in amounts of $100 or more. Since you then share in a portfolio of many T bills, etc., which are purchased at different periods of time, your earnings tend to reflect federal money-rate fluctuations. In this manner, you are not locked-in to a specific yield paid on a given date. Although the yield for the fund is not fixed, leaving no measure of price protection, most Treasury money market funds accrue dividends daily and are compounded monthly. Through a no-load fund there are no charges when you purchase or redeem shares, however, there are usually annual management fee charges. If you were to buy a T bill through a bank or broker, you would be charged a commission and probably a safekeeping fee.

As a shareholder in the fund, you can withdraw or redeem part or all of your shares at any time. If you buy a book-entry T bill, you cannot sell it until at least 20 days after its purchase or less than 20 days before maturity. Although you may redeem part of your T bill, the redemption must be in multiples of $5,000, and if the book-entry account is still to be maintained, a minimum balance of $10,000 is required (see Chapter 3).

Since they involve less risk, the yields of Treasury mutual funds are slightly lower than standard money market funds. However, since Treasury mutual funds generally enjoy check writing privilges, they are traditionally higher than the maximum rates permitted by "Notice of Withdrawal," or NOW accounts offered by banks and saving and loans. However, as of December 1982, subject to certain conditions, the interest rate ceiling on NOW accounts is removed and can be as high as external competition permits. In addition, NOW account rates can fluctuate on a daily basis or in some other fixed period determined by the savings institution.

As pointed out earlier, mutual funds, whether they are Treasury funds or money market funds, are not insured, even though the fund's investments are made in direct obligations of the U.S. government. At the present time, to my knowledge, no Treasury mutual fund has collapsed. One last point to be made is that dividends received are generally subject to state and local taxes, as well as federal taxes. This is in contrast to direct purchase of Treasury issues which are subject to federal taxes only. Specific tax treatments of these mutual funds are discussed in Chapter 9.

Treasury Futures

How would you like to control a $1 million T bill with an outlay of up to approximately $5,000? On the surface, it probably sounds too good to be true. In fact, what you would be doing is purchasing a *futures contract* to buy a $1 million T bill at a given price at a given future date. Like soybeans, plywood, and silver, T bills, notes, and bonds can be treated as *commodities.* Since buying or selling even a single futures contract involves a tremendous amount of risk, it is highly speculative, having been estimated that only 20 percent of all futures contracts make money. As a worthwhile caveat, *commodity futures are well beyond the limits of those primarily concerned with safety of principal or steady income.*

Reasons for Commodity Trading

Since there are substantial risks and the odds are against you, why, then, do people buy and sell futures contracts? In order to resolve this, let's consider the following situation.

Suppose your local bank bought a 29-year, $100,000 T bond directly from the Federal Reserve at par (100) with a coupon of 9 percent. If the interest rate of most money instruments later rises to 10 percent, for example, the open market value of this T bond will drop to approximately 90 percent of its par value. On the other hand, if the interest rates decrease to 8 percent, the T bond will be worth approximately 111 percent of its par value. Assume now that the bank needs some extra money. If the bank were to sell its T bond for less than par it would lose money. Banks as a rule prefer to have assets that are stable and predictable.

Since the bank is both a lender and borrower of money market funds, it *hedges* in Treasury futures as a *temporary substitute* for the actual lending or borrowing transaction that will be made at a future date. The hedgers then use the futures market to provide *forward price protection* for their anticipated transactions. Consequently, the bank takes one or more *positions* in the futures market to protect its positions or investments in the cash market.

For each position there has to be someone to take the opposite side of the contract. This may be a *speculator,* who seeks quick profits by buying or selling a given contract. If you have a twinge of greed and dream of making the "big kill" on the market, then you deserve to get all that is coming to you in addition to being labeled a speculator. Commodity trading as a speculator is akin to high-stakes gambling. The wheel of fortune operator yells, "Round and round she goes, where she stops, nobody knows." Furthermore, dealing in futures through a commodities dealer is like dealing with your local bookmaker; it really doesn't matter whether you win or lose, you still have to pay commissions.

Commodity Exchanges

Just as corporate stocks and bonds are traded daily on established and regulated stock exchanges, so are Treasury futures. Although there are over 30 different commodity exchanges in the United States, not all handle Treasury futures. At the present time, the major commodity exchanges trading T bill, note, and bond futures contracts are:

- American Board of Trade—T bills, notes, and bonds.
- Chicago Board of Trade—T bills, notes, and bonds.
- International Money Market—T bills and notes.
- Mid-America Commodity Exchange—T bills and bonds.
- New York Futures Exchange—T bills.

Each exchange, although regulated by the Commodity Futures Trading Commission (CFTC), a federal government agency, is also strictly self-regulated and has its own established rules. Even though several exchanges may trade T bills, for example, there are differences in contract size, trading hours, etc., among these exchanges.

1. T Bills. As an example, the International Money Market (IMM), a division of the Chicago Mercantile Exchange, trades 90-day T bills daily from 8 A.M. to 2 P.M. CST in a basic contract size of $1 million. The index used by the IMM for quoting prices is based on a par value of 100, and is simply the difference between the actual T bill yield and 100. This *IMM index* fits the traditional quotations used in futures trading and is contrary to the normal practice for trading stocks. For example, an IMM index of 91.50 is equivalent to a yield of 100 − 91.50, or 8.50 percent.

Unlike conventional stock and bond trading, there is a maximim price limit that T bill futures can move up or down in a given day. Presently, the IMM allows a maximum "normal" one-day trading limit of 0.60, or 60 points with a minimum price movement of 0.01 (1 point, or "tick"), where one point is worth $25. Consequently, the value of a T bill futures contract can change by as much as $1,500 in either direction from its opening quote. Suppose the opening price for a particular T bill futures contract is 91.50. At the close of that day's trading, the closing price can be either a maximum of 92.10 (up 60 points) or 90.90 (down 60 points) Chapter 7 discusses how to read quotations used by the International Money Market that appear in major daily newspapers.

However, the IMM allows this normal 60 tick limit to be expanded when certain conditions are met. If on two successive days, any month contract closes at the normal 60 tick limit in the same direction, but not necessarily the same month contract on both days, an expanded daily price limit schedule takes effect so that:

- 3d day—150 percent of normal limit (90 points, or $2,250).
- 4th day—200 percent of normal limit (120 points, or $3,000).
- 5th day—200 percent of normal limit (120 points, or $3,000).
- 6th day—normal limit (60 points, or $1,500) if previous day's price move did not reach 120 points; otherwise, the 120 point maximum swing continues until the 120 point limit is reached.

On the other hand, the Mid-America Commodity Exchange (MCE), originally incorporated as the Chicago Open Board of Trade, trades 90-day T bills daily from 8:00 A.M. to 2:15 P.M. CST, except on the last day of an expiring futures contract when trading hours are only from 8:00 A.M. to 10:10 A.M. The MCE trades T bill futures in a smaller basic contract size of $500,000, and the index used by the MCE (i.e., the *MCE index*) for quoting prices is the same as the IMM and is based on a par value of 100.

Presently, the MCE allows a maximum one-day trading limit of 0.60, or 60 points with a minimum price fluctuation of 0.01, or 1 point (tick), where one point is worth $12.50. Consequently, the value of a T bill futures contract traded on the MCE can change by as much as $750 in either direction from its opening quote.

2. T Notes and Bonds. As an example, the Chicago Board of Trade (CBT) trades both T notes and bonds daily from 8:00 A.M. to 2:00 P.M. CST in basic contract sizes of $100,000. The index used by the CBT for quoting prices is based on 1/32d of 1 percent, or $31.25, so that the 100 maximum scale, or par value, equals $100,000—the basic contract size traded by the CBT. The maximim daily price limit for a CBT T note or bond futures contract is 64/32ds, or 2 full points, which is equivalent to $2,000. However, like the IMM, this normal daily limit can be expanded.

Again for comparison, the MCE offers a smaller "mini-contract" size that is one half that of the CBT, or $50,000. T bond futures are traded daily on the MCE from 8:00 A.M. to 2:15 P.M. CST, except on the last day of an expiring futures contract when trading hours are from 8:00 A.M. to 12:15 P.M.

Advantages and Disadvantages

Although the various exchanges that trade contracts on Treasury futures have their own regulations about the conduct of its member firms, there are nevertheless a number of danger areas. Unlike stocks, which are regulated by the Securities and Exchange Commission, futures traders presently have no restriction on taking advantage of "inside information." In fact, it is the successful trader who takes advantage of information that is not public knowledge, or obtains such information well in advance of public disclosure.

A conflict of interest may arise since futures traders can place orders for the public and their own accounts at the same time. Consequently, some investors may pay either too much or receive not as much as they would have otherwise.

Perhaps the only advantage of buying and selling contracts in Treasury futures is the chance of making a nice profit with very little up-front money, whether you are a hedger or speculator. However, unlike the more conservative approaches discussed in this book, you cannot enter the futures game, sit back, and relax for several months. It must be constantly watched, either by you or by the commodity firm acting on your behalf.

Rules to Follow

Since trading futures is a high-stakes game and there are many brokers smooth enough to talk you into doing virtually anything, the following basic rules should be kept in mind if you plan to "ante up" and get into the game.

1. *Invest only money that you can well afford to lose.* If you cannot afford to lose, then you are certainly not in a position to win. Also, do not borrow money in order to invest in futures contracts.

2. *Choose your broker carefully.* Check their track record, their trading experience philosophy, whether or not they have a clean bill of health with the CFTC, as well as the exchanges they trade on. Never agree to open an account by telephone. Deal with a person whom you have met and talked with at your convenience. Get references from other individuals, particularly if they will be completely managing your account. In addition, commissions vary from broker to broker.

3. *Never meet a margin call.* If your broker calls you up needing more money to cover your positions, do not give in. Immediately sell your position and accept whatever losses you have sustained.

4. *Read as much as you can about the futures game before you invest.* This is paraphrased from the often quoted, but true axiom about coin collecting, "Buy the book before you buy the coin." A successful investor is a well-informed investor. In regard to Treasury futures, learn what factors influence prices.

For More Information

The addresses and telephone numbers of the major commodity exchanges are given if you desire more information about futures trading. Each exchange has its own printed pamphlets which are usually free and describe its policies and regulations, as well as including useful technical information. Some of these exchanges have toll-free numbers that may change from time to time but are usually listed in daily editions of *The Wall Street Journal*.

- American Board of Trade
  9 South William Street
  New York, NY 10004
  (212) 943-0100

- Chicago Board of Trade
  141 West Jackson Boulevard
  Chicago, IL 60604
  (312) 435-3558

- International Money Market
  (Chicago Mercantile Exchange)
  30 South Wacker Drive
  Chicago, IL 60606
  (312) 930-3000

- Mid-America Commodity Exchange
  175 West Jackson Boulevard
  Chicago, IL 60604
  (312) 435-0606

- New York Futures Exchange
  21 Broad Street
  New York, NY 10005
  (800) 221-7722

Treasury Options

What are Treasury Options?

Options in Treasury securities are in the middle between actual buying and selling of T bonds, for example, and trading T bond futures. Holders of options are permitted for a specified period of time to control a large face-valued T bond, typically $100,000, with a relatively small amount of money. An option on a specific Treasury security, in a class called *interest rate options*, is the right to buy or sell a given Treasury security at a specified, or *striking* price. The deadline when the option holder must exercise his option is termed the *expiration date*. Consequently, options are classified as diminishing assets as they pay no stated rate of interest. The closer the expiration date, the less time there is for the value of the option to either increase or decrease as the buyer anticipates.

Such Treasury or interest rate options listed by an exchange, in addition to its striking price, also specify the expiration date. Generally, this is the Saturday after the third Friday of the expiration month, and is every three months. The cost of the option is called the *premium*, and varies with the duration of the contract and market activity. In general, shorter term calls have smaller premiums. Chapter 7 discusses how Treasury options are quoted in major daily newspapers.

At the present time, options on Treasury securities are traded by two major exchanges:

- American Stock Exchange (AMEX): $200,000 13- and 26-week T bills; $20,000 T notes.

- Chicago Board of Options Exchange (CBOE): $20,000 and $100,000 T bonds.

Futures on Treasury Options—The Newest Game in Town

As if there were already not enough ways for you to invest your money, the newest game, which is a variation of several others, is called *futures options trading*. Simply stated, a futures option gives you the right to buy or sell a futures contract at a set price within a given period of time. The futures contract, in turn, calls for actual delivery of the commodity at a specified price and time in the future. At present, the only Treasury security being traded as a futures is the T bond, with a contract size of $100,000, and handled by the Chicago Board of Trade.

Temporarily banned by Congress in 1978 as a result of scandals and abuses, this type of trading again started on October 1, 1982, under a three-year pilot program approved by the CFTC. Like the T bond options discussed in the previous section, options on a T bond futures contract enables investors who want to speculate on where T bond prices are going to limit their risk, while at the same time gamble for potentially unlimited gains. However, they stand a very good chance of losing their entire investment.

In order to keep this pilot program above board, the CFTC now requires brokers to read to the investor extensive statements on likely investment risks. In addition to signing a standard form for trading commodities, the investor will receive a special 24-page statement of the risks in and the information on trading in futures options. Unlike the lack of screening potential investors for trading futures, brokers now require a statement of the investor's finances for futures options. Furthermore, all promotional material distributed by brokers must be cleared by the exchange (the CBOT for T bonds futures options) for accuracy.

For More Information

Like commodity exchanges, both the AMEX and CBOE have their own printed pamphlets, which are usually free and describe their policies and regulations, as well as useful technical information. In addition, the CFTC has free printed material about futures options.

- American Stock Exchange
  86 Trinity Place
  New York, NY 10006
  (212) 938-6000

- Chicago Board of Options Exchange
  141 West Jackson Boulevard
  Chicago, IL 60604
  (312) 431-5600

- Commodity Futures Trading Commission
  Education Office
  2033 K Street, N.W.
  Washington, DC 20581
  (202) 254-6387

The Tax Bracket Effect

How Tax Brackets Affect Your Effective Yield

One important point that you should always be aware of is that the interest earned from T bills, notes, and bonds are federally taxable as ordinary income, but *are exempt from state and local income taxes*. The problem then that you must consider is: "Is it worthwhile to invest in Treasury securities when I can get a little higher interest elsewhere but which is also liable for state and local taxes; or when I can purchase a tax-free municipal bond at a lower interest rate that may be exempt from state and local taxes as well as federal taxes?" The answer to this ever-present question among astute investors is determined by the federal, state, and/or local income tax brackets you are in. Whenever someone asks my advice as to whether a particular investment is a good one, I first determine the individual's tax bracket. Otherwise, we are analogous to being in a dark house groping around without a flashlight. Without it, we have virtually no sense of direction of where to go.

For example, suppose that you live in Maryland, which has a combined flat state and local tax rate of 7.5 percent, and you have determined (or were told by a tax expert) that you are in the 39 percent federal tax bracket. Which one of the three following investments would give you the highest percentage yield, assuming that you invested the same amount in all?

1. A 6-month (182-day) T bill at 12.236 percent.

2. A 6-month bank money market certificate at 12.843 percent.

3. A 20-year tax-free state of Maryland municipal bond at 7.25 percent.

For the T bill, which is liable only for federal income tax, the tax-free yield (TFY) is given by the simple formula:

$$TFY = TY \times (1 - FTB) \tag{6-1}$$

where:

FTB = Federal tax bracket
TY = Taxable yield

So that the 12.236 percent T bill now has an equivalent tax-free yield of:

$$
\begin{aligned}
TFY &= 12.236 \times (1 - 0.39) \\
&= 12.236 \times (0.61) \\
&= 7.464\%
\end{aligned}
$$

For the bank money market certificate, which is subject to federal, state, and local taxes, the tax-free yield is determined from:

$$TFY = TY \times (1 - (CSLTB + (FTB \times 1 - CSLTB))) \tag{6-2}$$

where:

CSLTB = Combined state and local tax bracket

Since the state and/or local taxes are deductible from federally taxable income, the above formula considers only the net reduction in federal taxes from the state and/or local exemption—not the entire federal tax bracket. Consequently, the 12.843 percent yield for the 6-month money market certificate has an equivalent tax-free yield of:

$$
\begin{aligned}
\text{TFY} &= 12.843 \times (1 - (0.075 + (0.39 \times 1 - 0.075))) \\
&= 12.843 \times (1 - (0.075 + (0.39 \times 0.925))) \\
&= 12.843 \times (1 - (0.075 + 0.361)) \\
&= 12.843 \times (1 - 0.436) \\
&= 12.843 \times (0.564) \\
&= 7.247\%
\end{aligned}
$$

Consequently, the overall tax bracket by this correct method is 43.6 percent rather than assuming the tax bracket is simply the sum of the federal and state rates, which in this case is 39 percent + 7.5 percent, or 46.5 percent. As summarized in Table 6–1, the 6-month T bill has the best tax-free yield at 7.464 percent. If you were in a lower federal tax bracket, for example 29 percent, then the T bill would be worth 8.688 percent, while the municipal bond would appear to be even worse than before as summarized in Table 6–2.

Table 6–1

Federal tax bracket = 39 percent
Combined Maryland state/local tax bracket = 7.5 percent

	Equivalent Rates	
	Taxable	Tax-Free
6-month T bill*	12.236%	7.464%
6-month MMC†	12.843	7.247
20-year Maryland bond	13.298‡	7.250

* Subject to federal tax only.
† Subject to federal, state, and local taxes.
‡ Assuming federal, state, and local tax liability.

Table 6–2

Federal tax bracket = 29 percent
Combined Maryland state/local tax bracket = 7.5 percent

	Equivalent Rates	
	Taxable	Tax-Free
6-month T bill*	12.236%	8.688%
6-month MMC†	12.843	8.435
20-year Maryland bond	11.419‡	7.250

* Subject to federal tax only.
† Subject to federal, state, and local taxes.
‡ Assuming federal, state, and local tax liability.

On the other hand, suppose you lived in Delaware, where you are determined to be in the 11 percent state tax bracket. In this case, the 6-month T bill has an equivalent tax-free yield (assuming a 39 percent federal tax bracket) of 7.464 percent as before, while the money market certificate now has a tax-free yield of 6.972 percent which is lower than the tax-free municipal bond offered. As is shown by these examples, the tax-free yield will be a function of which state you live in, as well as your federal tax bracket. Tabel 6–3 shows in percentage terms the added after-tax dollar interest earned on 6-month T bills compared with 6-month money market certificates (MMCs), taking into account that banks and savings and loan associations can pay an interest rate that is one fourth of a point (0.25 percent) higher than 6-month T bills.

Table 6–3   **Aftertax Edge of 6-Month T Bills**

| Interest Rate (%) | | State Tax Bracket | | | | | | | | | | | |
Bills	MMC	3%	4%	5%	6%	7%	8%	9%	10%	11%	12%	13%	14%
9.0	9.25	5.1	6.2	7.3	8.4	9.6	10.8	12.0	13.3	14.5	15.8	17.2	18.5
9.25	9.50	5.3	6.4	7.5	8.7	9.8	11.0	12.2	13.5	14.8	16.1	17.4	18.8
9.50	9.75	5.5	6.6	7.7	8.9	10.1	11.3	12.5	13.7	15.0	16.3	17.6	19.0
9.75	10.00	5.7	6.8	7.9	9.1	10.2	11.5	12.7	13.9	15.2	16.5	17.9	19.2
10.00	10.25	5.9	7.0	8.2	9.3	10.5	11.7	12.9	14.2	15.5	16.8	18.1	19.5
10.25	10.50	6.1	7.2	8.4	9.5	10.7	11.9	13.1	14.4	15.7	17.0	18.3	19.7
10.50	10.75	6.3	7.4	8.6	9.7	10.9	12.1	13.3	14.6	15.9	17.2	18.6	19.9
10.75	11.00	6.5	7.6	8.8	9.9	11.1	12.3	13.5	14.8	16.2	17.5	18.8	20.2
11.00	11.25	6.7	7.8	9.0	10.2	11.3	12.6	13.8	15.1	16.4	17.7	19.0	20.5
11.25	11.50	6.9	8.0	9.3	10.4	11.6	12.8	14.0	15.3	16.6	17.9	19.3	20.7
11.50	11.75	7.1	8.2	9.5	10.6	11.8	13.0	14.2	15.5	16.9	18.2	19.5	21.0
11.75	12.00	7.3	8.4	9.7	10.8	12.0	13.2	14.4	15.7	17.1	18.4	19.8	21.2
12.00	12.25	7.5	8.6	9.9	11.0	12.2	13.4	14.6	16.0	17.3	18.6	20.0	21.5
12.25	12.50	7.7	8.8	10.1	11.2	12.4	13.7	14.9	16.2	17.6	18.9	20.2	21.7
12.50	12.75	7.9	9.0	10.3	11.4	12.6	13.9	15.1	16.4	17.8	19.1	20.5	22.0
12.75	13.00	8.1	9.2	10.6	11.7	12.9	14.1	15.3	16.7	18.0	19.3	20.7	22.2
13.00	13.25	8.3	9.4	10.8	11.9	13.1	14.3	15.5	16.9	18.2	19.5	20.9	22.4
13.25	13.50	8.5	9.6	11.0	12.1	13.3	14.5	15.7	17.1	18.5	19.8	21.2	22.7
13.50	13.75	8.7	9.8	11.2	12.3	13.5	14.7	15.9	17.3	18.7	20.0	21.4	22.9
13.75	14.00	8.9	10.0	11.4	12.5	13.7	15.0	16.2	17.6	18.9	20.2	21.6	23.2
14.00	14.25	9.1	10.2	11.7	12.7	13.9	15.2	16.4	17.8	19.2	20.5	21.9	23.4
14.25	14.50	9.3	10.4	11.9	12.9	14.2	15.4	16.6	18.0	19.4	20.7	22.1	23.7
14.50	14.75	9.5	10.6	12.1	13.2	14.4	15.6	16.8	18.2	19.6	20.9	22.3	23.9
14.75	15.00	9.7	10.8	12.3	13.4	14.6	15.8	17.0	18.5	19.9	21.2	22.6	24.2
15.00	15.25	9.9	11.0	12.5	13.6	14.8	16.0	17.2	18.7	20.1	21.4	22.8	24.4

When interest rates are not the same for these three major types of investment instruments (i.e., those completely tax-free, those subject to both federal and state/local income taxes, and those subject only to federal income tax), there is no easy rule of thumb to determine which is the best deal. You will simply have to compute the tax-free yields for each case and compare them. These computations are easily carried on the simplest of nonscientific calculators. For those of you with access to computers, the BASIC and VisiCalc tax-bracket programs presented in Chapter 8 should be of interest.

How to Determine Your Tax Bracket

In the previous section we have seen how one's tax bracket affects the aftertax yield on Treasury securities and how to determine whether or not they offer a significant advantage over other forms of investments. Although attractive for some individuals, Treasury securities may not be advantageous for you.

The concept of the tax bracket must be carefully defined. One method, although incorrect, is to divide one's tax liability (i.e., the amount owed) by adjusted gross income. For example, suppose John Doe had an adjusted gross income of $25,000 and his tax liability on a joint return after taking various deductions and exemptions was $5,000. Using this simple rule, his tax bracket would appear to be $5,000/$25,000, or 20 percent. In actuality, John Doe's tax bracket is found by using the tax tables used to compute the tax return.

To determine your federal tax bracket, you find your taxable income in Table 6–4 for single taxpayers, Table 6–5 for married filing jointly, or Table 6–6 for married filing separately. You then read the corresponding tax bracket. In the case of John Doe, we find that he is actually in the 25 percent bracket, if married and filing a joint return.

Table 6–4

Federal Tax Brackets for Single Taxpayers (1984)

Taxable Income	Tax Bracket
Under $2,300	0
2,300–3,399	11%
3,400–4,399	12
4,400–6,499	14
6,500–8,499	15
8,500–10,799	16
10,800–12,899	18
12,900–14,999	20
15,000–18,199	23
18,200–23,499	26
23,500–28,799	30
28,800–34,099	34
34,100–41,499	38
41,500–55,299	42
55,300–81,799	48
Over 81,800	50

Table 6-5   **Federal Tax Brackets for Married Taxpayers**
                                          Filing Jointly (1984)

Taxable Income	Tax Bracket
Under $3,400	0
3,400–5,499	11%
5,500–7,599	12
7,600–11,899	14
11,900–15,999	16
16,000–20,199	18
20,200–24,599	22
24,600–29,899	25
29,900–35,199	28
35,200–45,799	33
45,800–59,999	38
60,000–85,599	42
85,600–109,399	45
109,400–162,399	49
Over 162,400	50

Table 6-6   **Federal Tax Brackets for Married Taxpayers**
                                         Filing Separately (1984)

Taxable Income	Tax Bracket
Under $1,700	0
1,700–2,749	11%
2,750–3,799	12
3,800–5,949	14
5,950–7,999	16
8,000–10,099	18
10,100–12,299	22
12,300–14,949	25
14,950–17,599	28
17,600–22,899	33
22,900–29,999	38
30,000–42,799	42
42,800–54,699	45
54,700–81,199	49
Over 82,200	50

In reality, this is not the end of the story. As we have seen in the previous section, most states levy income taxes and these also must be considered. Of course if you live in states such as Florida, Texas, New Hampshire, etc., which do not have state income taxes, then your total tax bracket is exactly the same as the federal bracket. Inclusion of the state tax bracket must be done in order to correctly determine the tax advantage (or disadvantage) of comparing certain types of investments.

Some states have a flat tax rate, while others have a graduated scale somewhat like the federal tax. As an example, Table 6–7 shows the graduated tax rate table for the state of Delaware which applies to all taxpayer statuses—married, single, head of household, etc.

Table   6–7

**State of Delaware
Tax Brackets (1984)**

Taxable Income	Tax Bracket
Under $1,000	1.4%
1,000–1,999	2.0
2,000–2,999	3.0
3,000–3,999	4.2
4,000–5,999	5.2
5,000–6,999	6.2
6,000–7,999	7.2
8,000–9,999	8.0
10,000–14,999	8.2
15,000–19,999	8.4
20,000–24,999	8.8
25,800–29,999	9.4
30,100–39,999	11.0
40,000–49,999	12.2
Over 59,000	13.5

How to Read Quotations and Determine Interest, Earnings, and Rate of Return on Treasury Securities

Introduction

Approximately $10 billion of U.S. government securities are traded or sold every business day. The bulk of these secondary market transactions in T bills, notes, and bonds is among bankers, commodity dealers, and brokers who buy and sell these securities after their original issuance, just like municipal or corporate bonds.

Every afternoon the Federal Reserve Bank of New York makes available a list of prices of marketable issues in its "Composite Closing Quotations for U.S. Government Securities" report. The prices listed for the T bills, notes, and bonds are obtained from five securities dealers, with one or more of these dealers being changed from time to time. The New York Fed then determines the listed price from the range of quotations received, although actual purchases or sales of these issues may have taken place at prices higher or lower than those listed by the Fed.

As most of us do not have daily access to the New York Fed or its reports, many of the nation's major daily newspapers, including *The Wall Street Journal*, carry these quotations in their next day's issue. As shown in Figure 7–1, the quotations separately list the trading prices of T bills from notes and bonds.

Reading Treasury Bill Quotations

Using the first T bill quote of August 25, 1982 (shown in Figure 7–1), as an example:

Mat. date	Bid	Asked Discount	Yield
–1982–			
9–2	6.02	5.78	5.87

The first column refers to the T bill's maturity date, which in this case is September 2, 1982. An investor's return on a given T bill is the difference between the purchase price and the subsequent sale price, or when held to maturity, the face value paid by the Treasury. Consequently, T bills are quoted at a discount from the face value, with the discount expressed as an annual rate based on a *360-day year*.

The *bid* quote of 6.02 percent is the annualized percentage return that the *buyer* is looking for. Since this quotation was made on August 25, 1982, or 8 days from the maturity date, the buyer, in order to receive a 5.87 percent annual return, would have to pay $9,986.62 for a $10,000 T bill that matures in 8 days. When it is held to maturity, the buyer will then receive $10,000, which is $13.38 more than he actually paid for it. The $13.38 represents a 5.87 percent annualized return on $10,000.

The *asked* quote of 5.78 percent is the annualized percentage return that the *seller* would like the buyer to accept.

Figure 7-1

**Daily Closing Market Quotations for Traded
Treasury Bills, Notes, and Bonds**

Treasury Issues
* * *
Bonds, Notes & Bills

Wednesday, August 25, 1982
Mid-afternoon Over-the-Counter quotations; sources on
request.
Decimals in bid-and-asked and bid changes represent
32nds; 101.1 means 101 1/32. e-Plus 1/64. b-Yield to call
date. d-Minus 1/64. n-Treasury notes.

Treasury Bonds and Notes

Rate	Mat. Date		Bid	Asked	Bid Chg.	Yld.
11⅝s,	1982	Aug n........ ,,,,	100.1	100.5	− .1	0.00
8⅞s,	1982	Sep n........... , ,	100.1	100.5	...	6.46
11⅜s,	1982	Sep n..........., ,,	100.11	100.13	...	7.13
12⅝s,	1982	Oct n........... , ,,	100.21	100.25	+ .1	7.36
7½s,	1982	Nov n........ , , ,	99.24	99.28	.	7.56
7⅞s,	1982	Nov n........	99.29	100.1	.	7.56
13⅞s,	1982	Nov n........	101.12	101.16	+ .1	7.73
9⅝s,	1982	Dec n........ ,	100.6	100.10	..	8.32
15⅝s,	1982	Dec n........ , ,	102.2	102.6	..	8.35
13⅜s,	1983	Jan n........	101.22	101.26	− .1	9.12
8s,	1983	Feb n........	99.11	99.15	− .1	9.16
13⅞s,	1983	Feb n........	102	102.4	− .1	9.51
9¼s,	1983	Mar n........	99.22	99.26	− .2	9.58
12⅝s,	1983	Mar n........	101.16	101.20	− .2	9.75
14½s,	1983	Apr n........	102.24	102.28	− .2	10.02
7⅞s,	1983	May n........	98.12	98.16	− .2	10.09
11⅜s,	1983	May n........	100.26	100.30	− .1	10.24
15⅝s,	1983	May n........ , , , ,	103.18	103.22	− .10	10.47
3¼s,	1978-83	Jun.	94.24	95.8	− .2	9.53
8⅞s,	1983	Jun n........	98.21	98.25	− .4	10.42
14⅜s,	1983	Jun n........	103.2	103.6	− .3	10.58
15⅜s,	1983	Jul n........	104.15	104.19	− .3	10.56
9¼s,	1983	Aug n........	98.23	98.27	− .3	10.54
11⅜s,	1983	Aug n........	101	101.4	− .2	10.62
16¼s,	1983	Aug n........	104.31	105.3	− .2	10.80
9⅜s,	1983	Sep n........	98.29	99.1	..	10.71
16s,	1983	Sep n........	104.25	105.1	− .1	11.00
15⅞s,	1983	Oct n........	104.18	104.26	− .1	11.04
7s,	1983	Nov n........	96.16	96.24	− .1	9.89
9⅞s,	1983	Nov n........	98.24	99	..	10.77
12⅛s,	1983	Nov n........	100.31	101.3	− .3	11.17
16½s,	1983	Dec n........	99.10	99.18	− .4	10.86
13s,	1983	Dec n........	101.28	102.4	− .2	11.25
15s,	1984	Jan n........	104.11	104.19	− .1	11.43
7¼s,	1984	Feb n........	95.15	95.23	− .1	10.47
15⅝s,	1984	Feb n........	104.18	104.26	− .2	11.57
14⅛s,	1984	Mar n........	103.16	103.20	....	11.57
14¼s,	1984	Mar n........	103.30	104.6	− .2	11.30
13⅞s,	1984	Apr n........	103.4	103.12	− .2	11.40
9¼s,	1984	May	97	97.8	+ .1	11.05
13¼s*	1984	May n........	102.12	102.20	− .4	11.52
1		n........	.2	102.10	− .4	11**
			.4	...		

U.S. Treas. Bills				Mat. date			
Mat. date	Bid	Asked	Yield		Bid	Asked	Yield
		Discount				Discount	
-1982-				-1982-			
9- 2	6.02	5.78	5.87	12-23	8.03	7.89	8.21
9- 9	6.37	6.09	6.19	12-30	8.12	8.00	8.34
9-16	6.49	6.27	6.38	-1983-			
9-23	5.78	5.52	5.62	1- 6	8.25	8.11	8.48
9-30	5.75	5.49	5.60	1-13	8.40	8.26	8.65
10- 7	6.78	6.56	6.70	1-20	8.55	8.41	8.83
10-14	6.79	6.57	6.72	1-27	8.64	8.50	8.94
10-21	6.90	6.68	6.84	2- 3	8.78	8.60	9.07
10-28	7.02	6.80	6.98	2-10	8.85	8.73	9.23
11- 4	7.18	7.02	7.22	2-17	8.87	8.77	9.29
11-12	7.26	7.16	7.37	2-24	8.92	8.84	9.38
11-18	7.36	7.24	7.47	3-24	9.13	9.07	9.65
11-26	7.42	7.34	7.58	4-21	9.33	9.21	9.83
12- 2	7.75	7.61	7.88	5-19	9.52	9.40	10.08
12- 9	7.80	7.66	7.94	6-16	9.61	9.49	10.23
12-16	7.96	7.82	8.13	7-14	9.71	9.59	10.40
				8-11	9.60	9.56	10.42

Courtesy The Wall Street Journal, *August 26, 1982*

Consequently, the seller would receive $9,987.16 for the $10,000 T bill if the buyer is willing to accept an annualized return of 5.87 percent. The bid quote is always higher than the asked quote for T bills, which in turn causes the asked price to be higher than the bid price.

The yield, based on the asked rate, is the annualized rate of return of the T bill if held to maturity and is also known as the equivalent coupon rate. As will soon be shown, the yield is calculated on the amount invested, not on the face value of the T bill. In this example, the investor receives $12.84 more eight days later at maturity than the price he paid on August 25, 1982.

Calculating T Bill Yields

From the published quotations, T bill prices and yields are calculated from knowing either the bid or asked quotes, and the exact number of days to maturity from the quote date. Other than manually counting the days on a calendar, using a "Julian" dated calendar or the table in Appendix H is faster, or for those of you who have access to personal computers (see Chapter 8), the determination is greatly simplified.

Using the bid rate of 6.02 percent, the bid dollar price is found from:

$$\text{PRICE} = \text{FV} - (\text{FV} \times \text{BR} \times \text{DM})/360 \qquad (7\text{--}1)$$

where:

FV = Face value   BR = Bid rate   DM = Number of days to maturity

So a $10,000 T bill maturing in eight days and having a bid of 6.02 percent would be:

$$
\begin{aligned}
\text{PRICE} &= \$10,000 - (10,000 \times 0.0602 \times 8)/360 \\
&= \$10,000 - (4,816.00)/360 = \$10,000 - \$13.38 \\
&= \$9,986.62
\end{aligned}
$$

Using the asked rate in place of the bid rate, we find that a $10,000 T bill with an asked rate of 5.78 percent has a price of:

$$
\begin{aligned}
\text{PRICE} &= \$10,000 - (10,000 \times 0.0578 \times 8)/360 \\
&= \$10,000 - (4,624.00)/360 = \$10,000 - \$12.84 \\
&= \$9,987.16
\end{aligned}
$$

The annualized yield rate is based on the asked quote, so that:

$$\text{YIELD} = (\text{FV} - \text{AP}) \times (365)/(\text{DM} \times \text{AP}) \qquad (7\text{--}2)$$

where:

FV = Face value   AP = Asked price   DM = Number of days to maturity

So a $10,000 T bill, purchased for $9,987.16 and maturing in eight days has an annualized yield of:

$$\text{YIELD} = (10,000 - 9,987.16) \times (365)/(8 \times 9,987.16)$$
$$= (12.84) \times (365)/(79,897.28) = 4,686.60/79,897.28$$
$$= 0.0587 \text{ or } 5.87\%$$

Reading Treasury Note and Bond Quotations

Treasury notes and bonds are quoted differently than T bills since they pay a stated rate of interest. Using the quotations from Figure 7–1, we have the following examples:

Rate	Mat.	Date	Bid	Asked	Bid Chg.	Yld.
16¼s	1983	Aug n ..	104.31	105.3 −	.2	10.80
3¼s	1978–83	Jun	94.24	95.8 −	.2	9.53
7¼s	1984	Aug n ..	94	94.8 −	.6	10.57
10¾s	1990	Aug n ..	93.22	93.30+	.2	11.94
14⅞s	1991	Aug n ..	111.30	112.6 −	.5	12.57

Numbers of the first column identify the issue by the coupon, or stated interest rate, 16¼ or 16.25 percent. The next two columns identify the maturity date, with the "n" indicating that the particular security is a Treasury note, while all others are bonds. Consequently, the first quotation above is often referred to as the "16¼s note of August 1983." If two years are shown, such as 1978–83, the first represents the *call date* while the latter is the maturity date.

The "bid" is the price a buyer is willing to pay for the issue, while "asked" is the price the seller is willing to accept. As with T bills, asked prices are always higher than bid prices. It should be noted that bid and asked quotes for notes and bonds are usually quoted in 32ds of a point. Therefore, a bid of 104.31 is 104 and 31/32ds of a point. If there is only one decimal place such as 101.1, then this is equal to 101 and 1/32ds of a point. For each $1,000 of face value, a full point is then equal to $10, while a 32d equals 31.25 cents. Thus, a quote of 104.31 means a price of:

$$\text{PRICE (104.31)} = (104 \times \$10) + (31 \times \$0.3125)$$
$$= \$1040.00 + \$9.69 = \$1049.69$$

Denominations other than $1,000 (3.g., $5,000) are quoted in multiples of this price.

As an aid, Table 7–1 gives the decimal equivalents of 32ds and 64ths per $100. For the above quote of 104.31 as an example, the table shows that 31/32ds has an equivalent decimal value of $.968750 (i.e., 96.875 cents) per $100. Since this quote is on a basis of $100, then the quote of 104.31 equals $104.968750. Consequently, a $1,000 bond has a price of 10 × $104.968750 or $1,049.6875 (or $1,049.69 when rounded up to the nearest cent).

Following the asked price is the change in the current day's bid price from the closing bid price of the preceding business day. This is also expressed as a 32d decimal. For the August 1983 note, the bid price was 2/32ds ($0.63) lower than the day before on a face value of $1,000.

Table 7–1   **Decimal Equivalents of 32ds and 64ths per $100**

32ds	64ths	Per $100	32ds	64ths	Per $100
+	1	$.015625	16+	33	$ .515625
1	2	.031250	17	34	.531250
1+	3	.046875	17+	35	.546875
2	4	.062500	18	36	.562500
2+	5	.078125	18+	37	.578125
3	6	.093750	19	38	.593750
3+	7	.109375	19+	39	.609375
4	8	.125000	20	40	.625000
4+	9	.140625	20+	41	.640625
5	10	.156250	21	42	.656250
5+	11	.171875	21+	43	.671875
6	12	.187500	22	44	.687500
6+	13	.203125	22+	45	.703125
7	14	.218750	23	46	.718750
7+	15	.234375	23+	47	.734375
8	16	.250000	24	48	.750000
8+	17	.265625	24+	49	.765625
9	18	.281250	25	50	.781250
9+	19	.296875	25+	51	.796875
10	20	.312500	26	52	.812500
10+	21	.328125	26+	53	.828125
11	22	.343750	27	54	.843750
11+	23	.359375	27+	55	.859375
12	24	.375000	28	56	.875000
12+	25	.390625	28+	57	.890625
13	26	.406250	29	58	.906250
13+	27	.428175	29+	59	.928175
14	28	.437500	30	60	.937500
14+	29	.453125	30+	61	.953125
15	30	.468750	31	62	.968750
15+	31	.484375	31+	63	.984375
16	32	.500000	32	64	1.000000

The yield, or equivalent coupon rate, is the annualized percentage return an investor receives if the note or bond is purchased on the day of the quotation at the asked price and then held to maturity. However, if the note or bond has a call provision, and the quotation date is earlier than the call date, the yield is termed *yield to call* rather than yield to maturity.

Calculating Note and Bond Yield to Maturity (or Call)

There exist several methods which may be used to calculate the yield of maturity (or call) for notes and bonds. The method given here is one of the simplest, yet gives answers that are within a 2 percent error of the quoted yields.

1. Determine the purchase (asked) price in dollars and cents.
2. Subtract the purchase price from the face value and divide the answer by the number of years to maturity (or call). This is the amount

of profit per year. If the purchase price is greater than the face value, than this is the amount of loss per year.

3. Add to the amount of yearly profit, or loss from Step 2, one year's interest based on the stated coupon rate. This is the amount of income you will receive each year.

4. Divide the yearly income from Step 3 by the purchase price from Step 1.

5. Divide the yearly income from Step 3 by the difference between the face value of the note or bond and the amount of profit (or loss) per year from Step 2.

6. Add the results in Steps 4 and 5 and divide by 2.

7. Multiply the result from Step 6 by 100 to express the yield in terms of a percentage.

As an example, consider the 10¾ percent note with an asked price of 93.30 maturing in August 1990, which is eight years away. The following calculations are then performed as described above:

1. Purchase price (93.30) = (93 × $10) + (30 × $.3125) = $939.38.

2. (1,000 − 939.38)/(8 years) = $7.58 per year.

3. $7.58 + (10.75%) × ($1,000) = $115.08.

4. $115.08/$939.38 = 0.1225.

5. $115.08/($1,000 − $7.58) = 0.1160.

6. (0.1225 + 0.1160)/2 = 0.1192.

7. 0.1192 × 100 = 11.92%.

Consequently, the yield to maturity is found to be 11.92 percent, which favorably compares with the 11.94 percent (a 0.17 percent difference) quoted in the newspaper.

The previous example illustrated the determination of the yield to maturity of a note selling at a discount, i.e., less than 100. Now let's take the 14⅞ note of August 1991, which matures in nine years and has an asked price of 112.6.

1. Purchase price (112.6) = (112 × $10) + (6 × $.3125) = $1,121.88.

2. (1,000 − 1,121.88)/9 = − $13.54 (i.e., loss per year).

3. − $13.54 + (14.875%) × ($1,000) = $135.21.

4. $135.21/$1,121.88 = 0.1205.

5. $135.21/($1,000 + $13.54) = 0.1334.

6. (0.1205 + 0.1334)/2 = 0.1270.

7. 0.1270 × 100 = 12.70%.

In this case, the purchase price of the note was at a premium, i.e., greater than 100 basis points, so that the yield to maturity is less than the stated coupon rate.

Reading Quotations on Treasury Futures

Futures quotations on Treasury securities are quoted daily in *The Wall Street Journal*, as well as a number of major daily newspapers such as *The New York Times*. A typical daily quotation for T bill futures traded on the International Money Market (IMM) might appear as shown in Table 7–2. The open, high, and low quotations, taking the March 1983 contract for a $1 million T bill as an example, are the respective prices (or yields) at which that contract first traded on that day (91.72, or 8.28 percent), its highest trade price (92.09, or 7.91 percent, and its lowest trade price (91.72, or 8.28 percent). Instead of quoting a closing price as is done with stocks, a *settlement price* is given. Since there are usually many trades made at the last minute of the trading day, it is virtually impossible to determine which trade was the last one made before the market closed. Consequently, the IMM averages out the prices at which all the last trades occurred, which is the settlement price.

In this example, the change in the settlement price from the previous day's trading was + 0.08, or up 8 IMM points. Each IMM point for T bills is equal to $25 so that the contract holder made 8 × $25, or $200 from one day to the next. Although the minimum price movement is .01 (1 point, or $25), the maximum normal IMM daily trading limit is 60 points up or down, which is equivalent to $1,500. As discussed in Chapter 5, this limit can be expanded when certain conditions are met.

The discount quotes for the "settle" and "change" columns are generally useless for the average speculator. For the March 1983 contract, the discount settlement yield of 8.12 percent is found from subtracting the settlement price from 100, so that 100 − 91.88 equals 8.12 percent. The *open interest* quotation is the number of contracts outstanding on

Table 7–2   **Typical International Money Market Quotations for 90-Day T Bill Futures**

Treasury Bills—$1 mil.; pts of 100 percent

	Open	High	Low	Settle	Change	Discount Settle	Discount Change	Open Interest
Mar83	91.72	92.09	91.72	91.88	+.08	8.12	−.08	25,604
June	91.59	91.94	91.58	91.76	+.12	8.24	−.12	12,784
Sept	91.26	91.54	91.26	91.42	+.10	8.58	−.10	4,267
Dec	90.98	91.19	90.97	91.07	+.08	8.93	−.08	2,016

that day. Consequently, T bill traders were holding over $25.6 billion worth of March 1983 T bill futures contracts.

The actual dollar value of a $1 million T bill quoted in terms of the IMM index can be easily determined. Taking the "open" price quote of 91.72 for the March 1983 contract again as an example:

1. Quote of 91.72 equals a yield of $100 - 91.72$, or 8.28%.

2. 8.28% equals 828 points.

3. 828 points $\times$ $25/point equals $20,700.

4. Price equals $1,000,000 less $20,700, or $979,300.

In terms of a simple formula, this four-step process becomes:

$$\text{Price} = \$1,000,000 - (100 - \text{IMM}) \times (2500) \qquad (7-3)$$

Using the above quote of 91.72, we have:

$$\begin{aligned}
\text{Price} &= \$1,000,000 - (100 - 91.72) \times (2500) \\
&= \$1,000,000 - (8.28) \times (2500) = \$1,000,000 - \$20,700 \\
&= \$979,300
\end{aligned}$$

Consequently, the price of the T bill for the March 1983 contract varied from $980,225 (92.09) and $979,300 (91.72), while settling at $979,300. This represents an increase of $200 over the previous day's trading. Normally a speculator is not interested in the actual price as much as he is in the *net point change*. If you bought a T bill contract at 90.05 (a yield of 9.95 percent) and sold it at 91.57 (8.43 percent), the net change is $90.05 - 91.57$, or $- 1.52$, which equals 152 points. At $25 a point, you lost $3,800.

Shown in Table 7–3 is a typical quotation for one day's activity on the Chicago Board of Trade (CBT) for 6½- to 10-year T notes, which is given in a format similar to that for T bills. The open, high, and low quotations have the same meaning as for the T bill quotations of Table 7–2, except that notes and bonds are quoted in 32ds of 1 percent. The "high" quote of 83–29 for the March 1983 contract means 83 and 29/32 points. This appears to be very low compared with T bill quotes on a scale of 100.

Table   7–3   **Typical Chicago Board of Trade Quotations for Treasury Notes Futures**

Treasury Notes—$100,000; pts 32ds of 100 percent

	Open	*High*	*Low*	*Settle*	*Change*	Discount *Settle*	Discount *Change*	*Open Interest*
Mar83	83–00	83–29	82–30	83–15	+10	10.738	−.059	7,864
June	82–00	82–31	82–00	82–16	+10	10.919	−.059	3,304

However, T note and bond contracts quoted by and traded on the CBT are based on a conversion factor so that the price of any note or bond will equal 8 percent when delivered. Consequently, the actual price of the security varies with the prevailing interest rate. In this case, the discount "settle yield" is quoted at 10.738 percent for the March 1983 contract which translates to a "standardized" yield of 8 percent.

Each 1/32d point for both CBT T note and bond futures is equal to $31.25 (i.e., 1,000 × 1/32), so that the 100 point maximum scale, or par value equals $100,000—the basic trading contract size. The minimum price movement allowed by the CBT is 1/32d point ($31.25), while the maximum daily limit is 64/32ds, or 2 points. This is equivalent to $2,000, although this limit may also be expanded.

The actual dollar value of any CBT quote is easily determined. Using the 83–29 quote as an example:

1. Quote of 83–29 equals 83–29/32.
2. (29) × ($31.25) = $906.25.
3. (83) × ($1,000) = $83,000.
4. Price = $83,000 + $906.25, or $83,906.25.

If you bought a T note contract at 83 16/32 and later sold it at 84 4/32, the net change is + 20/32 points. This represents a profit of 20 × $31.25, or $625.

Reading Quotations on Treasury Options

Treasury securities options traded by either the American Stock Exchange (AMEX) or the Chicago Board of Options Exchange (CBOE) are quoted in the same manner. As an example, the typical CBOE quotation of Table 7–4 is for the underlying issue of a T bond that is the 10⅜s issue of 2007–12. That is, this bond has a maturity of November, 2012 (i.e., the "11/12"), with a call date of November, 2007. The annual coupon rate is

---

Table 7–4   **Typical Chicago Board of Options Exchange Quotation for T Bonds**

U.S. Treasury Bond—$100,000 Principal Value

Underlying Issue	Strike Price	Calls-Last			Puts-Last		
		Mar	June	Sept	Mar	June	Sept
10⅜% bond due 11/12	96	3.22	3.30	....	....	....	....
	100	....	2.0	....	0.22	....	....
	104	....	0.17	....	....	....	....

10⅜ percent, so that the holder of this bond receives semiannual interest payments of $5,187.50 on the bond's $100,000 principal value.

Suppose this quotation was given at the close of trading on Thursday, March 3, 1983. One option to buy or sell such a $100,000 T bond is at the striking, or exercise price of 96 points, while other options are at prices of 100 and 104 points. Typically the striking price is quoted in intervals of 2 points, although the CBOE on occasion expands this interval to 4 points to reflect increased market volatility.

The premium, which is the cost of the option, is quoted in whole points and 32ds of a point for both call and put options. Each 1/32d point equals $31.25, so that each whole point equals $1,000 on a standard contract covering a $100,000 T bond as the underlying issue. At a striking price of 96 points, equivalent to $96,000, the March call contract had a premium price of 3.22, which means 3 22/32 points, or $3,687.50. Consequently, for $3,687.50 you can buy the option to purchase this particular $100,000 T bond at a price of $96,000. If this option is exercised by the Saturday following the third Friday of March 1983 (i.e., March 19th), then your total outlay for the T bond is the premium plus the strike price, or $99,687.50. This is in addition to having to pay the bond holder accrued interest, which would be approximately $3,458 for the four-month period from November 1982 to March 1983. For comparison, the average closing asked price on the open market for this T bond was quoted at 99.20 (i.e., 99 20/32), or $99,625.00. On the other hand, if you wanted to buy a June call option at a striking price of 96, then you would pay a premium of 3.30 points, or $3,937.50. At the strike price of 96 in this quotation, there was no market activity for contracts having September 1983 expirations.

Suppose you are lucky enough to own this particular T bond. You could only buy a put, or sell option for the March 1983 expiration at a strike price of par (100 points, or $100,000) for the premium price of 0.22, which is equivalent to 22 × $31.25, or $687.50. If you then exercise this option to sell your T bond, your net result is the strike price less the premium paid, or $99,312.50 in addition to receiving approximately four months worth of accrued interest on one semiannual coupon from November 1982 to March 1983.

Reinvesting the Interest from Notes or Bonds

Depending on what you do with the twice-a-year interest payments, the quoted or computed yield to maturity may not be what you will actually earn. It is very important that yield-to-maturity figures take into account that the periodic interest from the note or bond will be *reinvested upon receipt at a rate that equals the quoted yield to maturity at the time you purchased the security.* This is a very important and fundamental concept to remember. If these future reinvestments of periodic interest payments are made at a rate that is less than the stated yield to maturity at the time of purchase, then the true yield to maturity will be less than the stated yield. On the other hand, if these reinvestments are made at a higher rate, then the yield to maturity will be higher than the stated yield.

To illustrate how this is possible, let's assume that we purchased the 10¾ note of August 1990, whose face value is $1,000, at 93.30 (i.e., $939.38) on August 25, 1982, with a stated yield to maturity of 11.94 percent. Therefore, each coupon when redeemed will give us (10.75 percent) × $1,000/2, or $53.75 in interest. If we merely accumulate these 16 periodic interest payments, we will have $860 in interest after eight years when the note matures. The total value of our investment after eight years is then $1,860. The true realized yield to maturity can be then found from the formula:

$$i = \left(10^{\frac{1}{n} \log(S/P)} - 1\right) \times 100 \tag{7-4}$$

where:

i = True realized yield to maturity rate
n = Number of years to maturity
P = Purchase price (principal)
S = Value at maturity (future value)

Using the above information, we now find that the true realized yield to maturity is:

$$i = \left(10^{\frac{1}{8} \log(1860.00/939.38)} - 1\right) \times 100$$

$$= \left(10^{\frac{1}{8} (0.2967)} - 1\right) \times 100$$

$$= (1.0891 - 1) \times 100$$

$$= 8.91\%$$

This is about 25 percent less than the stated yield of 11.94 percent.

Now let's reinvest the 16 periodic interest payments of $53.75 at a 10.75 percent rate. The total amount earned from our reinvestments is found from:

$$S = P\frac{\left(1 + \frac{i}{2}\right)^n - 1}{i/2} \tag{7-5}$$

$$= (\$53.75)\frac{\left(1 + \frac{0.1075}{2}\right)^{16} - 1}{(0.1075/2)}$$

$$= \$1,311.01$$

The total value at maturity is therefore $2,311.01, so that the true realized yield to maturity is:

$$i = \left(10^{\frac{1}{8} \, \log \, (2311.01/939.38)} - 1\right)$$
$$= (1.1191 - 1) \times 100$$
$$= 11.91\%$$

This is essentially the quoted yield to maturity of 11.94 percent when the note was purchased on August 25, 1982.

Table 7–5 summarizes the above calculations for these and other interest rates up to 15 percent. It can now be seen that the true realized yield to maturity can possibly vary from 8.91 percent to 13.37 percent even though the stated yield to maturity at the time of purchase was 11.94 percent. Baron de Rothchild once exclaimed that compound interest was the "eighth wonder of the world." We have just shown how compound interest, or the lack of it, on our periodic reinvestments can either help or hurt our investment.

Table 7–5   **Effect of Reinvestment Rate on the True Realized Yield to Maturity**

Face value of note: $1,000
Coupon rate: 10.75 percent
Coupon payment: $53.75
Asked (purchase) price: 93.30 ($939.38)
Years to maturity: 8
Quoted yield to maturity at purchase: 11.94 percent

Reinvestment Interest Rate	Interest without Reinvestment	Interest Including Reinvestment*	Total Value Including Principal	True Realized Yield to Maturity†
0	$860.00	$ 860.00	$1860.00	8.91%
5	860.00	1041.69	2041.69	10.19
7	860.00	1127.16	2127.16	10.76
9	860.00	1221.16	2221.16	11.36
10	860.00	1271.59	2271.59	11.67
10.75	860.00	1311.01	2311.01	11.91
11	860.00	1324.46	2324.46	11.99
12	860.00	1379.90	2379.90	12.32
13	860.00	1438.03	2438.03	12.66
14	860.00	1498.98	2498.98	13.01
15	860.00	1562.90	2562.90	13.37

* Using Equation 7–4.
† Using Equation 7–5.

Amortization of Premiums

Under present regulations, all holders (except brokers and other dealers in Treasury securities) of those T notes and bonds bought at a premium can amortize the premium paid. Consequently, amortization reduces one's basis for determining the possible gain or loss when the security either is sold on the open market or matures.

When the purchase price of a T note or bond is higher than the value at maturity, the purchaser's capital can effectively be kept intact by setting aside a portion of the interest paid from the redeeming coupons so that the total of this amount will equal the amount of the premium at maturity (or call). The systematic method of computations is:

1. Compute the interest at the yield-to-maturity rate on the book value.
2. Subtract this from the interest of each coupon.
3. Apply this difference to periodically reducing the book value.

Consequently, this method gradually decreases the book value of the security so that, at maturity or call, the book value then equals the face value.

As an example, suppose a $1,000 Treasury note that has a 12¾ percent coupon was purchased at the asked price of 106.31. Furthermore, since the note matures in four years, the yield to maturity was quoted to be 10.57 percent.

The purchase price of the T note is $1,069.69, which is the initial investment on which a 10.57 percent yield is to be realized after eight semiannual interest payments of 6.375 percent times $1,000, or $63.75—still an annual rate of 12.75 percent. When the first coupon is redeemed, the buyer receives $63.75. However, the buyer actually receives 10.57/2 percent times the present book value, or purchase price, of $1,069.69, or $56.53 in interest, while the difference between this amount and the $63.75 coupon interest payment ($7.22) can be thought of as a *partial return* of the buyer's premium. Consequently, the $7.22 is capital for reinvestment and is no longer considered part of the investment in the bond. These partial returns of capital will equal the total premium, in this case $69.69, when the note matures (or is called), thereby keeping the buyer's capital intact. Each semiannual interest payment then shows a decreased note investment and an increased portion of the note's interest applied to the amortization of the premium. The money invested in the note at any time is termed the *book value* of the note. The amortization schedule in Table 7–6 shows how the book value finally equals the matured face value of the T note for this example.

An alternate but simpler method to amortize the premium paid on a T note or bond is used the *straight-line* method. By this method, the amortization amount of the premium is equally divided over the total number of interest payments. Using the previous example, the premium of $69.69 is then divided into eight semiannual amounts of $69.69/8, or $8.71 when rounded off to two decimal places. Table 7–7 shows the amortization schedule using the straight-line method.

Table 7-6   **Amortization Schedule of the Premium of a T Note**

Face value: $1,000
Purchase price: $1,069.69
Coupon rate: 12.75 percent per annum
Yield to maturity: 10.57 percent
Years to maturity: 4

Year	Payment	Interest on Book Value @10.57 percent pa*	Coupon Payment	Amount for Amortization of Premium	Book Value
					$1,069.69
1	1	$56.53	$63.75	$ 7.22	1,062.47
	2	56.15	63.75	7.60	1,054.87
2	3	55.75	63.75	8.00	1,046.87
	4	55.33	63.75	8.42	1,038.45
3	5	54.88	63.75	8.87	1,029.58
	6	54.41	63.75	9.34	1,020.24
4	7	53.92	63.75	9.83	1,010.41
	8	53.40	63.75	10.41†	1,000.00
Total				$69.69	

* All calculations rounded off to two decimal places before proceeding with the next calculation.
† This actual amortization amount is actually $10.35 which would result in a final book value of $1,000.07 The $0.07 is then added so that the book value at maturity equals the face value.

Table 7-7   **Amortization Schedule of the Premium of a T Note**
Using the Straight Line Method

Face value: $1,000
Purchase price: $1,069.69
Coupon rate: 12.75 percent per annum
Yield to maturity: 10.57 percent
Years to maturity: 4

Year	Payment	Amount for Amortization of Premium	Accumulated Amortization	Book Value
				$1,069.69
1	1	$8.71	$ 8.71	1,060.98
	2	8.71	17.42	1,052.27
2	3	8.71	26.13	1,043.56
	4	8.71	34.84	1,034.85
3	5	8.71	43.55	1,026.14
	6	8.71	52.26	1,017.43
4	7	8.71	60.97	1,008.72
	8	8.72	69.69	1,000.00

The tax consequences of the amortization of a note or bond premium
is discussed in Chapter 9.

Introduction

With the advent of the electronics revolution, many investors now own their own personal computer or have ready access to one. This chapter discusses several useful computer programs, both written in BASIC[1] and using VisiCalc®,[2] that can be used to assist you in the buying and selling of Treasury securities as well as other promising investments. Those programs written in BASIC can be run on virtually any computer having a BASIC interpreter and 16k (16,384 words) of "read/write" memory, such as the Radio Shack TRS-80, Apple II, Atari, Commodore's PET and CBM, IBM personal computer, etc.

Most of the BASIC programs presented are also able to be run using VisiCalc. As with the BASIC programs, the source listings and examples are also presented in the VisiCalc format. Whether using BASIC or Visi-Calc, this chapter is not meant to be a crash course in programming or to teach you how to use BASIC or VisiCalc, but rather presents a number of useful ready-to-run financial routines. In addition, this chapter discusses how computers can talk to other computer systems, such as the Dow Jones News Service and THE SOURCE, to obtain up to date financial information about Treasury securities.

Using BASIC

The following programs were written in "Microsoft" BASIC and were tested with the aid of both the Radio Shack TRS-80®[3] Model I and Model III computers. For the most part, these programs are compatible with other versions of BASIC. Individual statements on multiple statement lines in the BASIC source code listings presented in this chapter are separated by a colon (:), while exponentiation (the raising to a power) is indicated by the "up-arrow" character (↑). Since these programs are intended to be kept as simple and short as possible, there are no extensive error-trapping techniques used for input quantities, such as testing for unreal dates, invalid numbers, etc. For each program, both the BASIC source code listing and at least one sample printout are presented.

For those of you having a printer, all calculated results can be directed to the printer, providing a permanent record instead of the computer's video display. Since there are now literally dozens of computer systems available, the following discusses how these BASIC programs can be modified to give printer-oriented outputs on the TRS-80, Apple II, and

---

[1] BASIC is a computer language developed at Dartmouth College.

[2] VisiCalc is a registered trademark of VisiCorp.

[3] TRS-80 is a registered trademark of the Tandy Corporation.

IBM Personal Computer. For those of you with other systems, refer to your operator's manual.

1. Radio Shack TRS-80. All PRINT statement syntaxes can be changed to the corresponding LPRINT syntax, which then directs the output to the printer instead of the video display. This change works both with nondisk and all disk operating systems (DOS), such as TRSDOS, NEWDOS, DOSPLUS, LDOS, and VTOS. If this change is made, then no printed results appear on the screen other than those questions asked by INPUT statements. As an example, the statement

$$240 \text{ PRINT"CURRENT YIELD } = \text{ ";CY;"\%"}$$

is changed to

$$240 \text{ LPRINT"CURRENT YIELD } = \text{ ";CY;"\%"}$$

if this line is to be sent to the printer instead of the video display.

On the other hand, some operating systems have a "screen print" feature which allows the entire contents of the video display at a particular time to be copied by the printer simply by pressing two or more keys simultaneously. These are:

- TRSDOS 1.3 (Model III only): SHIFT-DOWN ARROW-*
  TRSDOS 2.0 (Model II only): type the command,
    SYSTEM "SCREEN".

- NEWDOS+, NEWDOS/80, VTOS, LDOS: J-K-L.

- DOSPLUS 3.4: SHIFT-CLEAR.

2. Apple II. For the Apple II system, the printer interface card is inserted into Slot 1. To enable the printer, the BASIC statement

$$\text{PRINT "PR\#1"}$$

must be inserted before the desired PRINT statement in the program. All program PRINT statements will then be printed until stopped by the inverse statement:

$$\text{PRINT "PR\#0"}$$

3. IBM Personal Computer. Like the TRS-80, all PRINT statement syntaxes can be changed to the corresponding LPRINT syntax. This change works both with nondisk and IBM's DOS (version 1.10). If this change is made, no printed results appear on the screen other than those questions asked by INPUT statements.

On the other hand, the IBM DOS does have a screen print feature which is activated by simultaneously pressing the "shift," or ↑ key, and the "PrtSc" key.

Determining the Number of Days between Two Dates

When buying, transferring, or selling Treasury securities, it is usually important to know how many days there are between two given dates. Using the simplest approach, we could take an ordinary calendar and manually count the days. However, we would probably tend to make an error in the count, especially if the number of days is greater than 60.

The DATE1 program of Figure 8–1 will determine the number of days between two dates, taking into account all leap years. For this program, all dates used as input information must be entered in the "extended date" form MM/DD/YYYY. For example, June 14, 1975, is to be entered as 06/14/1975, not 6/14/75.

Figure 8–1   **BASIC Source Listing for DATE1 Program**

```
100 REM      ---- DATE1 PROGRAM ----
110 DIM DM(12),WD$(7),MN$(12)
120 FOR I=1 TO 12: READ DM(I): NEXT
130 FOR J=1 TO 7: READ WD$(J): NEXT
140 FOR K=1 TO 12: READ MN$(K): NEXT
150 DATA 31,28,31,30,31,30,31,31,30,31,30,31
160 DATA "SUNDAY","MONDAY","TUESDAY","WEDNESDAY","THURSDAY",
    "FRIDAY","SATURDAY"
170 DATA "JANUARY","FEBRUARY","MARCH","APRIL","MAY","JUNE","JULY",
    "AUGUST","SEPTEMBER","OCTOBER","NOVEMBER","DECEMBER"
180 INPUT"EARLIER DATE (MM/DD/YYYY) ";D1$
190 Y1=VAL(RIGHT$(D1$,4)): M1=VAL(LEFT$(D1$,2)): D1=VAL(MID$(D1$,4,2))
200 Y=Y1:M=M1:D=D1: GOSUB 330 :GOSUB 370  :GOSUB 450
210 GOSUB 820
220 PRINT:INPUT"LATER DATE (MM/DD/YYYY) ";D2$
230 Y2=VAL(RIGHT$(D2$,4)):M2=VAL(LEFT$(D2$,2)):D2=VAL(MID$(D2$,4,2))
240 Y=Y2:M=M2:D=D2:GOSUB450
250 GOSUB820
260 GOSUB 540
270 PRINT:PRINT"THEN:":PRINT"NUMBER OF DAYS BETWEEN DATES =";N
280 F1=N/365: F2=N/366
290 F=(3*F1+F2)/4
300 FY=INT(F*100+.5)/100
310 PRINT"NUMBER OF YEARS BETWEEN DATES =";FY
320 END
330 L=0:IF INT(Y/4)*4<>Y THEN RETURN : REM  DETERMINE LEAP YEAR
340 IF INT(Y/100)*100<>Y THEN 360
350 IF INT(Y/400)*400<>Y THEN RETURN
360 L=1: RETURN
370 DX=0:IF M=1 THEN 390 : REM  CONVERT DATE TO JULIAN DATE
```

Figure 8–1 (*concluded*)

```
380 MX=M-1: FORI=1 TO MX: DX+=DX+DM(I):NEXT
390 DX=DX+D
400 IF M<3 THEN 440
410 GOSUB 330
420 IF L=0 THEN 440
430 DX=DX+1
440 YX=Y-INT(Y/100)*100: JD=YX*1000+DX:RETURN
450 GOSUB 330  : REM   DETERMINE DAY OF WEEK
460 IF L=0 THEN 470   ELSE DM(2)=29
470 W=Y-1751 + INT((Y-1753)/4)- INT((Y-1701)/100)
480 W=W+INT((Y-1601)/400)
490 W=W-INT((W-1)/7)*7
500 MX=M-1: IF MX=0 THEN 520
510 FORI=1 TO MX:W=W+DM(I):NEXT
520 W=W+D-1: W=W- INT((W-1)/7)*-
530 DM(2)=28: D$=WD$(W) : RETURN
540 M=M1:D=D1:Y=9999:GOSUB 370  : REM   DETERMINE # DAYS BETWEEN DATES
550 JY=JD-INT(JD/1000)*1000
560 M=M2:D=D2:GOSUB370
570 JZ=JD - INT(JD/1000)*1000
580 N=JZ - JY+365*(Y2-Y1)
590 L2=Y1
600 IF M1<=2 THEN 620
610 L2=Y1+1
620 L3=Y2
630 IF M2>=3 THEN 650
640 L3=Y2-1
650 IF L2>L3 THEN 710
660 FOR Y=L2 TO L3
670 GOSUB 330
680 IF L=0 THEN 700
690 N=N+1
700 NEXT Y
710 RETURN
720 Y3=INT(JD/1000): J4=JD-Y3*1000: GOSUB 330:
    REM   CONVERT TO GREGORIAN
730 IF L=0 THEN 760
740 IF J4<=59 THEN 760
750 J4=J4-1
760 D7=0
770 FOR MM=1 TO 12
780 D8=J4-D7
790 IF D8<=DM(MM) THEN 810
800 D7=D7+DM(MM):NEXTMM
810 RETURN
820 PRINT TAB(7);"WHICH IS: ";D$;" ";MN$(M);STR$(D);",";Y
830 RETURN
```

Suppose we want to determine how many days are between October 4, 1953, and March 8, 1981. As shown in the sample run of Figure 8–2, we find that there are 10,017 days between October 4, 1953, and March 8, 1981. When a specified date is either entered or calculated, the DATE1 program also determines and indicates the corresponding day of the week. In addition, the time between the two dates is also expressed in terms of years, which is useful for long-term calculations involving notes and bonds.

Figure 8–2   **Sample Results for DATE1 Program**

```
EARLIER DATE (MM/DD/YYYY) ? 10/04/1953
        WHICH IS: SUNDAY OCTOBER 4, 1953

LATER DATE (MM/DD/YYYY) ? 03/08/1981
        WHICH IS: SUNDAY MARCH 8, 1981

THEN:
NUMBER OF DAYS BETWEEN DATES = 10017
NUMBER OF YEARS BETWEEN DATES = 27.43
```

Computing a Calendar

Although the previous DATE1 program has the ability to determine the day of the week for a given date, there may be occasions when we want to know what an entire month looks like. The CALENDAR program listing of Figure 8–3 draws a calendar on the video display for a specified month and year.

When prompted, the month and year are entered together using the form MM/YYYY so that May, 1987, is entered as 05/1987. A sample printed run for October, 1992, is shown in Figure 8–4.

Calculating Yields

This section discusses four BASIC programs for the determination of yields for T bills, notes, and bonds.

1. TAXYLD1. The TAXYLD1 program of Figure 8–5 allows you to determine (1) the equivalent taxable yield of a tax-free security and (2) the

Figure 8-3   **BASIC Source Listing for CALENDAR Program**

```
100  REM      ---- CALENDAR PROGRAM ----
110  I=1
120  INPUT "INPUT MONTH AND YEAR IN THE FORM MM/YYYY ";D$(I)
130  M$(I)=LEFT$(D$(I),2):Y$(I)=RIGHT$(D$(I),4)
140  M(I)=VAL(M$(I)):  Y(I)=VAL(Y$(I))
150  D(I)=1
160  IF M(I)=1 OR M(I)=2 GOTO 200
170  A1=365*Y(I) + D(I)+31*(M(I)-1) - INT(.4*M(I)+2.3)
180  A2=INT(Y(I)/4)-INT(.75*(INT(Y(I)/100)+1))
190  GOTO 220
200  A1=365*Y(I)+D(I)+31*(M(I)-1)+INT((Y(I)-1)/4)
210  A2=-INT(.75*INT(((Y(I)-1)/100)+1))
220  F(I)=A1+A2
230  DAY(I)=F(I)-INT(F(I)/7)*7
240  FOR Z=0TO6:READ D$(Z):NEXT Z
250  DATA SATURDAY,SUNDAY,MONDAY,TUESDAY,WEDNESDAY,THURSDAY,FRIDAY
260  RESTORE
270  GOTO 280
280  IF M(I)=1   N=31:M$=" JANUARY"
290  IF M(I)=2 AND Y(I)/4=INT(Y(I)/4) N=29:M$="FEBRUARY"
300  IF M(I)=2 AND Y(I)/4<>INT(Y(I)/4) N=28:M$=" FEBRUARY"
310  IF M(I)=3 N=31:M$="    MARCH"
320  IF M(I)=4 N=30:M$="    APRIL"
330  IF M(I)=5 N=31:M$="      MAY"
340  IF M(I)=6 N=30:M$="     JUNE"
350  IF M(I)=7 N=31:M$="     JULY"
360  IF M(I)=8 N=31:M$="   AUGUST"
370  IF M(I)=9 N=30:M$="SEPTEMBER"
380  IF M(I)=10 N=31:M$="  OCTOBER"
390  IF M(I)=11 N=30:M$=" NOVEMBER"
400  IF M(I)=12 N=31:M$=" DECEMBER"
410  QQ=DAY(I)
420  IF DAY(I)=0 QQ=7
430  PRINT TAB(19) ;M$;" ";Y(I)
440  PRINT TAB(6)"S      M      T      W      T      F      S"
450  PRINT TAB(5)"===    ===    ===    ===    ===    ===    ==="
460  PRINT TAB(1+7*(QQ-1));
470  FOR L=1 TO N
480  IF L<=9 THEN PRINT "    ";L;
490  IF L>9 THEN PRINT"    ";L;
500  GOTO 520
510  PRINT"     ";L;
520  IF QQ/7=INT(QQ/7) PRINT:PRINT:PRINT" ";
530  QQ=QQ+1
540  NEXT L
550  PRINT:PRINT:PRINT:END
```

Figure 8–4   **Sample Results for CALENDAR Program**

```
INPUT MONTH AND YEAR IN THE FORM MM/YYYY ? 10/1992

                              OCTOBER   1992
             S      M      T      W      T      F      S
            ===    ===    ===    ===    ===    ===    ===
                                         1      2      3

             4      5      6      7      8      9     10

            11     12     13     14     15     16     17

            18     19     20     21     22     23     24

            25     26     27     28     29     30     31
```

Figure 8–5   **BASIC Source Listing for TAXYLD1 Program**

```
100 REM    ---- TAXYLD1 PROGRAM ----
110 PRINT"COMPARISON OF TAXABLE AND TAX-FREE YIELDS"
120 PRINT"ENTER:"
130 INPUT"YOUR FEDERAL % TAX BRACKET ";F
140 INPUT"YOUR STATE % TAX BRACKET ";S
150 INPUT"YOUR LOCAL % TAX BRACKET ";L
160 F=F/100:S=S/100:L=L/100
170 INPUT"IS YIELD <1> TAXABLE OR <2> TAX-FREE ";X
180 ON X GOTO 190,200
190 INPUT"TAXABLE % YIELD ";I: I=I/100 : GOTO 210
200 INPUT"TAX-FREE % YIELD   ";I: I=I/100
210 A=(1-(S+L+(F*(1-S+L)))): B=1/A
220 PRINT:PRINT"THEN: ";
230 ON X GOTO 260,240
240 PRINT"EQUIVALENT TAXABLE YIELD =";INT(B*I*1E5+.5)/1E3;"%"
250 END
260 PRINT"EQUIVALENT TAX-FREE YIELD =";INT(A*I*1E5+.5)/1E3;"%"
270 END
```

equivalent tax-free yield of a taxable security. Computations are based on the financial calculations presented in Chapter 6, which allow you to compare the yields of taxable and tax-free investments based on your federal, state, and local tax brackets, either individually or in any combination. All resultant yields are computed to three decimal places.

As an example, suppose you, a Delaware resident, are making a decision between buying:

- A 12½ percent Delaware municipal bond.
- A 14½ percent 3-month Treasury bill.
- A 13⅛ percent New York municipal bond.
- A 15 percent bank certificate of deposit.

In addition, you have determined that you are in the 39 percent federal, 8 percent state, and 0 percent local tax brackets. The Delaware bond, for Delaware residents, is free of both federal and state taxes; the T note is subject to federal taxes only; the New York bond is subject to Delaware state taxes only; and the certificate of deposit is subject to all taxes.

The four computer runs are presented in Figures 8–6, 8–7, 8–8, and 8–9, and summarized in Table 8–1. For these sets of conditions, the 12½ percent Delaware municipal bond has the best tax-free yield. However, there may be other considerations such as its rating or time to maturity, which may make this instrument unattractive.

Figure 8–6

**Sample Results for TAXYLD1 Program Showing
the Tax-Free Yield of a Municipal Bond**

```
COMPARISON OF TAXABLE AND TAX-FREE YIELDS
ENTER:
YOUR FEDERAL % TAX BRACKET ? 39
YOUR STATE % TAX BRACKET ? 8
YOUR LOCAL % TAX BRACKET ? 0
IS YIELD <1> TAXABLE OR <2> TAX-FREE ? 2
TAX-FREE % YIELD  ? 12.5

THEN: EQUIVALENT TAXABLE YIELD = 22.274 %
```

Figure 8–7

**Sample Results for TAXYLD1 Program Showing
the Tax-Free Yield of a Treasury Bill**

```
COMPARISON OF TAXABLE AND TAX-FREE YIELDS
ENTER:
YOUR FEDERAL % TAX BRACKET ? 39
YOUR STATE % TAX BRACKET ? 0
YOUR LOCAL % TAX BRACKET ? 0
IS YIELD <1> TAXABLE OR <2> TAX-FREE ? 1
TAXABLE % YIELD ? 14.5

THEN: EQUIVALENT TAX-FREE YIELD = 8.845 %
```

Figure 8−8

Sample Results for TAXYLD1 Program Showing the Tax-Free Yield of a Municipal Bond Subject to State Income Tax

```
COMPARISON OF TAXABLE AND TAX-FREE YIELDS
ENTER:
YOUR FEDERAL % TAX BRACKET ? 0
YOUR STATE % TAX BRACKET ? 8
YOUR LOCAL % TAX BRACKET ? 0
IS YIELD <1> TAXABLE OR <2> TAX-FREE ? 1
TAXABLE % YIELD ? 13.125

THEN: EQUIVALENT TAX-FREE YIELD = 12.075 %
```

Figure 8−9

Sample Results for TAXYLD1 Program Showing the Tax-Free Yield of a Bank Certificate of Deposit

```
COMPARISON OF TAXABLE AND TAX-FREE YIELDS
ENTER:
YOUR FEDERAL % TAX BRACKET ? 39
YOUR STATE % TAX BRACKET ? 8
YOUR LOCAL % TAX BRACKET ? 0
IS YIELD <1> TAXABLE OR <2> TAX-FREE ? 1
TAXABLE % YIELD ? 15.00

THEN: EQUIVALENT TAX-FREE YIELD = 8.418 %
```

Table 8−1

Federal Tax Bracket = 39 percent
State Tax Bracket = 8 percent

	Yields	
	Tax-Free	Taxable
Delaware bond	12.500%	22.274%
3-month T bill	8.845	14.500
NY bond	12.075	13.125
Bank CD	8.418	15.000

On the other hand, suppose we were in the 14 percent federal and 1.6 percent Delaware state tax brackets. Executing the TAXYLD1 program as

Table 8–2

Federal Tax Bracket = 14 percent
State Tax Bracket = 1.6 percent

	Yields	
	Tax-Free	*Taxable*
Delaware bond	12.500%	14.771%
3-month T bill	12.470	14.500
NY bond	12.915	13.125
Bank CD	12.694	15.000

before yields the results summarized in Table 8–2, which shows the marked effect of the tax bracket when compared with Table 8–1.

2. TBILL1. The TBILL1 program of Figure 8–10 consists of three separate analyses for T bill purchases, and is menu selectable, depending on what information is given. The first two analyses are applicable when buying a T bill as a new issue directly from a Federal Reserve bank, while the third analysis applies to quotations from the secondary or open market.

Figure 8–10   **BASIC Source Listing for TBILL1 Program**

```
100 REM     ---- TBILL1 PROGRAM ----
110 INPUT"T-BILL ANALYSIS BASED ON:
    <1> DISCOUNTED PURCHASE
    <2> QUOTED BASIS OF 100 POINTS
    <3> % BID/ASKED QUOTATIONS ";X
120 ON X GOTO 130,300,480
130 PRINT"T-BILL ANALYSIS #1: BASED ON DISCOUNTED PURCHASE"
140 PRINT:PRINT"ENTER THE FOLLOWING:"
150 INPUT"T-BILL FACE VALUE ";F
160 INPUT"NUMBER OF DAYS TO MATURITY ";N
170 INPUT"DISCOUNT AMOUNT ";D
180 INPUT"% FEDERAL TAX BRACKET ";T
190 P=(F-D)*100/F: P=INT(P*1000+.5)/1000
200 R=36000*D/(F*N): R=INT(R*1000+.5)/1000
210 C=(36500*D)/(N*(F-D)): C=INT(C*1000+.5)/1000
220 Y=(1-(T/100))*C: Y=INT(Y*1000+.5)/1000
230 PRINT:PRINT"THEN:"
240 PRINT"PURCHASE BASIS =";P
250 PRINT"DISCOUNT RATE =";R;"%"
260 PRINT"COUPON EQUIVALENT RATE =";C;"%"
270 PRINT"COUPON EQUIVALENT TAX-FREE YIELD =";Y;"%"
280 PRINT"PURCHASE PRICE = $";INT((F-D)*100+.5)/100
290 END
300 PRINT"T-BILL ANALYSIS #2: BASED ON QUOTED BASIS OF 100 POINTS"
```

Figure 8–10 (*concluded*)

```
310 PRINT:PRINT"ENTER THE FOLLOWING:"
320 INPUT"PURCHASE BASIS = ";PP
330 INPUT"T-BILL FACE VALUE = ";F
340 INPUT"NUMBER OF DAYS TO MATURITY = ";N
350 INPUT"% FEDERAL TAX BRACKET = ";T
360 D=F-(F*PP/100)
370 R=D*36000/(F*N): R=INT(R*1000+.5)/1000
380 C=D*36500/((F-D)*N)
390 Y=(1-(T/100))*C: Y=INT(Y*1000+.5)/1000
400 C=INT(C*1000+.5)/1000
410 PRINT:PRINT"THEN:"
420 PRINT"AMOUNT OF DISCOUNT = $";INT(D*100+.5)/100
430 PRINT"DISCOUNT RATE =";R;"%"
440 PRINT"COUPON EQUIVALENT RATE =";C;"%"
450 PRINT"COUPON EQUIVALENT TAX-FREE YIELD =";Y;"%"
460 PRINT"ACTUAL COST = $";INT((F-D)*1000+.5)/1000
470 END
480 PRINT"T-BILL ANALYSIS #3: BASED ON BID/ASKED QUOTATIONS"
490 PRINT:PRINT"ENTER THE FOLLOWING:"
500 INPUT"% BID QUOTATION ";B
510 INPUT"% ASKED QUOTATION ";A
520 INPUT"T-BILL FACE VALUE ";F
530 INPUT"NUMBER OF DAYS TO MATURITY ";N
540 INPUT"% FEDERAL TAX BRACKET ";T
550 SP=F-((F*B*N)/36000): SP=(SP*100+.5)/100
560 BP=F-((F*A*N)/36000): BP=(BP*100+.5)/100
570 Y=(F-BP)*36500/(N*BP)
580 E=(1-(T/100))*Y: E=INT(E*1000+.5)/1000
590 Y=INT(Y*1000+.5)/1000
600 PRINT:PRINT"THEN:"
610 PRINT"EQUIVALENT BID PRICE = $";SP
620 PRINT"EQUIVALENT ASKED PRICE = $";BP
630 PRINT"ANNUALIZED YIELD =";Y;"%"
640 PRINT"EQUIVALENT TAX-FREE YIELD =";E;"%"
650 END
```

As shown by the sample run of Figure 8–11, the "Analysis 1" section requires entry of:

- T bill face value.
- Number of days to maturity.
- Discount amount received.
- Your federal tax bracket.

From this information, the program computes the following quantities:

- Purchase basis as a percentage of par.

Figure 8–11   **Sample Results for TBILL1 Program Based on Knowing the Discount Amount**

```
T-BILL ANALYSIS BASED ON:
     <1> DISCOUNTED PURCHASE
     <2> QUOTED BASIS OF 100 POINTS
     <3> % BID/ASKED QUOTATIONS ? 1


T-BILL ANALYSIS #1: BASED ON DISCOUNTED PURCHASE

ENTER THE FOLLOWING:
T-BILL FACE VALUE ? 10000
NUMBER OF DAYS TO MATURITY ? 91
DISCOUNT AMOUNT ? 291.20
% FEDERAL TAX BRACKET ? 14

THEN:
PURCHASE BASIS = 97.088
DISCOUNT RATE = 11.52 %
COUPON EQUIVALENT RATE = 12.03 %
COUPON EQUIVALENT TAX-FREE YIELD = 10.346 %
PURCHASE PRICE = $ 9708.8
```

- Percentage discount rate.
- Coupon equivalent rate.
- Coupon equivalent tax-free yield.
- Actual discounted cost of the T bill.

For the example shown by the printout of Figure 8–11, suppose you are in the 14 percent federal tax bracket and have purchased a $10,000, 3-month (91 day) T bill, for which you received a discount check for the amount of $291.20 in the mail. Consequently, you then received a discount rate of 11.52 percent, which is equivalent to an annual coupon rate of 12.03 percent. Since you are in the 14 percent federal tax bracket, your equivalent tax-free yield is 10.346 percent.

The "Analysis 2" section of the TBILL1 program, of which sample results are shown in Figure 8–12, is based on having the purchase price quoted on the basis of 100 points par value. For this analysis, the results are determined by knowing:

- Purchase price.
- T bill face value.
- Number of days to maturity.
- Your federal tax bracket.

Figure   8-12   **Sample Results for TBILL1 Program Based on Knowing the Quoted Basis**

```
T-BILL ANALYSIS BASED ON:
    <1> DISCOUNTED PURCHASE
    <2> QUOTED BASIS OF 100 POINTS
    <3> % BID/ASKED QUOTATIONS ? 2


T-BILL ANALYSIS #2: BASED ON QUOTED BASIS OF 100 POINTS

ENTER THE FOLLOWING:
PURCHASE BASIS = ? 97.088
T-BILL FACE VALUE = ? 10000
NUMBER OF DAYS TO MATURITY = ? 91
% FEDERAL TAX BRACKET = ? 14

THEN:
AMOUNT OF DISCOUNT = $ 291.2
DISCOUNT RATE = 11.52 %
COUPON EQUIVALENT RATE = 12.03 %
COUPON EQUIVALENT TAX-FREE YIELD = 10.346 %
ACTUAL COST = $ 9708.8
```

Using this information, the program computes:

● Amount of discount to be received.

● Percentage discount rate.

● Coupon equivalent rate.

● Equivalent tax-free yield.

● Actual discounted cost of the T bill.

In this example, suppose you are in the 14 percent federal tax bracket and have purchased a 91-day, $10,000 T bill of which the purchase price was quoted in the Tuesday issue of *The Wall Street Journal* at 97.088, or 97.088 percent of par. From the results shown in Figure 8–12, you will receive a discount check for $291.20, having bought the $10,000 T bill at a discount of $9,708.80. This is equivalent to a discount rate of 11.52 percent, so that the annualized yield is 12.03 percent. Since you are in the 14 percent federal tax bracket, the equivalent tax-free yield is 10.346 percent.

The final section of the TBILL1 program analyzes bid and asked prices quoted for T bills on the open market. The information required is:

● Percentage bid quote.

● Percentage asked quote.

- T bill face value.
- Number of days to maturity.
- Your federal tax bracket.

As an example, suppose the respective open market bid and asked quotations for a given T bill are 6.02 percent and 5.78 percent. If you, being in the 39 percent federal tax bracket, have purchased a $10,000 T bill which will mature in eight days at the asked quote of 5.78 percent, the TBILL1 program will determine the following:

- Equivalent bid price.
- Equivalent asked price.
- Percentage annualized yield.
- Equivalent tax-free yield.

As shown in Figure 8–13, you would have to pay $9,987.16 for a $10,000 T bill maturing in eight days. At this price it represents an annual yield of 5.866 percent but is equivalent to a tax-free yield 3.578 percent.

Figure 8–13   **Sample Results for TBILL1 Program Based on Knowing Bid and Asked Prices**

```
T-BILL ANALYSIS BASED ON:
    <1> DISCOUNTED PURCHASE
    <2> QUOTED BASIS OF 100 POINTS
    <3> % BID/ASKED QUOTATIONS ? 3


T-BILL ANALYSIS #3: BASED ON BID/ASKED QUOTATIONS

ENTER THE FOLLOWING:
% BID QUOTATION ? 6.02
% ASKED QUOTATION ? 5.78
T-BILL FACE VALUE ? 10000
NUMBER OF DAYS TO MATURITY ? 8
% FEDERAL TAX BRACKET ? 39

THEN:
EQUIVALENT BID PRICE = $ 9986.63
EQUIVALENT ASKED PRICE = $ 9987.16
ANNUALIZED YIELD = 5.866 %
EQUIVALENT TAX-FREE YIELD = 3.578 %
```

---

3.   **TBOND1.**   The TBOND1 program of Figure 8–14 uses the same approximation method described in Chapter 7 in determining the equiv-

---

Figure   8-14   **BASIC Source Listing of TBOND1 Program**

```
100 REM     ---- TBOND1 PROGRAM ----
110 PRINT"YIELDS FOR T-NOTES AND BONDS"
120 INPUT"PURCHASE PRICE - WHOLE POINTS (BASIS OF 100) ";P1
130 INPUT"        1/32NDS ";P2
140 P2=P2/32 : P=P1+P2
150 INPUT"MATURITY, OR CALL DATE VALUE (BASIS OF 100) ";FV
160 INPUT"COUPON INTEREST RATE (%) ";CI: CI=CI/100
170 INPUT"YEARS TO MATURITY (OR CALL DATE) ";Y
180 NY=100000*CI/FV: NY=INT(NY*1000+.5)/1000
190 CY=10000*CI/P: CY=INT(CY*1000+.5)/1000
200 A=(FV-P)/Y: B=A+CI*FV : C=(B/P)+B/(FV-A): MY=50*C
210 MY=INT(MY*1000+.5)/1000
220 PRINT:PRINT"THEN:"
230 PRINT"BASED ON THE PURCHASE PRICE OF $";P
240 PRINT"CURRENT YIELD =";CY;"%"
250 PRINT"YIELD TO MATURITY (OR CALL) =";MY;"%"
260 END
```

---

alent coupon yield for notes and bonds. All that is required is the asked price, the face value at maturity (or call), the coupon interest rate, the time to maturity (or call) expressed in years, and your federal tax bracket. If you know the exact maturity date to the day, rather than only the month and year as given in most newspaper quotations, you can use the DATE1 program to determine the exact number of years, which is expressed as a 2-decimal number.

As in Chapter 7, first determine the equivalent coupon yield of a 12 percent T note maturing in five years with an asked quote of 94.17. Then determine the yield for a 15¾ percent note maturing in two years bought at a premium price of 103.11.

The run of Figure 8–15 shows the results for the 12 percent note, giving a yield of 13.545 percent, while Figure 8–16 shows the results for the 15¾ percent note with a yield of 13.735 percent. In both cases, the asked price is entered as a two-step process—whole points, followed by 1/32ds of a point.

4. SINKFND1. The quoted yield to maturity or equivalent coupon yield assumes the semiannual interest payment is reinvested at the identical coupon rate of the note or bond. In periods of rapidly fluctuating interest rates, it may not be possible to reinvest these payments into other instruments, such as money market funds, giving at least the same yield as the coupon rate. Consequently, the actual yield to maturity may be higher or lower than the calculated yield using the TBOND1 program.

Figure 8–15   **Sample Results for TBOND1 Program for a Bond Bought at a Discount**

```
YIELDS FOR T-NOTES AND BONDS
PURCHASE PRICE - WHOLE POINTS (BASIS OF 100) ? 94
      1/32NDS ? 17
MATURITY, OR CALL DATE VALUE (BASIS OF 100) ? 100
COUPON INTEREST RATE (%) ? 12
YEARS TO MATURITY (OR CALL DATE) ? 5

THEN:
BASED ON THE PURCHASE PRICE OF $ 94.5313
CURRENT YIELD = 12.694 %
YIELD TO MATURITY (OR CALL) = 13.545 %
```

Figure 8–16   **Sample Results for TBOND1 Program for a Bond Bought at a Premium**

```
YIELDS FOR T-NOTES AND BONDS
PURCHASE PRICE - WHOLE POINTS (BASIS OF 100) ? 103
      1/32NDS ? 11
MATURITY, OR CALL DATE VALUE (BASIS OF 100) ? 100
COUPON INTEREST RATE (%) ? 15.75
YEARS TO MATURITY (OR CALL DATE) ? 2

THEN:
BASED ON THE PURCHASE PRICE OF $ 103.344
CURRENT YIELD = 15.24 %
YIELD TO MATURITY (OR CALL) = 13.735 %
```

However, we may obtain some measure of how much money we will have after a given period of time with equal deposits at a stated interest rate.

The SINKFND1 program of Figure 8–17 requires the amount of each deposit, the nominal interest rate, the number of interest periods per year (i.e., the number of times interest is compounded yearly), and the number of interest periods between deposits. In addition, SINKFND1 needs to know if the fixed periodic deposits are made at the beginning or the end of the interest period.

As in Chapter 7, suppose we want to invest the semiannual interest from a 5-year, 13½ percent, $5,000 T note at our credit union, which pays an annual interest of 7 percent compounded quarterly. Consequently, we will have 10 regular deposits of $337.50. In addition, there are four interest periods per year and two interest periods between deposits. Figure

Figure 8-17 **BASIC Source Listing of SINKFND1 Program**

```
100 REM    ---- SINKFND1 PROGRAM ----
110  INPUT"AMOUNT OF PERIODIC DEPOSIT ";D
120 INPUT"ARE DEPOSITS MADE:
    <1> AT THE END OF EACH PERIOD
    <2> AT THE BEGINNING OF EACH PERIOD    ";X
130 INPUT"NUMBER OF DEPOSITS ";M
140 INPUT"NOMINAL INTEREST RATE (%) ";I:I=I/100
150 INPUT"NUMBER OF INTEREST PERIODS/YEAR ";Z:I=I/Z
160 INPUT"NUMBER OF INTEREST PERIODS/DEPOSIT ";N
170 S=D*((((I+1)↑(M*N)))-1)/(((I+1)↑N)-1)
180 IF X=1 THEN 190 ELSE S1=D*(((((I+1)↑(M*N)))-1):S=S+S1
190 PRINT"AMOUNT AFTER";M;"DEPOSITS =";INT(S*100+.5)/100
200 END
```

Figure 8-18 **Sample Results for SINKFND1 Program for Deposits
Made at the Start of an Interest Period**

```
AMOUNT OF PERIODIC DEPOSIT ? 337.50
ARE DEPOSITS MADE:
    <1> AT THE END OF EACH PERIOD
    <2> AT THE BEGINNING OF EACH PERIOD    ? 2
NUMBER OF DEPOSITS ? 10
NOMINAL INTEREST RATE (%) ? 7
NUMBER OF INTEREST PERIODS/YEAR ? 4
NUMBER OF INTEREST PERIODS/DEPOSIT ? 2
AMOUNT AFTER 10 DEPOSITS = 4104.94
```

Figure 8-19 **Sample Results for SINKFND1 Program for Deposits
Made at the End of an Interest Period**

```
AMOUNT OF PERIODIC DEPOSIT ? 337.50
ARE DEPOSITS MADE:
    <1> AT THE END OF EACH PERIOD
    <2> AT THE BEGINNING OF EACH PERIOD    ? 1
NUMBER OF DEPOSITS ? 10
NOMINAL INTEREST RATE (%) ? 7
NUMBER OF INTEREST PERIODS/YEAR ? 4
NUMBER OF INTEREST PERIODS/DEPOSIT ? 2
AMOUNT AFTER 10 DEPOSITS = 3964.95
```

8–18 shows $4,104.94 will be accumulated after five years when deposits are made at the beginning of an interest period, while Figure 8–19 shows only $3,964.94 in accumulated when deposits are made at the end of an interest period.

Using VisiCalc

The popular electronic spread sheet analysis program, VisiCalc, can be used to perform a "what if" analysis of most of the BASIC programs discussed in the previous section.

All of these programs were created with the TRS-80 version of the VisiCalc program but should work as well on other computer systems supported by VisiCorp, such as Apple II, Commodore's PET and CBM, and the IBM Personal Computer.

As with the BASIC programs, both a sample printout and VisiCalc source program listing is presented with each financial model. Each source code listing shows how to "key in" the results shown. Entries are provided by separate grid, or coordinate locations, where the greater than symbol (>) marks the beginning location; it is followed by the coordinates of the entry and a colon. For example, the entry

> D11: "TAX FREE

means the phrase TAX FREE is entered in location D11. *Formatted* entries, such as FR and FL, are preceeded by a slash symbol (/) and are used to left or right justify numerical entries or results. For example,

> A5: /FR9.012

means that the number 9.012 is displayed in a "flush right," or right justified format at coordinate location A5. *Global* formats, those preceeded by a slash character, are printed at the end of each source code listing. They are:

- /W1 (sets 1 window).
- /GOC (sets recalculation by columns).
- /GRA (sets automatic recalculation of entire sheet).
- /GC9 (sets 9 characters per column).

These need not be entered as they are the common VisiCalc default values assigned when the program is saved on disk. Each program contains sample data which can be used to check your results after entering the VisiCalc source code. When you are satisfied that your results are the same as in the illustrated examples, you are ready to perform a variety of "what if" calculations. For each printout example, all entered data is boxed.

Determining the Number of Days between Two Dates

The DATE2 program of Figure 8–20 determines the number of days between two dates, taking into account all leap years.

Figure 8–20   **VisiCalc Source Listing for DATE2 Program**

```
>E33:@LOOKUP(A99,E29...E31)          >A19:2
>E32:@LOOKUP(+A99,E26...E28)         >E18:+C18-D18
>E31:+E22*100                        >D18:@INT(C18)
>E30:+E21*100                        >C18:+F5/100
>E29:+E20*100                        >B18:0
>B29:334                             >A18:1
>A29:12                              >E17:+C17-D17
>E28:+E18*100                        >D17:@INT(C17)
>B28:304                             >C17:+F5/400
>A28:11                              >B17:/--
>E27:+E17*100                        >E16:+C16-D16
>B27:273                             >D16:@INT(C16)
>A27:10                              >C16:+F5/4
>E26:+E16*100                        >B16:"TEMP DATA
>B26:243                             >F15:/--
>A26:9                               >E15:/--
>E25:+D25+(365*F6)+D20+E6+1-D22+D21  >D15:/--
>D25:@LOOKUP(D6,A18...A29)           >C15:/--
>B25:212                             >B15:/--
>A25:8                               >A15:/--
>E24:+D24+(365*F5)+D16+E5+1-D18+D17  >E12:"THING.
>D24:@LOOKUP(D5,A18...A29)           >D12:"EN ADD NO
>B24:181                             >C12:"S = 0, TH
>A24:7                               >B12:"BOTH YEAR
>B23:151                             >G11:"   IF
>A23:6                               >F11:"ONTH > 2.
>E22:+C22-D22                        >E11:"ER DATE M
>D22:@INT(C22)                       >D11:" WHEN LAT
>C22:+F6/100                         >C11:"H < 3, OR
>B22:120                             >B11:"DATE MONT
>A22:5                               >G10:"RLIER
>E21:+C21-D21                        >F10:"S WHEN EA
>D21:@INT(C21)                       >E10:" TO # DAY
>C21:+F6/400                         >D10:"HEN ADD 1
>B21:90                              >C10:"R? = 0, T
>A21:4                               >B10:"IF LEAP Y
>E20:+C20-D20                        >F9:/FL@INT((F8*100/365)+.5)/100
>D20:@INT(C20)                       >E9:"# YEARS =
>C20:+F6/4                           >F8:/FL+E25-E24
>B20:59                              >E8:"# DAYS =
>A20:3                               >A8:/FL
>B19:31                              >G7:/-=
```

Figure 8−20 (*concluded*)

```
>F7:/-=
>E7:/-=
>D7:/-=
>G6:/FL+E33
>F6:/FL1981
>E6:/FL8
>D6:/FL3
>C6:"E:
>B6:"LATER DAT
>G5:/FL+E32
>F5:/FL1953
>E5:/FL4
>D5:/FL10
>C5:"ATE:
>B5:"EARLIER D
>G4:"-------
```

```
>F4:" ----
>E4:"----
>D4:"-----
>G3:"LEAP YR?
>F3:" YEAR
>E3:"DAY
>D3:"MONTH
>F1:"DATES
>E1:"WEEN TWO
>D1:" DAYS BET
>C1:"NUMBER OF
/W1
/GOC
/GRA
/GC9
/X>B1:>B1:
```

As an example, suppose we want to determine how many days are between October 4, 1953, and March 8, 1981. As shown in the sample run of Figure 8–21, we find that there are 10,017 days between October 4, 1953, and March 8, 1981. The "LEAP YEAR?" column is used to tell us whether we must add an extra day to our total. This feature must be

Figure 8−21   **Sample Results for DATE2 Program with No Leap Years**

```
         NUMBER OF DAYS BETWEEN TWO DATES


                   MONTH    DAY      YEAR    LEAP YR?

                   -----    ----     ----    --------

EARLIER DATE:      10       4        1953    NA
LATER DATE:        3        8        1981    NA

              ======================================
                    # DAYS =  10017
                    # YEARS = 27.44
     IF LEAP YR? = 0, THEN ADD 1 TO # DAYS WHEN EARLIER
     DATE MONTH < 3, OR WHEN LATER DATE MONTH > 2.  IF
     BOTH YEARS = 0, THEN ADD NOTHING.
```

added because although VisiCalc is a very powerful program, it nevertheless lacks some of the computational capabilities of BASIC. If this column reads 0, then add 1 to the total number of days only when the number of the earlier month is 1 or 2 (i.e., January or February), or when the number of the later date is 3 or more (i.e., March through December). If both dates have a 0 in this column add nothing. The "NA" (not applicable) designation indicates that that particular year is not a leap year.

As another example, Figure 8–22 shows that there are 886 days between October 4, 1953, and March 8, 1956, which is a leap year. The printouts of Figures 8–21 and 8–22 span the coordinates A1–M12.

Figure   8–22   **Sample Results for DATE2 Program with One Leap Year**

NUMBER OF DAYS BETWEEN TWO DATES

	MONTH	DAY	YEAR	LEAP YR?
	-----	----	----	--------
EARLIER DATE:	10	4	1953	NA
LATER DATE:	3	8	1956	0

=======================================

\# DAYS = 886

\# YEARS = 2.43

IF LEAP YR? = 0, THEN ADD 1 TO # DAYS WHEN EARLIER
DATE MONTH < 3, OR WHEN LATER DATE MONTH > 2. IF
BOTH YEARS = 0, THEN ADD NOTHING.

Calculating Yields

1. TAXYLD2. The TAXYLD2 program of Figure 8–23 allows you to determine (1) the equivalent taxable yield of a tax-free security and (2) the equivalent tax-free yield of a taxable security. Computations are based on the financial calculations presented in Chapter 6, which compare the yields of taxable and tax-free investments based on your federal, state, and local tax brackets, either individually or in any combination. All resultant yields are computed to a maximum of three decimal places.

Figure 8-23   **VisiCalc Source Listing for TAXYLD2 Program**

```
>B25:1/B24                              >C7:"LD:
>B24:(1-(B22+B23+(B21*(1-B22+B23)))) >B7:"ENTER YIE
>B23:+B6/100                            >D6:"E
>B22:+B5/100                            >C6:"% TAX RAT
>B21:+B4/100                            >B6:/FR0
>A20:"TEMP DATA                         >A6:"LOCAL:
>F12:"%                                 >D5:/FL"E
>E12:/FR@INT(B25*D8*1000+.5)/1000       >C5:"% TAX RAT
>D12:"TAXABLE                           >B5:/FR8
>C12:/FL"   (OR)                        >A5:"STATE:
>B12:/FL                                >D4:/FL"E
>A12:/FL                                >C4:"% TAX RAT
>F11:"%                                 >B4:/FR39
>E11:/FR@INT(B8*B24*1000+.5)/1000       >A4:"FEDERAL:
>D11:"TAX-FREE                          >E3:"Y:
>C11:/FL                                >D3:/FL"TAXABLE B
>A11:"                                  >C3:"CKETS IF
>C10:/FL"T YIELDS:                      >B3:"R TAX BRA
>B10:"EQUIVALEN                         >A3:"ENTER YOU
>F9:/--                                 >E1:"IELDS
>E9:/--                                 >D1:"AX-FREE Y
>D9:/--                                 >C1:"BLE AND T
>C9:/--                                 >B1:"N OF TAXA
>B9:/--                                 >A1:"COMPARISO
>A9:/--                                 /W1
>E8:"%                                  /GOC
>D8:/FR12.5                             /GRA
>C8:"% TAXFREE                          /GC9
>B8:/FR0                                /X>A1:>A1:
>A8:"TAXABLE
```

As an example, suppose you, a Delaware resident, are making a decision between buying:

- A 13½ percent Delaware municipal bond.
- A 14½ percent 3-month Treasury bill.
- A 13⅛ percent New York municipal bond.
- A 15 percent bank certificate of deposit.

In addition, you have determined that you are in the 39 percent federal, 8 percent state, 0 percent local tax brackets. The Delaware bond, for Delaware residents, is free of both federal and state taxes; the T note is subject to federal taxes only; the New York bond is subject to Delaware state taxes only; and the certificate of deposit is subject to all taxes.

Figure   8—24   **Sample Results for TAXYLD1 Program Showing the**
                                                  Tax-Free Yield of a Municipal Bond

```
COMPARISON OF TAXABLE AND TAX-FREE YIELDS


ENTER YOUR TAX BRACKETS IF TAXABLE BY:
FEDERAL:          39% TAX RATE
STATE:             8% TAX RATE
LOCAL:             0% TAX RATE
          ENTER YIELD:
TAXABLE           0% TAXFREE     12.5%
------------------------------------------------------------

          EQUIVALENT YIELDS:
                          TAX-FREE          0%
                  (OR)    TAXABLE        22.274%
```

Figure   8—25   **Sample Results for TAXYLD1 Program Showing the**
                                                  Tax-Free Yield of a Treasury Bill

```
COMPARISON OF TAXABLE AND TAX-FREE YIELDS


ENTER YOUR TAX BRACKETS IF TAXABLE BY:
FEDERAL:          39% TAX RATE
STATE:             0% TAX RATE
LOCAL:             0% TAX RATE
          ENTER YIELD:
TAXABLE         14.5% TAXFREE          0%
------------------------------------------------------------

          EQUIVALENT YIELDS:
                          TAX-FREE       8.845%
                  (OR)    TAXABLE           0%
```

Figure 8-26   **Sample Results for TAXYLD1 Program Showing the Tax-Free
Yield of a Municipal Bond Subject to State Income Tax**

```
COMPARISON OF TAXABLE AND TAX-FREE YIELDS

ENTER YOUR TAX BRACKETS IF TAXABLE BY:
FEDERAL:        0% TAX RATE
STATE:          8% TAX RATE
LOCAL:          0% TAX RATE
        ENTER YIELD:
TAXABLE    13.125% TAXFREE        0%
-------------------------------------------------------
        EQUIVALENT YIELDS:
                        TAX-FREE    12.075%
                (OR)    TAXABLE          0%
```

Figure 8-27   **Sample Results for TAXYLD1 Program Showing the
Tax-Free Yield of a Bank Certificate of Deposit**

```
COMPARISON OF TAXABLE AND TAX-FREE YIELDS

ENTER YOUR TAX BRACKETS IF TAXABLE BY:
FEDERAL:       39% TAX RATE
STATE:          8% TAX RATE
LOCAL:          0% TAX RATE
        ENTER YIELD:
TAXABLE    15% TAXFREE        0%
-------------------------------------------------------
        EQUIVALENT YIELDS:
                        TAX-FREE    8.418%
                (OR)    TAXABLE         0%
```

The four computer runs are shown in Figures 8–24, 8–25, 8–26, and 8–27, and summarized in Table 8–3. Each printout spans the coordinates A1–F12. For this set of circumstances, the 12½ percent Delaware municipal bond has the best tax-free yield. However, there may be other considerations, such as its rating or time to maturity, which may make this instrument unattractive.

Table 8–3

Federal Tax Bracket = 39 percent
State Tax Bracket = 8 percent

	Yield	
	Tax-Free	*Taxable*
Delaware bond	12.500%	22.274%
3-month T bill	8.845	14.500
NY bond	12.075	13.125
Bank CD	8.418	15.000

---

2. TBILL2. Like its BASIC version, the TBILL2 program of Figure 8–28 consists of three parts, depending on what information is given. The first two sections are applicable when buying a T bill as a new issue directly from a Federal Reserve bank, while the third section applies to transactions on the secondary or open market.

Figure 8–28   **VisiCalc Source Listing for TBILL2 Program**

```
>F41:/--
>E41:/--
>D41:/--
>C41:/--
>B41:/--
>A41:/--
>E40:"%
>D40:@INT(C39*(1-(C34/100))*1000+.5)/1000
>C40:"E YIELD =
>B40:"T TAX-FRE
>A40:"EQUIVALEN
>D39:"%
>C39:@INT(((C33-C38)*36500000/(C32*C38))+.5)/1000
>B39:"D YIELD =
>A39:"ANNUALIZE
>C38:/F$+C33-(C31*C33*C32/36000)
>B38:" =
```

Figure   8-28 (*continued*)

```
>A38:"BUY PRICE
>C37:/F$+C33-(C30*C33*C32/36000)
>B37:"E =
>A37:"SELL PRIC
>B36:"RESULTS
>D34:"% <
>C34:/FR39
>B34:"RACKET:
>A34:"FED TAX B
>D33:"  <
>C33:/FR10000
>B33:"NT:
>A33:"FACE AMOU
>D32:"  <
>C32:/FR8
>B32:"ATURITY:
>A32:"DAYS TO M
>D31:"% <
>C31:/FR5.78
>B31:"TE:
>A31:"ASKED QUO
>E30:/FR
>D30:"% <
>C30:/FR6.02
>B30:":
>A30:"BID QUOTE
>F29:"ONS
>E29:"D QUOTATI
>D29:" BID/ASKE
>C29:" BASED ON
>B29:"ALYSIS-3:
>A29:"T-BILL AN
>F27:/--
>E27:/--
>D27:/--
>C27:/--
>B27:/--
>A27:/--
>D26:"%
>C26:@INT(((C17-C25)*36000000/(C17*C18))+.5)/1000
>B26:"RATE =
>A26:"DISCOUNT
>F25:@INT(C24*1000*(1-(C19/100))+.5)/1000
>E25:"% YIELD =
>C25:/F$+C17-((100-C16)*C17/100)
>B25:"ST =
>A25:"ACTUAL CO
>E24:"TAX-FREE
>D24:"%
>C24:/FR@INT(36500000*C22/((C17-C22)*C18)+.5)/1000
>B24:"RATE =
>F23:"T
>E23:"EQUIVALEN
```

Figure 8-28 (*continued*)

```
>B23:"UIVALENT
>A23:"COUPON EQ
>E22:"COUPON
>C22:/F$+C17-(C16*C17/100)
>B22:"AMOUNT =
>A22:"DISCOUNT
>D21:"ULTS
>C21:"       RES
>D19:" <
>C19:/FR14
>B19:" BRACKET:
>A19:"% FED TAX
>D18:" <
>C18:/FR91
>B18:"ATURITY:
>A18:"DAYS TO M
>D17:" <
>C17:/FR10000
>B17:"E:
>A17:"FACE VALU
>D16:" <
>C16:/FR97.088
>B16:"PRICE:
>A16:"PURCHASE
>F15:"00 POINTS
>E15:"ASIS OF 1
>D15:" QUOTED B
>C15:" BASED ON
>B15:"ALYSIS-2:
>A15:"T-BILL AN
>F13:/--
>E13:/--
>D13:/--
>C13:/--
>B13:/--
>A13:/--
>M12:/FL@INT(J11*1000*(1-(J5/100))+.5)/1000
>J12:/F$
>F12:/FR@INT(C118*1000*(1-(C5/100))+.5)/1000
>E12:"% YIELD =
>C12:/F$+C2-C4
>B12:"ST =
>A12:"ACTUAL CO
>M11:"%
>J11:/FR
>E11:"TAX-FREE
>D11:"%
>C11:/FR@INT(36500000*C4/((C2-C4)*C3)+.5)/1000
>B11:"RATE =
>M10:"T
>F10:"T
>E10:"EQUIVALEN
>B10:"UIVALENT
```

Figure 8–28 (*concluded*)

```
>A10:"COUPON EQU
>J9:/F$
>E9:"COUPON
>D9:"%
>C9:/FR@INT((C4*36000000/(C2*C3))+.5)/1000
>B9:"RATE =
>A9:"DISCOUNT
>C8:/FR@INT(((C2-C4)*100000/C2)+.5)/1000
>B8:"POINTS =
>A8:"PURCHASE
>D7:"ULTS
>C7:"          RES
>J5:/FR
>D5:" <
>C5:/FR39
>B5:" BRACKET:
>A5:"% FED TAX
>J4:/FR
>D4:" <
>C4:/F$645.63
>B4:/FL"AMOUNT:
>A4:"DISCOUNT
>J3:/FR
>D3:" <
>C3:/FR182
>B3:"ATURITY:
>A3:"DAYS TO M
>J2:/FR
>D2:" <
>C2:/FR15000
>B2:"E:
>A2:"FACE VALU
>F1:"SE
>E1:"ED PURCHA
>D1:" DISCOUNT
>C1:" BASED ON
>B1:"ALYSIS-1:
>A1:"T-BILL AN
/W1
/GOC
/GRA
/GC9
/X>A1:>A1:
```

As shown in Figure 8–29, the "Analysis 1" section requires entry of:

- T bill face value.
- Number of days to maturity.
- Discount amount received.
- Your federal tax bracket.

From this information, the following quantities are determined:

- Percentage discount rate.
- Coupon equivalent rate.
- Coupon equivalent tax-free yield rate.
- Actual discounted cost of the T bill.

In this example, you are in the 39 percent federal tax bracket and have purchased a $15,000, 6-month (182 day) T bill, for which you later received a discount check in the mail for $645.63. Consequently, you received a discount rate of 8.514 percent, which is equivalent to an annual coupon rate of 9.02 percent. Since you are in the 39 percent federal tax bracket, your equivalent tax-free yield is 5.502 percent. This printout spans the coordinates A1–F13.

Figure 8–29   **Sample Results for TBILL2 Program Based on Knowing the Discount Amount**

```
T-BILL ANALYSIS-1: BASED ON DISCOUNTED PURCHASE
   FACE VALUE:          15000 <
   DAYS TO MATURITY:      182 <
   DISCOUNT AMOUNT:    645.63 <
   % FED TAX BRACKET:      39 <


                         RESULTS
   PURCHASE POINTS =    95.696
   DISCOUNT RATE =       8.514%        COUPON
   COUPON EQUIVALENT                   EQUIVALENT
            RATE =       9.02%         TAX-FREE
   ACTUAL COST =      14354.37         % YIELD =    5.502
   ----------------------------------------------------------
```

The "Analysis 2" section, shown in Figure 8–30, is based on having the purchase price quoted on the basis of par being 100 points. Information required is:

- Purchase price.
- Face value.
- Number of days to maturity.
- Federal tax bracket.

For this information the program computes:

- Amount of the discount.
- Discount rate.
- Coupon equivalent rate.
- Equivalent tax-free yield rate.
- Actual discounted cost of the T bill.

In this example, you are in the 14 percent federal tax bracket and have purchased a 91-day, $10,000 T bill of which the purchase price was quoted in the Tuesday issue of *The Wall Street Journal* at 97.088. You will then receive a check for $291.20, having bought the T bill at a discount of

---

Figure 8–30   **Sample Results for TBILL2 Program Based on Knowing the Quoted Basis**

```
T-BILL ANALYSIS-2: BASED ON QUOTED BASIS OF 100 POINTS
PURCHASE PRICE:      97.088 <
FACE VALUE:          10000 <
DAYS TO MATURITY:       91 <
% FED TAX BRACKET:      14 <


                        RESULTS
DISCOUNT AMOUNT =     291.20         COUPON
COUPON EQUIVALENT                    EQUIVALENT
        RATE =       12.03%          TAX-FREE
ACTUAL COST =        9708.80         % YIELD =   10.346
DISCOUNT RATE =      11.52%

------------------------------------------------------------
```

$9,708.80, or a discount rate of 11.52 percent. This is equivalent to an annualized yield of 12.03 percent. Since you are in the 14 percent federal tax bracket, this is equivalent to a tax-free yield of 10.346 percent. This printout spans the coordinates A15–F27.

The final section of the TBILL2 model analyzes bid and asked prices quoted for T bills on the open market. The information required is:

- Percentage bid quote.
- Percentage asked quote.
- T bill face value.
- Number of days to maturity.
- Your federal tax bracket.

As an example, suppose the respective open market bid and asked quotations for a given T bill are 6.02 percent and 5.78 percent. If you, being in the 39 percent federal tax bracket, were to purchase a $10,000 T bill which matures in eight days at the asked quote of 5.78 percent, the "Analysis 3" section will determine the following:

- Equivalent bid price.
- Equivalent asked price.

Figure 8–31   Sample Results for TBILL2 Program Based on Knowing Bid and Asked Prices

```
T-BILL ANALYSIS-3: BASED ON BID/ASKED QUOTATIONS
BID QUOTE:              6.02% <
ASKED QUOTE:            5.78% <
DAYS TO MATURITY:           8 <
FACE AMOUNT:            10000 <
FED TAX BRACKET:           39% <

          RESULTS
SELL PRICE =            9986.62
BUY PRICE =             9987.16
ANNUALIZED YIELD =       5.868%
EQUIVALENT TAX-FREE YIELD =      3.579%
```

- Percentage annualized yield.
- Equivalent tax-free yield.

For the results, as shown in Figure 8–31, you would have to pay $9,987.16 for a $10,000 T bill maturing in eight days. At this price it represents an annual yield of 5.868 percent but is equivalent to a tax-free yield of 3.579 percent.

3. TBOND2. The TBOND2 program of Figure 8–32 is applicable for both T notes and T bonds bought either as new issues or on the open market. The required information is:

- Asked price in terms of whole points and 1/32ds of a point.
- Face value at maturity, or value at the call date.
- Coupon interest rate.
- Number of years to maturity or call.
- Federal tax bracket.

In return, TBOND2 computes:

- Current yield.
- Yield to maturity, or call.
- Equivalent tax-free yield.
- Purchase price.

Figure 8–32   **VisiCalc Source Listing of TBOND2 Program**

```
>A29:50*A27                              >B12:"T TAX-FRE
>A28:10000*A23/A24                       >A12:"EQUIVALEN
>A27:(A26/A24)+(A26/(E4-A25))            >E11:"%
>A26:+A25+(A23*E4)                       >D11:@INT(A29*1000+.5)/1000
>A25:(E4-A24)/E6                         >C11:"OR CALL =
>A24:+E2+(E3/32)                         >B11:"MATURITY
>A23:+E5/100                             >A11;:"YIELD TO
>A22:/--                                 >F10:"RESULTS
>B21;:"ES                                >E10:"%
>A21:"TEMP VALU                          >D10:@INT(A28*1000+.5)/1000
>E14:/FI                                 >B10:"IELD =
>D13:/F$+A24*E7/100                      >A10:"CURRENT Y
>B13:"PRICE =                            >F9:/-=
>A13:"PURCHASE                           >E9:/-=
>E12:"%                                  >D9:/-=
>D12:@INT(D11*(1-(E8/100)*1000)+.5)/1000 >C9:/-=
>C12:"E YIELD =                          >B9:/-=
```

Figure 8–32 (*concluded*)

```
>A9:/-=                          >D4:"L):
>F8:"% <                         >C4:"UE AT CAL
>E8:/FR39                        >B4:"E (OR VAL
>C8:"T:                          >A4:"FACE VALU
>B8:"AX BRACKE                   >F3:" <
>A8:"FEDERAL T                   >E3:/FR6
>F7:" <                          >D3:":
>E7:/FR1000                      >C3:"D POINTS)
>B7:"E:                          >B3:"  (1/32N
>A7:"FACE VALU                   >F2:" <
>F6:" <                          >E2:/FR112
>E6:9                            >C2:" POINTS):
>D6:"DATE):                      >B2:"CE (WHOLE
>C6:"(OR CALL                    >A2:"ASKED PRI
>B6:"MATURITY                    >D1:"NALYSIS
>A6:"YEARS TO                    >C1:" T-BOND A
>F5:"% <                         >B1:" T-NOTE &
>E5:/FR14.875                    /W1
>C5:"TE:                         /GOC
>B5:"TEREST RA                   /GRA
>A5:"COUPON IN                   /GC9
>F4:" <                          /X>A1:>A1:
>E4:/FR100
```

Using the example printout of Figure 8–33, we want to buy a $1,000 T bond on the secondary market having a coupon interest rate of 14⅞ percent. The asked price is 112.6, meaning 112 6/32 points, and the bond will mature in nine years at par (i.e., 100). In addition, we are fortunate to be in the 39 percent federal tax bracket. We will have to pay $1,121.88 for this $1,000 bond, which will have a current yield of 13.259 percent and a yield to maturity of 12.696 percent. This is equivalent to a tax-free yield of 7.745 percent. This printout spans the coordinates A1–F13.

4. SINKFND2. The SINKFND2 program of Figure 8–34, which is a sinking fund analysis model, requires the following information:

- The amount of each deposit.
- The nominal interest rate.
- The number of interest periods per year (i.e., the number of times interest is compounded yearly).
- The number of interest periods between deposits.

In addition, SINKFND2 needs to know if the fixed periodic deposits are made at the beginning or end of the interest period.

Figure   8-33   **Sample Results for TBOND2 Program for a Bond Bought at a Premium**

```
                    T-NOTE & T-BOND ANALYSIS
        ASKED PRICE (WHOLE POINTS):              112  <
                       (1/32ND POINTS):            6  <
        FACE VALUE (OR VALUE AT CALL):           100  <
        COUPON INTEREST RATE:                 14.875% <
        YEARS TO MATURITY (OR CALL DATE):         9  <
        FACE VALUE:                             1000  <
        FEDERAL TAX BRACKET:                     39% <

        ============================================================
        CURRENT YIELD =                 13.259%         RESULTS
        YIELD TO MATURITY OR CALL =     12.696%
        EQUIVALENT TAX-FREE YIELD =      7.745%
        PURCHASE PRICE =               1121.88
```

Figure   8-34   **VisiCalc Source Listing of SINKFND2 Program**

```
>A28:+D3*D6                                    >A9:"IF DEPOSI
>A27:+A26+1                                    >C8:"RESULTS
>A26:+A25/D5                                   >F7:/--
>A25:+D4/100                                   >E7:/--
>A24:/--                                       >D7:/--
>A23:"TEMP DATA                                >C7:/--
>D12:"   <----<<                               >B7:/--
>C12:/F$+C10+(D2*((A27↑A28)-1))                >A7:/--
>B12:" DUE =                                   >E6:"  <
>A12:"   AMOUNT                                >D6:/FI2
>F11:"IOD:                                     >C6:"/DEPOSIT:
>E11:" EACH PER                                >B6:"T PERIODS
>D11:"INNING OF                                >A6:"# INTERES
>C11:"DE AT BEG                                >E5:"  <
>B11:"TS ARE MA                                >D5:/FI4
>A11:"IF DEPOSI                                >C5:"/YEAR:
>D10:"   <----<<                               >B5:"T PERIODS
>C10:/F$+D2*((A27)↑(A28)-1)/((A27↑(D6))-1)     >A5:"# INTERES
>B10:" DUE =                                   >E4:"% <
>A10:"   AMOUNT                                >D4:/FR7
>E9:"PERIOD:                                   >C4:"TE:
>D9:" OF EACH                                  >B4:"TEREST RA
>C9:"DE AT END                                 >A4:"ANNUAL IN
>B9:"TS ARE MA"                                >E3:"  <
```

Figure 8—34 (*concluded*)

```
>D3:/FI10                           >A2:"AMOUNT OF
>C3:":                              >D1:"ANALYSIS
>B3:" DEPOSITS                      >C1:"SINKFUND
>A3:"NUMBER OF                      /W1
>E2:"  <                            /GOC
>D2:/F$337.5                        /GRA
>C2:" DEPOSIT:                      /GC9
>B2:" PERIODIC                      /X>A1:>A1:
```

As an example, suppose we want to invest the semiannual interest from a 5-year, 13½ percent, $5,000 T note at our credit union, which pays an annual interest of 7 percent compounded quarterly. Consequently, we will have 10 regular deposits of $337.50. In addition, there are four interest periods per year and two interest periods between deposits. Figure 8–35 shows that $4,104.94 will be accumulated after five years when deposits are made at the beginning of the interest period, while only $3,964.95 is accumulated when deposits are made at the end of the interest period. This printout spans the coordinates A1–F12.

Figure 8—35   **Sample Results for SINKFND2 Program**

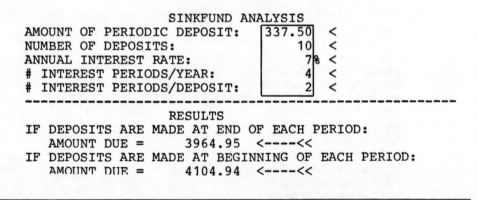

```
                    SINKFUND ANALYSIS
AMOUNT OF PERIODIC DEPOSIT:    337.50   <
NUMBER OF DEPOSITS:                10   <
ANNUAL INTEREST RATE:               7%  <
# INTEREST PERIODS/YEAR:            4   <
# INTEREST PERIODS/DEPOSIT:         2   <
------------------------------------------------------------
                       RESULTS
IF DEPOSITS ARE MADE AT END OF EACH PERIOD:
    AMOUNT DUE =       3964.95   <----<<
IF DEPOSITS ARE MADE AT BEGINNING OF EACH PERIOD:
    AMOUNT DUE =       4104.94   <----<<
```

The Computer and the Telephone

Data Retrieval Services

Unless you religiously read sources of financial information, such as *The Wall Street Journal*, *Barrons*, or various specialized private newsletters, or constantly phone your broker, it is very difficult to keep your finger on the pulse of the Treasury securities market. This is particularly true when trying to inquire about current information, as well as information that may be several weeks to up to 90 days old.

Besides being able to perform financial calculations regarding Treasury securities, most personal home computers have provisions for talking with other computer systems via what is referred to as *information retrieval services.* By merely dialing a telephone number, an average investor can "tie into" one of several financial service networks that provide capsulations of financial news as well as up to date quotations of specific Treasury issues.

In order for your computer to "talk" with a data retrieval service, which is simply a big computerized data bank, you must have a *MODEM*, which is an acronym for modulator-demodulator. The MODEM then allows your computer to be coupled to the telephone line, either directly or acoustically. Furthermore, you must have some type of "terminal," or "communications" computer program package specifically designed for your computer which primarily permits the control of sending and receiving data. Advanced communication programs allow the information to be outputted to a printer for a hard-copy record as well as for the video display, or the information can be transferred to diskettes for storage.

Unlike public libraries, data retrieval services are not free. Some require a one-time initiation, application, or membership fee. However, all charge the user either a per minute or per hour time charge. These time charges usually have a two-tiered fee structure—a prime rate during business hours, and a less expensive off-hours rate. Service users are each issued an *identification number* and a *password.* The latter should be kept secret but usually can be changed at any time by the subscriber so that only authorized subscribers gain access to a particular data retrieval service.

Once a subscriber accrues a significant amount of time charges, the service then bills the subscriber in one of two ways. For corporations and qualified individuals, billing is done directly by the service. For most individuals, billing is done via one of the major credit card firms. Furthermore, the cost of subscribing to and using an information retrieval service is wholly tax deductible if the service is used solely to manage your portfolio.

Dow Jones News/Retrieval Service

One such information retrieval service of interest to individuals concerned with Treasury issues is the Dow Jones News/Retrieval Service.[4]

---

[4] Sample printouts are reprinted by permission of the Dow Jones News/Retrieval Service, © Dow Jones & Company, Inc., 1982. All rights reserved.

Operating between 6 A.M. and 3 A.M. eastern time, this service allows the display of specific news stories from the Dow Jones News Service, as well as specific quotations on Treasury bonds and notes, of which bid and asked prices are updated each day at 6 P.M.

The Dow Jones system uses a series of coded symbols for the acquisition of specific information. For example, Figure 8–36 shows a list of 4-character codes reserved for specific Treasury notes and bonds, which is periodically revised to delete matured issues as well as adding new issues. Figure 8–37 shows the printout of a typical computer inquiry of June 10, 1982, from 8:07 to 8:16 P.M. for which current quotations for the following issues were requested:

Treasury Issue	Assigned Symbol
13¾% May 1986 T note	BAVB
3% February 1995 T bond	BGME
15¾% May 1984 T note	BARX
4% February 1988–93 T bond	BFCA

For each request, the bid and asked prices are in 1/32ds, while the yield to maturity is in percent.

On the other hand, retrieval of specific news items issued by *The Wall Street Journal, Barrons,* or the Dow Jones News Service can be selected from a menu of headlines each having its own two-letter code, as shown by the printout of Figure 8–38. Further information on the Dow Jones News/Retrieval can be obtained from:

Dow Jones & Company, Inc.
Information Services
P.O. Box 300
Princeton, NJ 08540
Telephone: 800-257-5144 (except New Jersey)
609-452-1511 (New Jersey only)

THE SOURCE

Besides the Dow Jones News/Retrieval Service, another major low-cost information retrieval system is THE SOURCE^SM, a subsidiary of *Reader's Digest.*[5] Its UNISTOX data base service can provide regularly updated quotations on Treasury rates. Secondary market bid and asked prices for traded T bills, notes, and bonds can be requested for any single issue or, as shown by the printouts of Figures 8–39 and 8–40, the entire list of a given security. Futures prices can be requested either as an hourly sum-

---

[5] THE SOURCE is a service mark of Source Telecomputing Corporation, which has applied to register THE SOURCE in the U.S. Patent and Trademark Office as a computer time-sharing information and communications service. Printouts are reprinted by permission.

Figure 8–36 4-Letter Codes Used by Dow Jones News/Retrieval Service to Identify a Given Treasury Note or Bond

U.S. Treasury Issues

U.S. TREASURY NOTES & BONDS

rate name	symbol
9¾% May 1981 N	BALC
6¾% June 1981 N	BALD
9⅛% June 1981 N	BALE
9⅜% July 1981 N	BALK
7% August 1981	BALT
7⅝% August 1981 N	BALY
8⅜% August 1981 N	BAMA
9⅝% August 1981 N	BAMB
6¾% September 1981 N	BAMC
10⅛% September 1981 N	BAMD
12⅝% October 1981 N	BAMF
7% November 1981 N	BAME
7¾% November 1981 N	BAMG
12⅛% November 1981 N	BAMH
7¼% December 1981 N	BAMK
11⅜% December 1981 N	BANL
11½% January 1982 N	BANN
6⅛% February 1982 N	BANA
6⅜% February 1982	BANE
13⅞% February 1982 N	BANC
7⅞% March 1982 N	BANK
15% March 1982 N	BANO
11⅜% April 1982 N	BAND
7% May 1982 N	BANM
8% May 1982 N	BANP
9¼% May 1982 N	BANQ
9⅜% May 1982 N	BANS
8¼% June 1982 N	BANR
8⅝% June 1982 N	BANT
8⅞% July 1982 N	BANU
8⅛% August 1982 N	BANY
9% August 1982 N	BANZ
11⅛% August 1982 N	BAPB
8⅜% September 1982 N	BAPA
11⅞% September 1982 N	BAPD
12⅛% October 1982 N	BAPF
7⅛% November 1982 N	BAPL
7⅞% November 1982 N	BAPM
13⅞% November 1982 N	BAPO
9⅜% December 1982 N	BAPS
15⅛% December 1982 N	BAPU
13⅝% January 1983 N	BAPW
8% February 1983 N	BAQE
13⅞% February 1983 n	BAQF
9¼% March 1983 N	BAQG
12% March 1983 N	BAQI
14½% April 1983N	BAQJ
7⅞% May 1983 N	BAQH
11⅝% May 1983 N	BAQK
3¼% June 1978-83	BAQN
8⅞% June 1983 N	BAQR
11⅞% August 1983 N	BAQS
9¼% August 1983 N	BAQU
9¾% Septemer 1983 N	BAQT
7% November 1983 N	BARE
9⅞% November 1983 N	BARJ
10½% December 1983 N	BARH

U.S. TREASURY NOTES & BONDS

rate name	symbol
7¼% February 1984 N	BARN
14¼% March 1984 N	BARO
9¼% May 1984 N	BARR
13¼% May 1984 N	BART
15¾% May 1984 N	BARX
8⅞% June 1984 N	BARV
6⅜% August 1984	BASE
7¼% August 1984 N	BASH
13¼ August 1984 N	BASI
12⅛% September 1984 N	BBASJ
14% December 1984 N	BASK
8% February 1985 N	BAST
13⅜% March 1985 N	BASU
3¼% May 1985	BATE
4¼% May 1975-85	BATN
10⅜% May 1985 N	BATO
14⅜% May 1985 N	BATQ
8¼% August 1985 N	BATP
9⅝% August 1985 N	BATR
11¾% November 1985	BATU
13½% February 1986 N	BATW
7⅞% May 1986 N	BAVA
13¾% May 1986 N	BAVB
8% August 1986 N	BAVN
6⅛% November 1986	BAXE
9% February 1987 N	BAXF
12% May 1987 N	BAXL
7⅝ November 1987 N	BAXK
12⅜% January 1988 N	BAXM
13¼% April 1988 N	BAXO
8¼% May 1988 N	BAYE
8¾% November 1988 N	BAYH
9¼% May 1989 N	BAYR
10¾% November 1989 N	BAZA
3½% February 1990	BEDE
8¼% May 1990	BEDU
10¾% August 1990 N	BEDW
13% November 1990 N	BEDX
4¼% August 1987-92	BFBE
14.42 May 1991 N	BEDZ
7¼% August 1992	BFBH
4% February 1988-93	BFCA
6¾% February 1993	BFCU
7⅞% February 1993	BFCW
7½ August 1988-93	BFDK
8⅝% August 1993	BFDN
8⅝% November 1993	BFDR
9% February 1994	BFKA
4⅛% May 1989-94	BGEL
8¾% August 1994	BGER
10⅛% November 1994	BGEV
3% February 1995	BGME
10½% February 1995	BGMG
12⅝% May 1995	BGMJ
10⅜% May 1995	BGMO
7% May 1993-98	BLDE
3½% November 1998	BLDU

U.S. TREASURY NOTES & BONDS

rate name	symbol
8½% May 1994-99	BLFE
7⅞% February 1995-00	BLGA
8⅜% August 1995-00	BLGN
8% August 1996-01	BLHU
8¼% May 2000-05	BNCA
11¾% February 2001	BLGP
13⅛% May 2001	BLGR
7⅝% February 2002-07	BNKA
7⅞% November 2002-07	BNKU
8⅜% August 2003-08	BNLE
8¾% November 2003-08	BNLH
9⅛% May 2004-09	BNLP
10⅜% Novembar 2004-09	BNLS
11¾% February 2005-10	BNLV
10% May 2005-10	BNLX
12¾% November 2005-10	BNLZ
13⅞% May 2006	BLGT

N-Notes.

Figure 8–37   **Sample Quotation Requests**

```
            DOW JONES NEWS/RETRIEVAL
               COPYRIGHT (C) 1982
            DOW JONES & COMPANY, INC.
               ALL RIGHTS RESERVED.

     ENTER QUERY
        #BAVB

     DOW JONES STOCK
     QUOTE REPORTER SERVICE
     STOCK QUOTES DELAYED
     OVER 15 MINUTES
     * = CLOSE ADJ. FOR EX-DIVIDEND

     STOCK          BAVB
     BID            99.03
     ASKED          99.07
     YIELD          14.02


        #BGME


     STOCK          BGME
     BID            83.04
     ASKED          83.20
     YIELD          4.73


        #BARX


     STOCK          BARX
     BID            102.26
     ASKED          102.30
     YIELD          13.96


        #BFCA


     STOCK          BFCA
     BID            82.28
     ASKED          83.12
     YIELD          6.15


     DISC


     LOG ON: 20 07  LOG OFF: 20 16  EASTERN TIME
     JUNE 10, 1982
```

Courtesy Dow Jones News/Retrieval Service

Figure 8–38   **Sample News Stories Concerning Treasury Securities**

```
        DOW JONES NEWS/RETRIEVAL
           COPYRIGHT (C) 1982
        DOW JONES & COMPANY, INC.
           ALL RIGHTS RESERVED.


  N  G/TRE     04/43  HR 1/3
//FIN BON/TRE
      TREASURY TO SELL 2-YEAR
 06/09  NOTES JUNE 16, 4-YEAR
 (DW )  NOTES JUNE 23
     WASHN -DJ- THE TREASURY PLANS
TO RAISE $2.53 BILLION IN FRESH
CASH NEXT WITH THE SALE OF $5.5
BILLION IN TWO-YEAR NOTES ON
JUNE 16 AND $4 BILLION IN
FOUR-YEAR NOTES JUNE 23.
     THE BALANCE OF THE PROCEEDS
OF BOTH ISSUES WILL BE USED TO
REDEEM $6.97 BILLION IN MATURING
NOTES.


  N  G/TRE     04/43  HR 2/3
     BOTH ISSUES WILL BE DATED
JUNE 30. THE TWO-YEAR NOTES WILL
MATURE JUNE 30 1984 AND THE
FOUR-YEAR NOTES WILL MATURE JUNE
30 1986.
     TENDERS FOR THE TWO-YEAR
NOTES AVAILABLE IN MINIMUM
DENOMINATIONS OF $5 000 MUST BE
RECEIVED BY 1 30 P.M. EDT JUNE
16 AT THE TREASURY OR AT FEDERAL
RESERVE BANKS OR BRANCHES.
     TENDERS FOR THE FOUR-YEAR
NOTES AVAILABLE IN MINIMUM
DENOMINATIONS OF $1 000  MUST BE
RECEIVED BY 1 30 PM EDT JUNE 23


  N  G/TRE     04/43  HR 3/3
AT THE TREASURY OR AT FEDERAL
RESERVE BANKS OR BRANCHES.
     THE TREASURY SAID IT WILL
POSTPONE THE FOUR- YEAR NOTE
AUCTION UNLESS IT HAS ASSURANCE
OF CONGRESSIONAL ACTION ON
LEGISLATION TO RAISE THE DEBT
CEILING BEFORE THE SCHEDULED
AUCTION DATE.
     4 07 PM
                DISC


LOG ON: 21 09  LOG OFF: 21 18   EASTERN TIME
JUNE 10, 1982
```

Courtesy Dow Jones News/Retrieval Service

Figure 8–39   **Closing Treasury Bill Quotations**

```
(C) COPYRIGHT SOURCE TELECOMPUTING CORPORATION 1983.
UNISTOX

ENTER KEYWORDS, ONE PER LINE, AND PRESS RETURN TWICE,
OR PRESS RETURN ONCE FOR THE ENTIRE REPORT.

FRI, FEB 18 1983

     New York (UPI)
   Closing U.S.
Treasury Bills for
Friday.
   Maturity     # Bid#Ask
         #  *#  *  Discount
 Feb  24/83  8.00 7.90
 Mar   3     8.00 7.90
 Mar  10     7.85 7.75
 Mar  17     7.75 7.65
 Mar  24     7.85 7.75
 Mar  31     7.85 7.75
 Apr   7     7.85 7.75
 Apr  14     7.95 7.85
 Apr  21     8.05 7.95
 Apr  28     8.05 7.95
 May   5     8.05 7.95
 May  12     8.05 7.95
 May  19     7.98 7.94
 May  26     7.95 7.85
 Jun   2     8.05 7.95
 Jun   9     8.05 7.95
 Jun  16     8.10 8.00
 Jun  23     8.05 7.95
 Jun  30     8.10 8.00
 Jly   7     8.15 8.05
 Jly  14     8.15 8.05
 Jly  21     8.15 8.05
 Jly  28     8.20 8.10
 Aug   4     8.20 8.10
 Aug  11     8.20 8.10
 Aug  18     8.13 8.09
 Sep   8     8.10 8.00
 Oct   6     8.15 8.05
 Nov   3     8.20 8.10
 Dec   1     8.20 8.10
 Dec  29     8.25 8.15
 Jan  26/84  8.22 8.18
```

Courtesy THE SOURCE

Figure 8–40   **Closing Treasury Bond Quotations**

```
(C) COPYRIGHT SOURCE TELECOMPUTING CORPORATION 1983.
UNISTOX

ENTER KEYWORDS, ONE PER LINE, AND PRESS RETURN TWICE,
OR PRESS RETURN ONCE FOR THE ENTIRE REPORT.

FRI, FEB 18 1983
     TREASURY BONDS
     NEW YORK (UPI)  Closing Over-the-
Counter U.S. Government Treasury
Bonds Friday. Prices quoted in dollars
and 32nds.
          #   *#   *#  *#   *   # Bid*Ask*Chg*Yld
   7 7-8s 2000    Feb      77.17 77.25+ .23 10.75
   8 3-8s 2000    Aug      80.29 81.05+ .27 10.79
  11 3-4s 2001    Feb     104.30 105.06+ .23 11.07
  13 1-8s 2001    May     114.28 115.04+1.01 11.16
   8s   2001      Aug      77.30 78.06+ .23 10.73
  13 3-8s 2001    Aug     116.24 117.00+ .29 11.18
  15 3-4s 2001    Nov     135.02 135.18+1.04 11.18
  14 1-4s 2002    Feb     123.27 124.03+1.03 11.17
  11 5-8s 2002    Nov     104.14 104.22+ .26 11.03
  10 3-4s 2003    Feb      98.24 99.00+ .29 10.88
   8 1-4s 2005    May      79.18 80.02+ .23 10.59
   7 5-8s 2007    Feb      74.19 74.29+ .25 10.51
   7 7-8s 2007    Nov      76.14 76.22+ .21 10.54
   8 3-8s 2008    Aug      79.26 80.02+ .18 10.66
   8 3-4s 2008    Nov      82.24 83.00+ .24 10.70
   9 1-8s 2009    May      85.27 86.03+ .29 10.72
  10 3-8s 2009    Nov      95.24 96.00+ .23 10.84
  11 3-4s 2010    Feb     105.23 105.31+ .25 11.02
  10s   2010      May      92.28 93.04+ .28 10.79
  12 3-4s 2010    Nov     113.08 113.16+ .26 11.11
  13 7-8s 2011    May     122.11 122.19+1.00 11.14
  14s   2011      Nov     123.26 124.02+ .30 11.11
  10 3-8s 2012    Nov      96.16 96.20+ .24 10.76
     Source: Federal Reserve Bank of New York.
```

Courtesy THE SOURCE

mary (see Figure 8–41), a current report, the previous day's closing prices (see Figure 8–42), or last week's closing prices.

THE SOURCE also has an option, called COMPUDEX, which is a library of computer application programs. For those interested in Treasury securities, COMPUDEX can determine:

- The price of accrued interest for a T note or bond.
- The aftertax yield to maturity of a T note or bond.
- Amortization schedules.

as well as other useful investment situations. Further information about THE SOURCE can be obtained from:

> Source Telecomputing Corporation
> 1616 Anderson Road
> McLean, VA 22102
> Telephone: 703-734-7500
> 800-336-3366 (except Virginia)
> 800-572-2070 (Virginia only)

Figure 8–41   **Hourly Summary Quotations on 13-Week Treasury Bill Futures
Traded on the International Monetary Market**

```
(C) COPYRIGHT SOURCE TELECOMPUTING CORPORATION 1983.
UNISTOX

IMM - 13-WK T-BILLS

1   CURRENT REPORT
2   HOURLY SUMMARY
3   TODAY'S OPEN
4   CLOSING PRICES
5   LAST WEEK'S CLOSE

Enter item number or HELP: 2

1346 CST FUTURES PRICES
      HIGH      LOW       LAST      CHANGE
    IMM 13-WK T-BILLS
  MAR 9218      9204      9210      UP   11
  JUN 9208      9193      9201      UP   11
  SEP 9171      9158      9165A
  DEC 9133      9122      9128      UP   10
  MAR 9093      9087A     9089      UP   5
```

Courtesy THE SOURCE

Figure 8–42   **Treasury Bill and Bond Futures Closing Prices**

```
(C) COPYRIGHT SOURCE TELECOMPUTING CORPORATION 1983.
UNISTOX

ENTER KEYWORDS, ONE PER LINE, AND PRESS RETURN TWICE,
OR PRESS RETURN ONCE FOR THE ENTIRE REPORT.

FRI, FEB 18 1983
   90-DAY TREASURY BILLS
   CHICAGO (UPI)  International
Monetary Market 90-day Treasury bill
futures closing range of prices Friday.
90-DAY U.S. TREASURY BILLS:
Mercex $1 million; pts of 100 pc
```

	#	*#	* Open#	High*Low*	Close	Prev.
Mar		92.04	92.18	92.04	92.09	91.99
Jun		91.93	92.08	91.93	92.00	91.90
Sep		91.58	91.71	91.58	91.64	91.53
Dec		91.24	91.33	91.22	91.25	91.18
Mar		90.08	90.93	90.87	90.89	90.84
Jun		90.60	90.61	90.60	90.61	90.57
Sep		90.33	90.33	90.32	90.32	90.31
Dec		90.10	90.10	90.10	90.10	90.06

```
   Open interest: 46,362 up 93.
   Total volume: 20,920 contracts.


   TREASURY BOND FUTURES
   CHICAGO (UPI)   Long-term Treasury bond futures closing
range of prices Friday:

LONG-TERM TREASURY BONDS:
Bd Trade   8 pc; $100,000 prin;
points and 32nds of 100 pc
```

	#	*#	* Open#	High*Low*	Close	Prev.
Mar		75.05	75.27	75.05	75.23	75.01
Jun		74.14	75.01	74.13	74.31	74.08
Sep		73.25	74.11	73.25	74.10	73.20
Dec		73.10	73.28	73.10	73.28	73.05
Mar		72.30	73.14	72.30	73.10	72.25
Jun		72.22	73.04	72.22	72.30	72.16
Sep		72.16	72.28	72.16	72.23	72.09
Dec		72.10	72.21	72.10	72.20	72.03
Mar	**	**	**	72.15	71.30	
Jun	**	**	**	72.10	71.26	
Sep	**	**	**	72.06	71.22	

```
   Open interest: 161,424 off 3,575.
   Total volume: 62,380 contracts.
```

Courtesy THE SOURCE

A friend of mine once told me, "We don't have as much to fear from the Russians as we do from the IRS." Well, I admit that the IRS does on occasion make its presence felt. Although this chapter is not designed to be a discussion on how to avoid the IRS or evade paying taxes, I am not going to bury my head in the sand and deny that there are techniques used to minimize one's visibility to the IRS. This chapter discusses your legal tax consequences when dealing with Treasury securities—whether purchased directly or indirectly as zero coupon securities, through mutual funds, options, or commodity futures. When in doubt, always seek the advice of a competent tax advisor—it's tax deductible.

Your Tax Liability

By law, all interest from T bills, notes, and bonds is subject to federal income tax as ordinary income, but is entirely exempt from all state and local taxes. This is reported on Part 1, Schedule B of Form 1040 when you prepare your income tax return.

T Bills

If you purchase T bills at auction directly from the Treasury, at the beginning of the following year you will receive an IBM-style card or other facsimile from the Federal Reserve bank where you submitted your tender. This card, which is a substitute for the IRS Form 1099-INT, indicates the amount of interest paid on a particular T bill issue. If you purchased five different T bills during the year, you will receive five different notices. The interest need only be reported for the year that the T bill matured. For example, suppose you purchased a 13-week T bill in November of 1981 and received a discount check for $250. Since the T bill actually matures in February 1982, the $250 in interest earned on this bill is declared on your *1982* Federal tax return.

If, on the other hand, you purchased your T bill on the open market through a bank or broker and let it mature, you will receive the 1099-INT form directly from them instead of the Treasury. However, if you sell the T bill on the open market before it matures, the difference between the purchase price and the selling price is treated as ordinary income (i.e., interest) and is reported on Part 1 of Schedule B. Of course this assumes that you sell the T bill for more than you paid for it, either on the open market or at a discount at auction. If you sell a T bill for less than you paid for it, then this is treated as a *short-term capital loss* and is reported on Schedule D.

Since, in all cases, the government has your taxpayer identification number when the purchase was made, there is no way you can escape reporting the interest.

T Notes and Bonds

Because of the manner T notes and bonds are issued, they present different circumstances. To purchase *bearer* T notes and bonds before 1983, a taxpayer identification number was not required. Consequently, for tax purposes, the Treasury did not really know who held the certificates. However, as of January 1, 1983, when you cash interest coupons at either the Federal Reserve bank or a local bank, the teller will fill out an IRS Form 1099-INT (see Figure 9–1) for the amount of interest paid. In addition, your taxpayer identification number will be required for the completion of this form.

On the other hand, the ownership of registered T notes and bonds are recorded by the Treasury. Consequently, they and the IRS have the taxpayer identifying number(s) of the owner(s).

Normally, T bonds, when owned by a person who later dies, become part of the decedent's estate. However, certain T bond issues may, at the request of the estate's executor or administrator, be redeemed at par value only if the U.S. Treasury is instructed to apply the proceeds to federal estate taxes. Because of the nature of these deeply discounted T bonds, they have often been referred to as *flower bonds*, but they are no longer

Figure 9–1   **IRS Form 1099-INT**

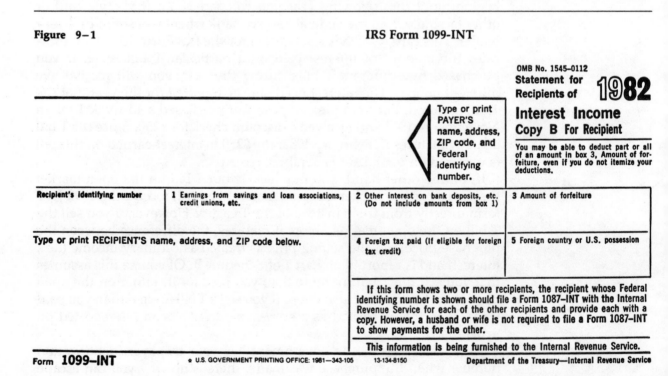

available as new issues. As of 1983, the outstanding issues still carrying this provision are listed in Table 9–1.

Table 9–1	Outstanding Flower Bonds (1983)	
	3¼%	May 15, 1985
	4¼%	August 15, 1987–92
	4%	February 15, 1988–93
	4⅛%	May 15, 1989–94
	3½%	February 15, 1990
	3%	February 15, 1995
	3½%	November 15, 1998

Capital Gain or Loss

T bills, which are normally bought at a discount, are not normally subject to capital gains treatment. On the other hand, if T notes or bonds are bought and then later sold before maturity on the open market, you must report the gain (or loss) on this exchange as *capital* gain or (loss) on Schedule D of your tax return. At the present time, the gain is taxed at a 40 percent rate when the security is held longer than one year (i.e., a long-term gain); otherwise, short-term gains are taxed fully at 100 percent. This "holding period" for T notes and bonds sold at auction starts the day after the subscription letter or tender is submitted. For specific details as to whether your capital gain deduction may be subject to preferential tax treatments, such as the alternative tax for individuals, it is strongly recommended that you consult with a person well versed in the tax law.

Zero Coupon Securities

Holders of zero coupon securities are required to declare each year the accrued interest that was earned even though no interest was paid. As an example, suppose you bought one of E. F. Hutton Group Inc.'s TBRs maturing in 10 years for $200, even though the principal face value is $1,000. If you hold this bond to maturity, you would realize a gain of $1,000 − $200, or $800. Consequently, the yearly taxable interest is then $800/10 or $80, which is reported on Part 1 of Schedule B of your tax return.

On the other hand, suppose you decide to sell the TBR on the open market after holding it for five years. To first determine your current cost basis, multiply the $80 annual taxable interest by the five years the bond was held, or $400. Then you add this to the original TBR purchase price of $200, or a current cost basis of $600. If you sell the TBR for more than the $600 current cost basis, for example $700, the $100 difference is treated as a *long term capital gain*. However, if you sell the TBR at $450, you achieve a $600 − $450, or a $150 capital loss which is then used to offset other gains or ordinary income. Like any other capital gain or loss, this is reported on Schedule D of your tax return.

If the zero coupon bond discount is more than $10, the securities dealer from whom you purchased a discounted zero coupon bond will give you a copy of Form 1099-OID, or Statement for Recipients of Original Issue Discount (see Figure 9–2) for the calendar year in which you purchased the bond.

Figure 9–2   **IRS Form 1099-OID**

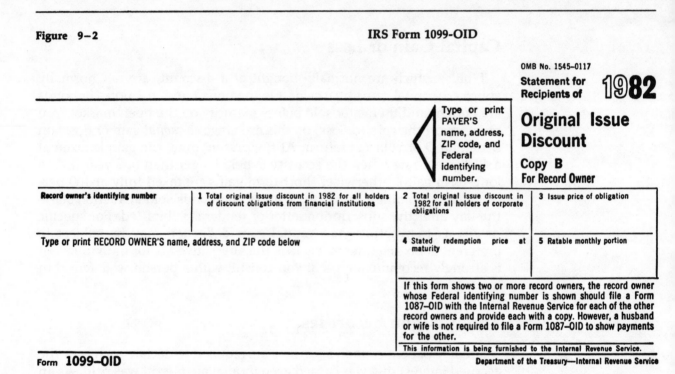

Treasury Money Market Mutual Funds

By the IRS Code, a money market mutual fund is a "regulated investment company" and does not pay any taxes on the net income and capital gains it pays to its shareholders. In general, "Treasury" money market mutual funds qualify for this tax status as long as they meet certain requirements.

Figure 9–3   IRS Form 1099-DIV

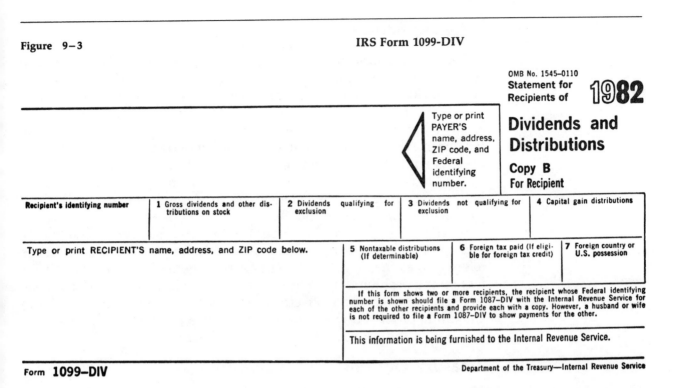

Mutual funds make payments to shareholders from their net investment income in the form of dividend payments, which generally
include any net short-term capital gains. These payments are taxable as
ordinary income, whether received in cash or reinvested in additional
shares. The mutual fund sends you a copy of IRS Form 1099-DIV (see
Figure 9–3), indicating the amount of your dividends. This is reported on
Part 2 of Schedule B of your tax return. In general, no portion of any
mutual fund's dividend is eligible for the "dividends received" exclusion
available to individual taxpayers, or the 85 percent deduction for dividends received by corporations.

Capital gain distributions made are taxable as long-term capital gains,
regardless of how long you held the shares. Furthermore, capital gain
distributions are not eligible for the dividends received from individual
exclusion or corporate deduction.

Even though a Treasury mutual fund's income may have been derived
from interest on U.S. government securities which normally would be
exempt from state and local income taxes if purchased directly from the
Treasury, the dividends may still be subject to certain state and local
income taxes. Although the mutual fund should notify shareholders
about the tax status of its dividends and distributions, you should nevertheless consult a competent tax advisor as to the application of state and
local taxes on Treasury mutual funds.

Treasury Futures

Gains and losses on hedging contracts purchased in the ordinary course of a business, such as a bank, are treated as ordinary business gains and losses. On the other hand, gains and losses on Treasury futures contracts held as capital investments by speculators, are generally treated as any other capital gain or loss and are reported on Schedule D of your tax return. The exception is that the holding period for long-term treatment is six months instead of the present one-year period generally applied to capital gains and losses. "Round turn" commissions paid to brokers are not deductible, but are used to determine the cost basis of the contract for capital gains and losses.

Special rules apply to the amount of loss you may deduct on one or more positions of a *straddle*, or any set of offsetting positions (sometimes referred to as the "legs" of the straddle). In general, you may deduct a loss on the position only to the extent that the loss exceeds any unrealized gain you have on offsetting positions. An *unrealized gain* is the amount of profit you would have if you sold a position on the last business day of the tax year at its fair market value.

Treasury Options

At the present, all option premiums, gains, and losses are considered to be short-term capital gains and losses and are reported on Schedule D of your tax return. This is because Treasury options by their nature have a maximum expiration of less than one year, so there can be no long-term capital gain.

If the option is exercised, the entire transaction is treated as either a purchase or sale of the underlying Treasury security, for example, a T bill. You must add this payment to any other amounts you receive to determine the amount you realized on the sale of the underlying securities. The holding period of the option cannot be added to that of the security when determining the holding period for capital gains and losses. On the other hand, if you own an option and it expires unexercised, its value is zero. You therefore have a short-term capital loss.

If you exercise a *call*, or buy option, you add its cost to the basis of the Treasury security you bought. If you exercised a *put*, or sell option, you subtract its cost from the amount realized on the sale of the underlying security.

What about Deductions?

In your pursuit to acquire those investments which will hopefully be profitable, the IRS does allow you to deduct certain "ordinary and necessary" expenses when preparing your tax return. The following most common deductions that apply to investors concerned with T bills, notes, and bonds are entered as *miscellaneous deductions* on Schedule A of your tax return.

Amortization of Premiums

Under present regulations, all holders (except brokers and other dealers in Treasury securities) of those T notes and bonds bought at a premium can amortize the premium paid. Consequently, amortization reduces one's basis for determining the possible gain or loss when the security either is sold on the open market or matures. The advantage of amortization is that the amount being amortized in a given tax year is allowed as a deduction, and the basis for the T note or bond is reduced accordingly. This deduction is entered as a miscellaneous deduction on Schedule A of your tax return.

When the purchase price of either a T note or bond is higher than the value at maturity, the purchaser's capital can effectively be kept intact by setting aside a portion of the interest paid from the redeeming coupons so that the total of this amount will equal the amount of the premium at maturity (or call). The period of amortization is from the date of purchase to the maturity or call date, whichever is applicable. If the T note or bond is called before maturity, any unamortized premium is amortized at the time of the call, to the extent that this unused amount plus the tax basis for the note or bond exceeds the amount received on redemption at call.

The actual amortization used may be any one of several which are "customary, reasonable, and consistent with proper accounting procedures." The two most common methods are the *straight-line* method and one that is built around equations used to compute those yield tables that appear in many books on finance. Examples for determining the amortization schedule are discussed in Chapter 7.

Investment Counsel and Advice

You may deduct fees paid for counsel and advice about Treasury securities since these types of securities are generally intended to earn income that is taxable. Other than those fees paid to lawyers, certified public accountants, and other tax and investment advisors, you may, for example, deduct the purchase price of this book, charges for computer data retrieval services, computer investment software, and subscriptions for investment and financial magazines, newsletters, and newspapers, such as *The Wall Street Journal, Barrons, and Forbes.*

Safe Deposit Box Rental

If you use a safe deposit box to store T notes and bonds (whether registered or bearer issues), zero coupon Treasury securities, receipts for book-entry T bill accounts, or receipts from banks or security firms holding T bills, notes, or bonds for you, you are entitled to deduct the box rental paid. However, if you also use a safe deposit box to store personal items and tax-exempt securities, then you can only deduct part of the rental fee.

Unless you have a large safe deposit box where the rental fee is greater than about $50, I have found that a significant number of people tend not to deduct safe deposit box rental fees. This is probably done to reduce one's visibility to the tax collector, especially when certain liquid assets may be subject to estate taxes upon the death of the owner.

Custody Fees

If you purchase a T bill on the open market through a bank or securities dealer, you will usually be charged a commission in addition to a "safekeeping" fee. The safekeeping fee can be deducted, while the commission paid for the purchase or sale of the T bill must be used to determine the cost basis of the T bill.

If a bank or securities dealer purchases a T note or bond on the open market, they will generally hold the certificate, while also collecting the semiannual coupon interest payments for you. If you prefer to have possession of the security certificate instead of the bank or securities dealer, you will usually pay a "transfer" fee which is deductible as a miscellaneous deduction. The commission charged for the purchase or sale of a T note or bond is not deductible, but must be used to determine the cost basis of the note or bond. Any fees charged for the collection and payment of interest is also deductible.

Interest Paid

If you borrow money in order to buy Treasury securities, you can deduct the interest paid to the lender only on your federal tax return (Schedule A). Since the income from Treasury securities is generally exempt from state and local taxes, this interest expense is not generally able to be used as a deduction on state and local tax returns. However, this interest deduction is limited to the *net investment income* plus $10,000 for a joint return ($5,000 for single individuals or married filing separately).

Postage

If you purchase Treasury securities directly from the Treasury and use certified mail for mailing your subscription or tender letter or for sending matured securities by registered mail, the cost of postage can be deducted as a miscellaneous deduction.

Transportation

In general, you are not able to deduct transportation and other traveling expenses incurred in order to attend a stockholder's meeting of a Treasury mutual fund in which you have no interest other than owning shares. This is true even though you may take the position that your attendance is to obtain information that would be useful in making future investments.

The 1970 Bank Secrecy Act and IRS Form 4789

Most U.S. citizens who frequently travel abroad probably know of the provision of Public Law 91-508 which prohibits one from legally taking out or bringing into the United States an amount over $5,000 at one time, without it being declared to the Customs Department and consequently to the IRS. This includes U.S. currency, foreign currency, traveler's checks, money orders, or bearer form negotiable securities, whether physically or by mail. If such is the case, one must fill out IRS Form 4790 on the spot and give it to the customs officer.

On the other hand, more people use banks every day than those who travel, but very few know of several other provisions of Public Law 91-508, formerly called the Currency and Foreign Transactions Reporting Act. This act is presently referred to as the 1970 Bank Secrecy Act and frequently requires the completion of IRS Form 4789. In fact, when the provisions of this act apply, you are not the one who fills out this form!

Basically, the Secrecy Act states that any financial institution must report to the IRS on Form 4789 (see Figure 9–4) any transaction for amounts over $10,000. Such transactions include deposits, withdrawals, exchanges of currency, cashing of checks, cashier's/treasurer's checks purchased, bank transfers, etc. Furthermore, multiple transactions by or for any person where the one-day total is more than $10,000 at a given institution, such as a bank with its branch offices, is to be treated as if it were a single transaction.

Figure 9-4   IRS Form 4789 for Reporting Transactions over $10,000

Currency Transaction Report

Form 4789
(Rev. Sept. 1980)
Department of the Treasury
Internal Revenue Service

File a separate report for each transaction
(Complete all applicable parts—see instructions)

Part I   Identity of individual who conducted this transaction with the financial institution

Name (Last)	First		Middle Initial	Social Security Number
Number and Street				Business, occupation, or profession
City	State	ZIP code	Country (If not U.S.)	

Method of verifying identification:
☐ Driver's permit _____(State)_____ _____(Number)_____   ☐ Alien ID card _____(Country)_____ _____(Number)_____
☐ Passport _____(Country)_____ _____(Number)_____   ☐ Other (specify) _____

Part II   Individual or organization for whom this transaction was completed (Complete only if different from Part I)

Name	Identifying number
Number and Street	Business, occupation, or profession

City	State	ZIP code	Country (If not U.S.)

Part III   Customer's account number

☐ Savings account _____(Number)_____   ☐ Share account _____(Number)_____   ☐ Safety deposit box _____(Number)_____
☐ Checking account _____(Number)_____   ☐ Loan account _____(Number)_____   ☐ Other (specify) _____

Part IV   Description of transaction. If more space is needed, attach a separate schedule and check this box ☐

1. Nature of transaction (check the applicable boxes)
☐ Deposit   ☐ Check Cashed   ⎫   ☐ Currency Exchange
☐ Withdrawal   ☐ Check Purchased ⎬ See item 6   ☐ Mail/Night Deposit
                                                                   ☐ Other (specify)

2. Total amount of currency transaction (in U.S. dollars)	3. Amount in denominations of $100 or higher	4. Date of transaction (Month, day, and year)

5. If other than U.S. currency is involved, please furnish the following information:

Currency name	Country	Total amount of each foreign currency (in U.S. dollars)

6. If a check was involved in this transaction, please furnish the following information (See Instructions):

Date of check	Amount of check (in U.S. dollars)	Payee
Drawer of check		Drawee bank and City

Part V   Financial institution reporting the financial transaction

Name and Address	Identifying number (EIN or SSN)
	Business activity

Sign here ► _____(Authorized Signature)_____   _____(Title)_____   _____(Date)_____

Type or print name of authorized signer ►

As with any rule, there are exceptions. Without going into the gory details, Form 4789 does not have to be filed if the individual or business is routinely involved in the transaction of large sums of money. However, a record of these customers must be maintained. For obvious reasons in the IRS's favor, the word *routine* has not been precisely defined by them. Banks have been fined as much as $250,000 for failing to report such transactions to the IRS within 15 days. If the implications of the Bank Secrecy Act are not apparent, you probably have nothing to hide from the "big bad wolf."

Glossary

Common Terms Used with
Treasury Securities and Other
Money Market Instruments

ABT: American Board of Trade, an options exchange.

Accretion (of a discount):   In portfolio accounting, a straight-line accumulation of capital gains on discount bonds in anticipation of receipt of par at maturity.

Accrued interest: Interest due from issue or from the last coupon date to the present on an interest-bearing security. The buyer of the security pays the quoted dollar price plus accrued interest.

Active: A market in which there is much trading.

Actuals: The cash commodity as opposed to the futures contract.

Add-on rate: A specific rate of interest to be paid. Stands in contrast to the rate on a discount security, such as a Treasury bill, that pays *no* interest.

Aftertax real rate of return: Money aftertax rate of return minus the inflation rate.

Agent: A firm that executes orders for or otherwise acts on behalf of another (the principal) and is subject to its control and authority. The agent may receive a fee or commission.

Amortize: In portfolio accounting, periodic charges made against interest income on premium bonds in anticipation of receipt of the call price at call or of par value at maturity.

Arbitrage: Strictly defined, buying something where it is cheap and selling it where it is dear; e.g., a bank buys 3-month CD money in the U.S. market and sells 3-month money at a higher rate in the Eurodollar market. In the money market, often refers: (1) to a situation in which a trader buys one security and sells a similar security in the expectation that the spread in yields between the two instruments will narrow or widen to his profit, (2) to a swap between two similar issues based on an anticipated change in yield spreads, and (3) to situations where a higher return (or lower cost) can be achieved in the money market for one currency by utilizing another currency and swapping it on a fully hedged basis through the foreign exchange market.

Asked: The price at which securities are offered.

Away: A trade, quote, or market that does not originate with the dealer in question, e.g., "the bid is 98-10 away (from me)."

Back contracts: Futures contracts farthest from expiration.

Back up: (1) When yields rise and prices fall, the market is said to back up. (2) When an investor swaps out of one security into another of shorter current maturity (e.g., out of a 2-year note into an 18-month note), he is said to back up.

Bank discount rate: Yield basis on which short-term, non-interest-bearing money market securities are quoted. A rate quoted on a discount basis understands bond equivalent yield. That must be calculated when comparing return against coupon securities.

Bank wire: A computer message system linking major banks. It is used not for effecting payments, but as a mechanism to advise the receiving bank of some action that has occurred, e.g., the payment by a customer of funds into that bank's account.

Basis: (1) Number of days in the coupon period. (2) In *commodities* jargon, basis is the spread between a futures price and some other price. A money market participant would talk about *spread* rather than basis.

Basis point: One one hundredth of 1% (0.01%).

Basis price: Price expressed in terms of yield to maturity or annual rate of return.

Bear market: A declining market or a period of pessimism when declines in the market are anticipated. (A way to remember: "Bear down.")

Bearer security: A security the owner of which is not registered on the books of the issuer. A bearer security is payable to the holder.

Bid: The price offered for securities.

Block: A large amount of securities, normally much more than what constitutes a round lot in the market in question.

Book-entry securities: The Treasury and federal agencies are moving to a book-entry system in which securities are not represented by engraved pieces of paper but are maintained in computerized records at the Fed in the names of member banks, which, in turn, keep records of the securities they own as well as those they are holding for customers. In the case of other securities for which there is a book-entry system, engraved securities do exist somewhere in quite a few cases. These securities do not move from holder to holder but are usually kept in a central clearinghouse or by another agent.

Book value: The value at which a debt security is shown on the holder's balance sheet. Book value is often acquisition cost ± amortization/accretion, which may differ markedly from market value. It can be further defined as "tax book," "accreted book," or "amortized book" value.

Broker: A broker brings buyers and sellers together for a commission paid by the initiator of the transaction or by both sides; he does not position. In the money market, brokers are active in markets in which banks buy and sell money and in interdealer markets.

Bull market: A period of optimism when increases in market prices are anticipated. (A way to remember: "Bull ahead.")

Buy a spread: Buy a near futures contract and sell a far one.

Buy-back: Another term for a repurchase agreement.

Calendar: List of new bond issues scheduled to come to market soon.

Call: An option that gives the holder the right to buy the underlying security at a specified price during a fixed time period.

Call money: Interest-bearing bank deposits that can be withdrawn on 24-hours notice. Many Eurodeposits take the form of call money.

Callable bond: A bond that the issuer has the right to redeem prior to maturity by paying some specified call price.

Cash commodity or security: The actual commodity or security as opposed to futures contracts for it.

Cash management bill: Very short-maturity bills that the Treasury occasionally sells because its cash balances are down and it needs money for a few days.

Cash market: Traditionally, this term has been used to denote the market in which commodities were traded, for immediate delivery, against cash. Since the inception of futures markets for T bills and other debt securities, a distinction has been made between the cash markets in which these securities trade for immediate delivery and the futures markets in which they trade for future delivery.

Cash price: Price quotation in the cash market.

CATS: Certificates of Accrual on Treasury Securities. Zero coupon Treasury bonds sold by Salomon Brothers/Bache.

CBOE: Chicago Board Options Exchange.

CBT: Chicago Board of Trade, a futures exchange.

Certificate of deposit (CD):   A time deposit with a specific maturity evidenced by a certificate. Large-denomination CDs are typically negotiable.

CFTC: Commodity Futures Trading Commission. An agency created by Congress which regulates futures trading.

Commercial paper: An unsecured promissory note with a fixed maturity of no more than 270 days. Commercial paper is normally sold at a discount from face value.

Competitive bid: (1) Bid tendered in a Treasury action for a specific amount of securities at a specific yield or price. (2) Issuers, municipal and public utilities, often sell new issues by asking for competitive bids from one or more syndicates.

Confirmation: A memorandum to the other side of a trade describing all relevant data.

Corporate bond equivalent: See **Equivalent bond yield.**

Corporate taxable equivalent: Rate of return required on a par bond to produce the same aftertax yield to maturity that the premium or discount bond quoted would.

Coupon: (1) The annual rate of interest on the bond's face value that a bond's issuer promises to pay the bondholder. (2) A certificate attached to a bond evidencing interest due on a payment date.

Cover: Eliminating a short position by buying the securities shorted.

Covered call write: Selling calls against securities owned by the call seller.

Cross hedge: Hedging a risk in a cash market security by buying or selling a futures contract for a similar but not identical instrument.

CRTs: Abbreviation for the cathode-ray tubes used to display market quotes.

Current coupon: A bond selling at or close to par; that is, a bond with a coupon close to the yield currently offered on new bonds of similar maturity and credit risk.

Current issue: In Treasury bills and notes, the most recently auctioned issue. Trading is more active in current issues than in off-the-run issues.

Current maturity: Current time to maturity on an outstanding note, bond, or other money market instrument; for example, a 5-year note 1 year after issue has a current maturity of 4 years.

Current yield: Coupon payments on a security as a percentage of the security's market price. In many instances the price should be *gross* of accrued interest, particularly on instruments where no coupon is left to be paid until maturity.

Cushion bonds: High-coupon bonds that sell at only a moderate premium because they are callable at a price below that at which a comparable noncallable bond would sell. Cushion bonds offer considerable downside protection in a falling market.

CUSIP: Committee of Uniform Securities Identification Procedures.

Day trading: Intraday trading in securities for profit as opposed to investing for profit.

Dealer: A dealer, as opposed to a broker, acts as a principal in all transactions, buying and selling for his own account.

Debenture: A bond secured only by the general credit of the issuer.

Debt securities: IOUs created through loan-type transactions—commercial paper, bank CDs, bills, bonds, and other instruments.

Default: Failure to make timely payment of interest or principal on a debt security or to otherwise comply with the provisions of a bond indenture.

Delivery month: A month in which a futures contract expires and delivery may be taken or made.

Discount bond: A bond selling below par.

Discount rate: The rate of interest charged by the Fed to member banks that borrow at the discount window. The discount rate is an add-on rate.

Discount securities: Non-interest-bearing money market instruments that are issued at a discount and redeemed at maturity for full face value; e.g., U.S. Treasury bills.

Discount window: Facility provided by the Fed enabling member banks to borrow reserves against collateral in the form of governments or other acceptable paper.

Disintermediation: The investing of funds that would normally have been placed with a bank or other financial intermediary directly into debt securities issued by ultimate borrowers; e.g., into bills or bonds.

Distributed: After a Treasury auction, there will be many new issues in dealers' hands. As those securities are sold to retail, the issue is said to be distributed.

Dollar price of a bond: Percentage of face value at which a bond is quoted.

Due bill: An instrument evidencing the obligation of a seller to deliver securities sold to the buyer. Occasionally used in the bill market.

Dutch auction: Auction in which the lowest price necessary to sell the entire offering becomes the price at which all securities offered are sold. This technique has been used in Treasury auctions.

Elbow: The elbow in the yield curve is the maturity area considered to provide the most attractive short-term investment; e.g., the maturity range in which to initiate a ride along the yield curve.

Equivalent bond yield: Annual yield on a short-term, non-interest-bearing security calculated so as to be comparable to yields quoted on coupon securities.

Equivalent taxable yield: The yield on a taxable security that would leave the investor with the same aftertax return he would earn by holding a tax-exempt municipal; for example, for an investor taxed at a 50 percent marginal rate, equivalent taxable yield on a muni note issued at 3 percent would be 6 percent.

ETR: Easy-growth Treasury Receipts. Zero coupon Treasury bonds sold by Dean Witter.

Euro bonds: Bonds issued in Europe outside the confines of any national capital market. A Euro bond may or may not be denominated in the currency of the issuer.

Euro CDs: CDs issued by a U.S. bank branch or foreign bank located outside the United States. Almost all Euro CDs are issued in London.

Eurodollars: U.S. dollars deposited in a U.S. bank branch or a foreign bank located outside the United States.

Exchange offering: A Treasury sale when specific Treasury notes and bonds may be issued in exchange for other outstanding Treasury notes or bonds.

Exempt securities: Instruments exempt from the registration requirements of the Securities Act of 1933 or the margin requirements of the Securities and Exchange Act of 1934. Such securities include governments, agencies, municipal securities, commercial paper, and private placements.

Exercise: To invoke the right to buy or sell granted under terms of a listed options contract.

Exercise price: The price at which an option holder may buy or sell the underlying security. Also called the striking price.

Expiration date: The deadline when the holder of an option must exercise this option.

Extension swap: Extending maturity through a swap, e.g., selling a 2-year note and buying one with a slightly longer current maturity.

Fail: A trade is said to fail if on settlement date either the seller fails to deliver securities in proper form or the buyer fails to deliver funds in proper form.

Fed funds: See **Federal funds.**

Fed wire: A computer system linking member banks to the Fed, used for making interbank payments of Fed funds and for making deliveries of and payments for Treasury and agency securities.

Federal Deposit Insurance Corporation (FDIC): A federal institution that insures bank deposits, currently up to $100,000 per deposit.

Federal funds: (1) Non-interest-bearing deposits held by member banks at the Federal Reserve. (2) Used to denote "immediately available" funds in the clearing sense.

Federal funds rate: The rate of interest at which Fed funds are traded. This rate is currently pegged by the Federal Reserve through open-market operations.

Figuring the tail: Calculating the yield at which a future money market instrument (one available some period hence) is purchased when that future security is created by buying an existing instrument and financing the initial portion of life with a term RP.

Flat trades: (1) A bond in default trades flat; that is, the price quoted covers both principal and unpaid, accrued interest. (2) Any security that trades without accrued interest or at a price that includes accrued interest is said to trade flat.

Float: The difference between the credits given by the Fed to banks' reserve accounts on checks being cleared through the Fed and the debits made to banks' reserve accounts on the same checks. Float is always positive, because in the clearing of a check, the credit sometimes precedes the debit. Float adds to the money supply.

Flower bonds: Government bonds that are acceptable at par in payment of federal estate taxes when owned by the decedent at the time of death.

Full-coupon bond: A bond with a coupon equal to the going market rate and consequently selling at or near par.

Futures market: A market in which contracts for future delivery of a commodity or a security are bought and sold.

General obligation bonds: Municipal securities secured by the issuer's pledge of its full faith, credit, and taxing power.

Give up: The loss in yield that occurs when a block of bonds is swapped for another block of lower-coupon bonds. Can also be referred to as "aftertax give up" when the implications of the profit (loss) on taxes are considered.

Go-around: When the Fed offers to buy securities, to sell securities, to do repo, or to do reverses, it solicits competitive bids or offers, as the case may be, from all primary dealers. This procedure is known as a go-around.

Good funds: A market expression for immediately available money; i.e., Fed funds.

Good trader: A Treasury coupon issue that can readily be bought and sold in size. If a trader can short $10 or $20 million of an issue and sleep at night, that issue is said to be a good trader.

Governments: Negotiable U.S. Treasury securities.

Gross spread: The difference between the price that the issuer receives for its securities and the price that investors pay for them. This spread equals the selling concession plus the management and underwriting fees.

Handle: The whole-dollar price of a bid or offer is referred to as the *handle*. For example, if a security is quoted 101-10 bid and 101-11 offered, 101 is the handle. Traders are assumed to know the handle, so a trader would quote that market to another by saying he was at 10-11. (The 10 and 11 refer to 32ds.)

Hedge: To reduce risk, (1) by taking a position in futures equal and opposite to an existing or anticipated cash position, or (2) by shorting a security similar to one in which a long position has been established.

Hit: A dealer who agrees to sell at the bid price quoted by another dealer is said to *hit* that bid.

IMM: International Monetary Market, a futures exchange.

In-the-money option: An option selling at a price such that it has intrinsic value.

Interest rate exposure: Risk of gain or loss to which an institution is exposed due to possible changes in interest rate levels.

Junk bonds: High-risk bonds that have low credit ratings or are in default.

Lifting a leg: Closing out one side of a long-short arbitrage before the other is closed.

LION: Lehman Investment Opportunity Notes. Zero coupon Treasury bonds sold by Lehman Brothers.

Liquidity: A liquid asset is one that can be converted easily and rapidly into cash without a substantial loss of value. In the money market, a security is said to be liquid if the spread between bid and asked prices is narrow and reasonable size can be done at those quotes.

Locked market: A market is said to be locked if the bid price equals the asked price. This can occur, for example, if the market is brokered and brokerage is paid by one side only, the initiator of the transaction.

Long: (1) Owning a debt security, stock, or other asset. (2) Owning more than one has contracted to deliver.

Long bonds: Bonds with a long current maturity.

Long coupons: (1) Bonds or notes with a long current maturity. (2) A bond on which one of the coupon periods, usually the first, is longer than the others or than standard.

Long hedge: *Purchase* of a *futures* contract to lock in the yield at which an anticipated cash inflow can be invested.

Make a market: A dealer is said to make a market when he quotes bid and offered prices at which he stands ready to buy and sell.

Margin: (1) In an RP or a reverse repurchase transaction, the amount by which the market value of the securities collateralizing the transaction exceeds the amount lent. (2) In futures markets, money buyers and seller must put up to assure performance on the contracts. (3) In options, similar meaning as in futures for sellers of put and call options.

Marginal tax rate: The tax rate that would have to be paid on any additional dollars of taxable income earned.

Market value: The price at which a security is trading and could presumably be purchased or sold.

Marketability: A negotiable security is said to have good marketability if there is an active secondary market in which it can easily be resold.

MCE: Mid-America Commodity Exchange, a futures exchange.

Money market: The market in which short-term debt instruments (bills, commerical paper, bankers' acceptances, etc.) are issued and traded.

Money market (center) bank: A bank that is one of the nation's largest and consequently plays an active and important role in every sector of the money market.

Money Market Certificates (MMCs):   Six-month certificates of deposit with a minimum denomination of $10,000 on which banks and thrifts may pay a maximum rate tied to the rate at which the U.S. Treasury has most recently auctioned six-month bills.

Money market fund: Mutual fund that invests solely in money market instruments.

Money rate of return: Annual return as a percentage of asset value.

Money supply definitions used by the Fed in January 1983:
   M-1:   Currency in circulation plus demand deposits plus other checkable deposits including NOW accounts.

M-2: M-1 plus money market deposit accounts plus overnight RPs and money market funds and savings and small (less than $100,000) time deposits at all depository institutions plus over night RPs at banks plus overnight Euros held by nonbank U.S. depositors in the Caribbean branches of U.S. banks plus balances at money funds (excluding institutions-only funds).

M-3: M-2 plus large (over $100,000) time deposits at all depository institutions, term RPs at banks and S&Ls plus balances at institutions-only money funds.

L: M-3 plus other liquid assets such as term Eurodollars held by nonbank U.S. residents, bankers' acceptances, commercial paper, Treasury bills and other liquid governments, and U.S. savings bonds.

Municipal (muni) notes: Short-term notes issued by municipalities in anticipation of tax receipts, proceeds from a bond issue, or other revenues.

Municipals: Securities issued by state and local governments and their agencies.

Naked option position: An unhedged sale of a put or call option.

Naked position: An unhedged long or short position.

Nearby contract: Futures contracts nearest to expiration.

Negotiable certificate of deposit: A large-denomination (generally $1 million) CD that can be sold but cannot be cashed in before maturity.

New money: In a Treasury refunding, the amount by which the par value of the securities offered exceeds that of those maturity.

Nob: Note-bonds spread in futures contracts.

Noncompetitive bid: In a Treasury auction, bidding for a specific amount of securities at the price, whatever it may turn out to be, equal to the average price of the accepted competitive bids.

Note: Coupon issues with a relatively short original maturity are often called *notes*. Muni notes, however, have maturities ranging from a month to a year and pay interest only at maturity. Treasury notes are coupon securities that have an original maturity of up to 10 years.

NOW (Negotiable order of withdrawal) accounts: These amount to checking accounts on which depository institutions (banks and thrifts) may pay a rate of interest subject to federal rate lids.

NYFE: New York Futures Exchange, a futures exchange and division of the New York Stock Exchange.

OCC: Options Clearing Corporation, the issuer of all listed options trading on national options exchanges.

Odd lot: Less than a round lot.

Off-the-run issue: In Treasuries and agencies, an issue that is not included in dealer or broker runs. With bills and notes, normally only current issues are quoted.

Offer: Price asked by a seller of securities.

One-man picture: The price quoted is said to be a one-man picture if both the bid and ask come from the same source.

One-sided (one-way) market: A market in which only one side, the bid or the asked, is quoted or firm.

Option: (1) **Call option:** A contract sold for a price that gives the holder the right to buy from the writer of the option, over a specified period, a specified amount of securities at a specified price. (2) **Put option:** A contract sold for a price that gives the holder the right to sell to the writer of the contract, over a specified period, a specified amount of securities at a specified price.

Original maturity: Maturity at issue. For example, a 5-year note has an original maturity at issue of 5 years; 1 year later, it has a current maturity of 4 years.

Over-the-counter (OTC) market: Market created by dealer trading as opposed to the auction market prevailing on organized exchanges.

Paper: Money market instruments, commercial paper, and other.

Paper gain (loss):   Unrealized capital gain (loss) on securities held in portfolio, based on a comparison of current market price and original cost.

Par: (1) Price of 100%. (2) The principal amount at which the issuer of a debt security contracts to redeem that security at maturity, *face value*.

Par bond: A bond selling at par.

Paydown: In a Treasury refunding, the amount by which the par value of the securities maturing exceeds that of those sold.

Pay-up: (1) The loss of cash resulting from a swap into higher-price bonds. (2) The need (or willingness) of a bank or other borrower to pay a higher rate to get funds.

Pickup: The gain in yield that occurs when a block of bonds is swapped for another block of higher-coupon bonds.

Picture: The bid and asked prices quoted by a broker for a given security.

Plus: Dealers in governments normally quote bids and offers in 32ds. To quote a bid or offer in 64ths, they use pluses; for example, a dealer who bids 4+ is bidding the handle plus 4/32 + 1/64, which equals the handle plus 9/64.

Point: (1) 100 basis points = 1%. (2) One percent of the face value of a note or bond. (3) In the foreign exchange market, the lowest level at which the currency is priced. Example: "One point" is the difference between sterling prices of $1.8080 and $1.8081.

Portfolio: Collection of securities held by an investor.

Position: (1) To go long or short in a security. (2) The amount of securities owned (long position) or owed (short position).

Premium: (1) The amount by which the price at which an issue is trading exceeds the issue's par value. (2) The amount that must be paid in excess of par to call or refund an issue before maturity. (3) In money market parlance, the fact that a particular bank's CDs trade at a rate higher than others of its class, or that a bank has to pay up to acquire funds.

Premium bond: Bond selling above par.

Prepayment: A payment made ahead of the scheduled payment date.

Presold issue: An issue that is sold out before the coupon announcement.

Price risk: The risk that a debt security's price may change due to a rise or fall in the going level of interest rates.

Prime rate: The rate at which banks lend to their best (prime) customers. The all-in cost of a bank loan to a prime credit equals the prime rate plus the cost of holding compensating balances.

Principal: (1) The face amount or par value of a debt security. (2) One who acts as a dealer buying and selling for his own account.

Prospectus: A detailed statement prepared by an issuer and filed with the SEC prior to the sale of a new issue. The prospectus gives detailed information on the issue and on the issuer's condition and prospects.

Put: An option that gives the holder the right to sell the underlying security at a specified price during a fixed time period.

Ratings: An evaluation given by Moody's, Standard & Poor's, Fitch, or other rating services of a security's credit worthiness.

"Red" futures contract month: A futures contract in a month more than 12 months away; e.g., in November, the Dec (pronounced Dees) bond contract would mature one month later, the red Dec contract 13 months later.

Red herring: A preliminary prospectus containing all the information required by the Securities and Exchange Commission except the offering price and coupon of a new issue.

Refunding: Redemption of securities by funds raised through the sale of a new issue.

Registered bond: A bond whose owner is registered with the issuer.

Regular way settlement: In the money and bond markets, the regular basis on which some security trades are settled is that delivery of the securities purchased is made against payment in Fed funds on the day following the transaction.

Reinvestment rate: (1) The rate at which an investor assumes interest payments made on a debt security can be reinvested over the life of that security. (2) Also, the rate at which funds from a maturity or sale of a security can be reinvested. Often used in comparison to *give up* yield.

Reopen an issue: The Treasury, when it wants to sell additional securities, will occasionally sell more of an existing issue (reopen it) rather than offer a new issue.

Repo: See **Repurchase agreement.**

Repurchase agreement (RP or repo):   A holder of securities sells these securities to an investor with an agreement to repurchase them at a fixed price on a fixed date. The security "buyer" in effect lends the "seller" money for the period of the agreement, and the terms of the agreement are structured to compensate him for this. Dealers use RP extensively to finance their positions. Exception: When the Fed is said to be doing RP, it is lending money, that is, increasing bank reserves.

Retail: Individual and institutional customers as opposed to dealers and brokers.

Revenue bond: A municipal bond secured by revenue from tolls, user charges, or rents derived from the facility financed.

Reverse: See **Reverse repurchase agreement.**

Reverse repurchase agreement: Most typically, a repurchase agreement initiated by the lender of funds. Reverses are used by dealers to borrow securities they have shorted. Exception: When the Fed is said to be doing reverses, it is borrowing money, that is; absorbing reserves.

Risk: Degree of uncertainty of return on an asset.

Roll over: Reinvest funds received from a maturing security in a new issue of the same or a similar security.

Round lot: In the money market, round lot refers to the minimum amount for which dealers' quotes are good. This may range from $100,000 to $5 million, depending on the size and liquidity of the issue traded.

RP: See **Repurchase agreement.**

Run: A run consists of a series of bid and asked quotes for different securities or maturities. Dealers give to and ask for runs from each other.

Safekeep: For a fee, banks will safekeep (i.e., hold in their vault, clip coupons on, and present for payment at maturity) bonds and money market instruments.

Sale repurchase agreement: See **Repurchase agreement.**

Savings deposit: Interest-bearing deposit at a savings institution that has no specific maturity.

Scalper: A speculator who actively trades a futures contract in the hope of making small profits off transitory upticks and downticks in price.

Seasoned issue: An issue that has been well distributed and trades well in the secondary market.

Secondary market: The market in which previously issued securities are traded.

Securities and Exchange Commission (SEC):   Agency created by Congress to protect investors in securities transactions by administering securities legislation.

Sell a spread: Sell a nearby futures contract and buy a far one.

Serial bonds: A bond issue in which maturities are staggered over a number of years.

Settlement date: The date on which trade is cleared by delivery of securities against funds. The settlement date may be the trade date or a later date.

Shopping: Seeking to obtain the best bid or offer available by calling a number of dealers and/or brokers.

Short: A market participant assumes a short position by selling a security he does not own. The seller makes delivery by borrowing the security sold or reversing it in.

Short bonds: Bonds with a short current maturity.

Short coupons: Bonds or notes with a short current maturity.

Short the Board: Sell GNMA or T bond futures on the CBT.

Short hedge: Sale of a *futures* contract to hedge, for example, a position in cash securities or an anticipated borrowing need.

Short sale: The sale of securities not owned by the seller in the expectation that the price of these securities will fall or as part of an arbitrage. A short sale must eventually be covered by a purchase of the securities sold.

Sinking fund: Indentures on corporate issues often require that the issuer make annual payments to a sinking fund, the proceeds of which are used to retire randomly selected bonds in the issue.

Size: Large in size, as in "size offering" or "in there for size." What constitutes size varies with the sector of the market.

Skip-day settlement: The trade is settled one business day beyond what is normal.

Specific issues market: The market in which dealers reverse in securities they want to short.

Spread: (1) Difference between bid and asked prices on a security. (2) Difference between yields on or prices of two securities of differing sorts or differing maturities. (3) In underwriting, difference between price realized by the issuer and price paid by the investor. (4) Difference between two prices or two rates. What a commodities trader would refer to as the *basis*.

Spreading: In the futures market, buying one futures contract and selling a nearby one to profit from an anticipated narrowing or widening of the spread over time.

Stop-out price: The lowest price (highest yield) accepted by the Treasury in an auction of a new issue.

Striking price: See **Exercise price.**

Subject: Refers to a bid or offer that cannot be executed without confirmation from the customer.

Swap: (1) In securities, selling one issue and buying another. (2) In foreign exchange, buying a currency spot and simultaneously selling it forward.

TABs (tax anticipation bills): Special bills that the Treasury occasionally issues. They mature on corporate quarterly income tax dates and can be used at face value by corporations to pay their tax liabilities.

Tail: (1) The difference between the average price in Treasury auctions and the stop-out price. (2) A *future* money market instrument (one available some period hence) created by buying an existing instrument and financing the initial portion of its life with term RP.

Take-out: (1) A cash surplus generated by the sale of one block of securities and the purchase of another, e.g., selling a block of bonds at 99 and buying another block at 95. (2) A bid made to a seller of a security that is designed (and generally agreed) to take him out of the market.

TBR: Treasury Bond Receipts. Zero coupon Treasury bond issues sold by E. F. Hutton.

TED: A spread trade: T bill futures to CD futures.

Tender: A formal application offer to buy Treasury bills, notes, or bonds.

Tenor: Maturity.

Term bonds: A bond issue in which all bonds mature at the same time.

Term RP (repo): RP borrowings for a period longer than overnight, may be 30, 60, or even 90 days.

Thin market: A market in which trading volume is low and in which consequently bid and asked quotes are wide and the liquidity of the instrument traded is low.

Tick: Minimum price movement on a futures contract.

Tight market: A tight market, as opposed to a thin market, is one in which volume is large, trading is active and highly competitive, and spreads between bid and ask prices are narrow.

TIGR: Treasury Investment Growth Receipts. Zero coupon Treasury bond issues sold by Merrill Lynch.

Time deposit: Interest-bearing deposit at a savings institution that has a specific maturity.

Trade date: The date on which a transaction is initiated. The settlement date may be the trade date or a later date.

Treasurer's check: A check issued by a bank to make a payment. Treasurer's checks outstanding are counted as part of a bank's reservable deposits and as part of the money supply.

Treasury bill: A non-interest-bearing discount security issued by the U.S. Treasury to finance the national debt. Most bills are issued to mature in 3 months, 6 months, or 1 year.

Turnaround: Securities bought and sold for settlement on the same day.

Turnaround time: The time available or needed to effect a turnaround.

Two-sided market: A market in which both bid and asked prices, good for the standard unit of trading, are quoted.

Two-way market: Market in which both a bid and an asked price are quoted.

Variable-price security: A security, such as stocks or bonds, that sells at a fluctuating, market-determined price.

When-issued trades: Typically there is a lag between the time a new bond is announced and sold and the time it is actually issued. During this interval, the security trades, **wi,** "when, as, and if issued."

Wi: When, as, and if issued. See **When-issued trades.**

Wi wi: T bills trade on a wi basis between the day they are announced and the day they are settled. Late Tuesday and on Wednesday, two bills will trade wi, the bill just auctioned and the bill just announced. The latter used to be called the wi wi bill. However, now it is common for dealers to speak of the just auctioned bill as the 3-month bill and of the newly announced bill as the wi bill. This change in jargon resulted from a change in the way interdealer brokers of bills list bills on their screens. Cantor Fitz still lists a new bill as the wi bill until it is settled.

Without: If 70 were bid in the market and there was no offer, the quote would be "70 bid without." The expression *without* indicates a one-way market.

Write: To sell an option.

Yield curve: A graph showing, for securities that all expose the investor to the same credit risk, the relationship at a given point in time between yield and current maturity. Yield curves are typically drawn using yields on governments of various maturities.

Yield to maturity: The rate of return yielded by a debt security held to maturity when both interest payments and the investor's capital gain or loss on the security are taken into account.

Zero coupon bonds: Corporate, municipal, or Treasury bonds where the owner separates the interest-bearing coupons and sells the remaining principal certificate, usually at a substantial price below its face value.

Appendix *A*

**Useful Addresses and
Telephone Numbers
Concerning Treasury
Securities**

The Federal Reserve System

Federal Reserve Bank District/Branch	Address and Phone Number
Board of Governors	20th and Constitution Ave., N.W., Washington, DC 20551 (202) 452-3000
1. Boston	600 Atlantic Ave. Boston, MA 02106 (617) 973-3800
2. New York	33 Liberty St. (Federal Reserve P.O. Station) New York, NY 10045 (212) 791-5000 or 791-6619 (212) 791-5823 or 791-7773—24 hr recording
Buffalo Branch	160 Delaware Ave. (P.O. Box 961) Buffalo, NY 14240 (716) 849-5046
3. Philadelphia	100 N. 6th St., Philadelphia, PA 19106 (P.O. Box 66, Philadelphia, PA 19105) (215) 574-6580
4. Cleveland	1455 E. 6th St. (P.O. Box 6387) Cleveland, OH 44101 (216) 241-2800
Cincinnati Branch	150 E. 4th St. (P.O. Box 999) Cincinnati, OH 45201 (513) 721-4787
Pittsburgh Branch	717 Grant St. (P.O. Box 867) Pittsburgh, PA 15230 (412) 261-7864
5. Richmond	701 E. Byrd St. (P.O. Box 27622) Richmond, VA 23261 (804) 643-1250
Baltimore Branch	114–120 E. Lexington St. (P.O. Box 1378) Baltimore, MD 21203 (301) 576-3300
Charlotte Branch	401 S. Tryon St. (P.O. Box 300) Charlotte, NC 28230 (704) 373-0200
6. Atlanta	104 Marietta St. N.W., Atlanta, GA 30303 (404) 586-8657

Federal Reserve Bank District/Branch	Address and Phone Number
Birmingham Branch	1801 5th Ave., North (P.O. Box 10447) Birmingham, AL 35202 (205) 252-3141, ext 215
Jacksonville Branch	515 Julia St. Jacksonville, FL 32203 (904) 632-4400
Miami Branch	9100 N.W. 36th St. Extension, Miami, FL 33178 (P.O. Box 520847, Miami, FL 33152) (305) 593-9923
Nashville Branch	301 8th Ave., North Nashville, TN 37203 (615) 259-4006
New Orleans Branch	525 St. Charles Ave. (P.O. Box 61630) New Orleans, LA 70161 (504) 586-1505
7. Chicago	230 S. LaSalle St. (P.O. Box 834) Chicago, IL 60690 (312) ~~922-3196~~ 322-5322 322-5369 (FORMS)
Detroit Branch	160 Fort St., West (P.O. Box 1059) Detroit, MI 48231 (313) 961-6880
8. St. Louis	411 Locust St. (P.O. Box 442) St. louis, MO 63166 (314) 444-8444
Little Rock Branch	325 W. Capitol Ave. (P.O. Box 1261) Little Rock, AR 72203 (501) 372-5451
Louisville Branch	410 S. 5th St. (P.O. Box 899) Louisville, KY 40201 (502) 587-7351
Memphis Branch	200 N. Main St. (P.O. Box 407) Memphis, TN 38101 (901) 523-7171
9. Minneapolis	250 Marquette Ave. Minneapolis, MN 55480 (612) 340-2345
Helena Branch	400 N. Park Ave. Helena, MT 59601 (406) 442-3860

	Federal Reserve Bank District/Branch	*Address and Phone Number*
10.	Kansas City	925 Grand Ave. (Federal Reserve System) Kansas City, MO 64198 (816) 881-2783
	Denver Branch	1020 16th St. (P.O. Box 5228, Terminal Annex) Denver, CO 80217 (303) 292-4020
	Oklahoma City Branch	226 N.W. 3rd St. (P.O. Box 25129) Oklahoma City, OK 73125 (405) 235-1721
	Omaha Branch	102 S. 17th St. Omaha, NE 68102 (402) 341-3610
11.	Dallas	400 S. Akard St. (Station K) Dallas, TX 75222 (214) 651-6111
	El Paso Branch	301 E. Main St. (P.O. Box 100) El Paso, TX 79999 (915) 544-4730
	Houston Branch	1701 San Jacinto St. (P.O. Box 2578) Houston, TX 77001 (713) 659-4433
	San Antonio Branch	126 E. Nueva St. (P.O. Box 1471) San Antonio, TX 78295 (512) 224-2141
12.	San Francisco	400 Sansome St. (P.O. Box 7702) San Francisco, CA 94120 (415) 544-2000
	Los Angeles Branch	409 W. Olympic Blvd. (P.O. Box 2077, Terminal Annex) Los Angeles, CA 90051 (213) 683-8323
	Portland Branch	915 S.W. Stark St. (P.O. Box 3436) Portland, OR 97208 (503) 221-5931
	Salt Lake City Branch	120 S. State St. (P.O. Box 780) Salt Lake City, UT 84110 (801) 322-7924
	Seattle Branch	1015 2nd Ave. (P.O. Box 3567) Seattle, WA 98124 (206) 442-1650

Bureau of the Public Debt*

Purpose	Address
1. Mail tender for T bills.	Bureau of the Public Debt Securities Transactions Branch Room 2134, Main Treasury Washington, DC 20226
2. Exemptions from or cancellation of withholding on Treasury securities.	Bureau of the Public Debt Department B (for T bills) (or) Department C (for T notes and bonds) Washington, DC 20226
3. Transactions in established T bill accounts.	Bureau of the Public Debt Department X Washington, DC 20226
4. Discount & redemption check information, forms, and general information.	Bureau of the Public Debt Department W (or Department F) Washington, DC 20226

Telephone Number	Type of Information
(202) 287-4113.	Analysts are available to answer questions about your T bill, note, or bond account 9:00 A.M. to 4:30 P.M. (Monday–Friday).
(202) 287-4097.	Telecommunication device for the deaf.
(202) 287-4100.	Recorded message about current T bill, note, and bond offerings, and the latest auction results.
(202) 287-4088.	Recorded message containing general information on Treasury notes and bonds.
(202) 287-4091.	Recorded message containing general information about T bills.
(202) 287-4217.	Recorded message on buying securities in person at the Main Treasury Building in Washington, DC.

* For those calling from outside the metropolitan Washington, D.C., calling area, long distance telephone toll charges are in effect. The Bureau of the Public Debt cannot accept collect calls.

Appendix B

*Proper Forms of Registration
for Transferable Treasury
Securities*

Accounts may be maintained in the name(s) of individuals, executors, trustees, partners, officers of corporations or unincorporated associations, natural or voluntary guardians, etc. The following examples illustrate the proper format for various forms of registration.

Social security and employee identification numbers (sometimes called taxpayer identifying numbers)[1] are not required for foreign governments, nonresident aliens not engaged in trade or business within the United States, international organizations, foreign corporations not engaged in trade or business and not having an office or place of business or financial or paying agent within the United States, and other persons or organizations as may be exempt according to IRS regulations.

A. Natural Persons in Their Own Right

Natural persons in their own right are defined as those natural persons who are not under any legal disability. Registration may be made either in the name of a single person, or two or more persons as follows.

1. One Person.   For a registration in a single name only, the following examples with and without titles are applicable:

1.   John A. Doe (123-45-6789).

2.   (Mr., etc.) John A. Doe (123-45-6789).

3.   Jane C. Doe (987-65-4321).

4.   (Miss, etc.) Jane C. Doe (987-65-4321).

On the other hand, if you are the sole proprietor of a business conducted under a trade name, you may include a reference to the trade name, as shown by the following examples:

1.   John A. Doe, doing business as Doe's Hardware Store (12-3456789).

2.   John A. Doe (123-45-6789), doing business as Doe's Hardware Store.

Notice that in the first example, Doe's employee identification number is used for his business, while the second example uses Doe's own social security number.

2. Two or More Persons.   Regulations prohibit an account for Treasury securities to be maintained in the name of a single person payable to a second person after the death of the first. The account cannot be in following format:

---

[1] The social security number used as an example is 123-45-6789; the employee identification number example is 12-3456789.

John A. Doe and Mrs. Jane C. Doe, or either of them.

Registrations in this form will be treated as though the phrase "or either of them" did not appear. The taxpayer identifying number of any of the joint owners must be shown on Treasury security accounts in joint ownership form. As examples:

1. John A. Doe (123-45-6789) and Mrs. Jane C. Doe.
2. John A. Doe and Mrs. Jane C. Doe (987-65-4321).

a. With Right of Survivorship.   Registration may be accomplished in the names of two or more persons with right of survivorship, as shown by the following examples:

1. John A. Doe (123-45-6789) or Mrs. Jane C. Doe or the survivor.
2. John A. Doe (123-45-6789) or Mrs. Jane C. Doe or Miss Judy Elaine Doe or the survivor or survivors.
3. John A. Doe (123-45-6789) and Mrs. Jane C. Doe.
4. John A. Doe (123-45-6789) or Mrs. Jane C. Doe.
5. John A. Doe (123-45-6789) and Mrs. Jane C. Doe as joint tenants with right of survivorship and not as tenants in common.

On the other hand, a registration limited to a husband and wife may appear as:

John A. Doe (123-45-6789) and Mrs. Jane C. Doe, as tenants in common.

b. Without Right of Survivorship.   To preclude the right of survivorship, registration may be in two or more individuals using the following examples:

1. John A. Doe (123-45-6789) and Jack B. Smith as tenants in common.
2. John A. Doe as natural guardian of William F. Doe, a minor, and Robert C. Doe (123-45-6789) without right of survivorship.

On the other hand, registration limited to a husband and his wife may properly appear as:

John A. Doe (123-45-6789) and Jane C. Doe, as partners in community.

B. Minors and Incompetents

1. Natural Guardians of Minors.   A Treasury security may be registered in the name of a natural guardian of a minor for whose estate no legal guardian or similar representative has been legally appointed by a court. As examples:

1. Jack B. Doe as natural guardian of John A. Doe, a minor (123-45-6789).

2. William D. Smith as appointed guardian of John A. Doe, a minor (123-45-6789).

In both cases, the taxpayer identifying number is the social security number of the minor. The parent with whom the minor child resides, or if the minor child does not reside with either parent then the person who furnishes the chief support of the minor, will be recognized as the guardian and will be considered a fiduciary. Registration of Treasury securities in the name of a minor child in his or her own right is not authorized, and will be treated as if registered in the name of the natural guardian acting in that capacity.

2. Custodian under Gifts to Minors Acts Statutes. Treasury securities may be purchased as a gift to a minor under the "Gifts to Minors" statute that is in effect in the State in which either the donor or the minor resides. The registration must then be done in the form identifying the statute, as shown by the following examples:

1. Jack B. Doe, as custodian for John A. Doe, a minor (123-45-6789), under the Delaware Uniform Gifts to Minors Act.

2. William D. Smith, as custodian for John A. Doe, a minor (123-45-6789), under the Delaware Uniform Gifts to Minors Act.

3. William D. Smith, as custodian for John A. Doe, a minor (123-45-6789), under the laws of Delaware; Ch. 48–3, Code of Del. Anno.

3. Incompetents Not under Guardianship. Registration in the form:

John A. Doe, an incompetent (123-45-6789), under voluntary guardianship

is possible *only on reissue after a voluntary guardian has qualified, and only for the purpose of collecting the interest on the Treasury security.* Otherwise, the Treasury will not recognize the registration in the name of an incompetent not under legal guardianship.

C. Executors, Administrators, Guardians, and Similar Representatives or Fiduciaries

Treasury security accounts may be registered in the names of legally qualified executors, administrators, guardians, and representatives or fiduciaries of a single estate. The names and capacities of all the representatives or fiduciaries, as shown in their letters of appointment by the court, *must be included in the registration and must be followed by an adequate identifying reference to the estate*, as illustrated by the following examples:

1. Jack D. Smith, executor of will of John A. Doe, deceased (12-3456789).

2. Jack D. Smith, administrator of estate of John A. Doe, deceased (12-3456789).

3. Jack D. Smith, guardian of estate of John A. Doe, a minor (123-45-6789).

4. Jack D. Smith, conservator of estate of John A. Doe, an incompetent (123-45-6789).

D. Life Tenant under Will

Accounts may be registered in the name of a life tenant, followed by an adequate identifying reference to the will, using the form:

Jane C. Doe, life tenant under the will of John A. Doe, deceased (12-3456789).

In this case, the life tenant will be considered a fiduciary.

E. Private Trust Estates

Accounts may be maintained in the name and title of the trustee(s) of a single private trust, followed by an adequate identifying reference to the authority governing the trust, as illustrated by the examples:

1. John A. Doe and American Trust Co., Wilmington, Delaware, trustees under the will of Jane C. Doe, deceased (12-3456789).

2. John A. Doe and Jack B. Smith, trustees under agreement with Robert Jones, dated June 5, 1974 (12-3456789).

As illustrated in the above examples, the names of *all* the trustees, in the form used in the trust instrument (agreement), must be included in the registration. However, two exceptions to this provision are as follows:

1. If there are several trustees designated as a board, or authorized to act as a unit, their names should be omitted and the phrase "Board of Trustees" be substituted for the word "trustees," as illustrated by the following example:

Board of Trustees of American Trust Co. Retirement Fund, under the collective bargaining agreement dated June 5, 1974 (12-3456789).

2. If the trustees do not constitute a board or otherwise act as a unit, or are either too numerous to be designated by their names and title or serve for limited terms, then some or all of the names may be omitted, as illustrated by the following examples:

1. John A. Doe, Jack Smith, et al., trustees under will of Jane C. Doe, deceased (12-3456789).

2. Trustees under the will of Jane C. Doe, deceased (12-3456789).

3. Trustees of Retirement Fund of Ajax Trading Co., under directors' resolution of June 30, 1950 (12-3456789).

F. Corporations, Unincorporated Associations, and Partnerships

Accounts may be maintained in the name of any private corporation, unincorporated association, or partnership, including a nominee which is treated as the owner of a given Treasury security. When registered as such, the full name of the organization as set forth in its charter, articles of incorporation, constitution, partnership agreement, or other authority from which its powers are derived, must be stated. In addition, the organization's name may be followed by a reference to a particular account or fund (other than a trust fund) if desired.

1. Corporations. The following examples illustrate the account registration format for business, fraternal, religious, or other private corporations. The organization name must also include words indicating the corporate status, unless the term "corporation" or a legal abbreviation, such as AB, AG, A/S, BV, Cie, Co., Corp., GmbH, Inc., Ltd., NV, PVBA, SA, Sarl, SpA, SPRL, SRL, etc., is the name of that corporation or association organized under federal law (e.g., a national bank or federal savings and loan association).

1. John A. Doe & Co., a corporation (12-3456789).

2. John Doe Corp. (12-3456789).

3. A. C. Schultz, Gmbh.

4. Doe's Hardware Store, Inc. (12-3456789).

5. Doe and Smith, Ltd.—Depreciation Acct. (12-3456789).

6. 1st National Bank of Wilmington (12-3456789).

7. XYZ & Co., Inc., a nominee corporation (12-3456789).

Note that, in example 3, a foreign corporation does not require a taxpayer identifying number.

2. Unincorporated Associations. The following examples illustrate the account registration format for names of a lodge, club, labor union, religious society, or similar *self-governing* organizations which are not incorporated (even though they may or may not be chartered by or affiliated with a parent organization which itself is incorporated) must be followed by the phrase: "an unincorporated association." This phrase should not be used to describe a trust fund, partnership, or a business that is conducted under a trade name.

Accounts should not be maintained in the name of an unincorporated association if the legal title to its property or to the funds with which the Treasury securities are to be purchased is held by trustees. In this case, registration must be maintained as is described under "Private Trust Estates."

1. American Legion Post #1234, an unincorporated association (12-3456789).

2. Local Union No. 1234, International Brotherhood of Electrical Workers, an unincorporated association (12-3456789).

3. Partnerships. In the case of partnerships, accounts must state the name of the partnership followed by the phrase: "a partnership," as shown below:

1. Doe & Jones, a partnership (12-3456789).

2. XYZ Co., a limited partnership (12-3456789).

3. Doe & Co., a nominee partnership (12-3456789).

G. States, Public Bodies, and Corporations and Public Officers

The following examples illustrate how Treasury securities may be properly registered in the name of a state, county, city, town, village, school district, or other political entity, public body, or corporation established by law which is an owner or official custodian of public funds (other than trust funds), or in the full legal title of the public officer having custody of such funds.

1. State of Delaware.

2. Delaware State Highway Administration.

3. Comptroller, City of Wilmington, Delaware.

4. Treasurer of the State of Delaware—State Pension Fund.

H. States, Public Officers, Corporations or Bodies as Trustees

The following examples illustrate how Treasury securities may be properly registered in the name of the title of a public officer, or in the name of a State, county, or public body acting as trustee under express authority of law. An appropriate reference to the statute creating the trust may be included in the registration.

1. Insurance Commissioner of the state of Delaware trustee for benefit of policyholders of Ace Insurance Co. (12-3456789), under Sec. 32.7, Delaware Stats.

2. Cherry Island Investment Commission, trustee of General Sinking Fund under Ch. 26, Gen. Laws of Delaware.

3. State of Delaware in trust for Delaware Redevelopment Authority.

Appendix **C**

Summary of Forms Used in Conjunction with Treasury Securities

The following special forms are used and required by the Bureau of the Public Debt for various actions concerning U.S. Treasury securities.

Form	*Title and Purpose*
PD 345.	Description of Registered Securities. Used to change the address of the owner of registered T notes and bonds (see Figure C–1).
PD 1001.	Power of Attorney by Individual Authorizing Disposition of Registered Transferable Securities. Used to show that an individual has appointed another as his attorney-in-fact to act on his behalf (see Figure C–2).
PD 1003.	Power of Attorney by Corporation or Unincorporated Association Authorizing Disposition of Registered Transferable Securities. Used to show that a corporation or unincorporated association has appointed someone other than one of its officers as their attorney-in-fact to act on their behalf (see Figure C–3).
PD 1006.	Specific Power of Substitution Under Power of Attorney Granted to an Individual to Dispose of Registered Securities. Used as a power of substitution to show that an individual acting under power of attorney has appointed a substitute to act on their behalf (see Figure C–4).
PD 1008.	Specific Power of Substitution Under Power of Attorney Granted to Corporation to Dispose of Registered Sceurities. Used as a power of substitution to show that a corporation acting under power of attorney has appointed a substitute to act on their behalf (see Figure C–5).
PD 1010.	Resolution by Governing Body of an Organization Authorizing Assignment and Disposition of Specified Securities Owned in Its Own Right or in a Fiduciary Capacity. Used to authorize certain officers of an organization to act on their behalf (see Figure C–6).
PD 1014.	Certificate of Incumbency of Officers (Corporation or unincorporated association). Used to certify the incumbency, or holder of the various offices of either a corporation or unincorporated association (see Figure C–7).
PD 1071.	Certificate of Ownership of United States Bearer Securities. Used to substantiate ownership of bearer Treasury securities when requesting payment of principal after (a) three months past maturity on T notes of less than seven years or (b) six months past maturity on T notes and bonds of more than seven years (see Figure C–8).
PD 1461.	Application for Recognition as Voluntary Guardian of Incompetent Owner of Registered Securities and for Disposition of the

Securities or Interest Thereon. Used to apply for recognition as a voluntary guardian of a person owning registered Treasury securities, who is incompetent to manage his or her own affairs, or for whose estate no legal guardian or representative has been appointed (see Figure C–9).

PD 1646.   Application for Disposition—United States Registered Securities and Related Checks Without Administration of Deceased Owner's Estate. Used by the heirs and others entitled to share in a decedent's estate, not formally administered, to apply for the disposition of registered Treasury securities. In addition, Form PD 1646 may be also used to support the redemption of flower bonds, discussed in Chapter 9 (see Figure C–10).

PD 1782.   Application for Redemption at Par of United States Treasury Bonds Eligible for Payment of Federal Estate Tax. Used to request the par redemption of flower Treasury bonds (see Chapter 9) for the payment of federal estate taxes owed (see Figure C–11).

PD 1832.   Special Form of Detached Assignment for United States Registered Securities. Used to transfer registration of Treasury securities (see Figure C–12).

PD 2446.   Certificate of Incumbency for Fiduciaries. Used to certify the incumbency of the fiduciaries of any trust estate, public or private committee, or other body not appointed by a court and designated by name in the registration of registered Treasury Securities (see Figure C–13).

PD 2481.   Application for Recognition as Natural Guardian of Minor not under Legal Guardianship and for Disposition of Minor's Interest in Registered Securities. Used to apply for disposition of registered Treasury securities belonging to a minor for whose estate no legal representative has been appointed. In addition, Form PD 2481 is used to qualify as a natural guardian when a designated natural guardian is no longer acting, either by death or incompetency (see Figure C–14).

PD 3905.   Request for Securities Transaction. Used to redeem, exchange registered securities for coupon issues, or exchange coupon securities for registered issues (see Figure C–15).

PD 4632–1.   Tender for Treasury Bills in Book-Entry Form at the Department of the Treasury (52-week bills). Used to purchase 52-week T bills at public auction.

PD 4632–2.   Tender for Treasury Bills in Book-Entry Form at the Department of the Treasury (26-week bills only). Used to purchase 26-week T bills at public auction (see Figure 3–2).

PD 4632–3.   Tender for Treasury Bills in Book-Entry Form at the Department

	of the Treasury (13-week bills). Used to purchase 13-week T bills at public auction.
PD 4633.	Request for Transactions in Book-Entry Treasury Bills Maintained by the Bureau of the Public Debt (see Figure 3–8).
PD 4633–1.	Request for Reinvestment of Book-Entry Treasury Bills. Used to request reinvestment of either 13-, 26-, or 52-week book-entry T bills (see Figure C–16).
PD 4633–2.	Request for Reinvestment of Book-Entry Treasury Bills (IBM card). Same use as Form PD 4633–1 (see Figure 3–7).
PD 4949.	Statement of Account for Treasury Bills. Used to describe your book-entry T bill account (see Figure 3–6).

Figure   C–1   **Form PD 345**

FORM PD 345
Dept. of the Treasury
Bur. of the Public Debt
(Rev. Aug. 1975)

DESCRIPTION OF REGISTERED SECURITIES

To   Bureau of the Public Debt, Division of Securities Operations, Washington, D.C. 20226 (For United States securities and those of agencies for which the Treasury acts as transfer agent.)

The undersigned owner of the registered securities described below hereby —

(Check appropriate box to show purpose for which form is being used.)   ☐ Gives notice of change of address.
☐ Describes holdings for identification of accounts.

TITLE OF SECURITY (Identify securities by interest rate, type, series, call and maturity dates)	DENOMINATION (Face Amount)	SERIAL NUMBER	REGISTRATION (Exact inscription including Taxpayer Identifying Number(s) as shown on the face of each security. If no such numbers appear in the registration, complete the block below as appropriate.)

(If space is insufficient, describe additional bonds on the reverse.)

(If not shown above)
Taxpayer Identifying Number: ☐☐☐ – ☐☐ – ☐☐☐☐   or   ☐☐ – ☐☐☐☐☐☐☐
(See Instruction No. 2 on reverse side)   *(Social Security Account Number)*   *(Employer Identification Number)*

Former address _____
                                   (Number and street or rural route)

_____
      (City or town)   *(State)*   *(ZIP code)*

New address _____
                                   (Number and street or rural route)

_____
      (City or town)   *(State)*   *(ZIP code)*

_____   _____
(Signature of registered owner, representative, or fiduciary)   *(Date)*

NOTE - Send prompt notice of any change of address. Address changes received just prior to the interest-payment date may not be reflected on the interest check for that payment date. A registered owner's signature should be in the same form in which his name appears on the security. The signature of a representative or fiduciary should be in the same form as that given in the court papers or other evidence of his authority and should be followed by the proper title and reference to the estate or trust; for example: "John W. Smith, administrator of the estate of Henry L. Smith, deceased", or "John Doe, attorney-in-fact for Mary Doe". A copy of the appropriate document, properly certified, should be forwarded with this form.

Figure　C–2　　　　　　　　　　　　　　　**Form PD 1001**

Form PD 1001
Dept. of the Treasury
Bureau of the Public Debt
(Rev. Oct. 1974)

POWER OF ATTORNEY BY INDIVIDUAL AUTHORIZING
DISPOSITION OF REGISTERED TRANSFERABLE SECURITIES

> **IMPORTANT. – Follow instructions on the reverse in completing this form.**

KNOW ALL MEN BY THESE PRESENTS:

That _____ hereby
　　　　　　　　　　(Name of grantor)

appoints _____, of _____ ,
　　　　(Name of grantee)　　　　　　　　　　　(Post office address)

his attorney in fact to assign, or to sell, or to otherwise dispose of

> **STRIKE OUT ITEM 1 OR 2 – SEE INSTRUCTION 2**

1. the following-described registered transferable United States securities or securities for which the Treasury Department acts as transfer agency which he owns individually or holds in a fiduciary capacity, with authority to appoint one or more substitutes for such purpose:

LOAN TITLE (Include interest rate, call and maturity dates)	DENOMINATION	SERIAL NUMBER	REGISTRATION (Exact inscription on each security)

(If space is insufficient, list additional securities on back. Any separate list must refer to this document expressly.)

2. any and all registered transferable United States securities or securities for which the Treasury Department acts as transfer agency now or hereafter owned by him, with authority to appoint one or more substitutes for such purpose.

The undersigned hereby ratifies any and all action as herein authorized previously taken by his above-named attorney in fact.

_____
(Signature and fiduciary capacity, if any, of grantor)

_____
(Complete address)

I CERTIFY that the above-named person as described, whose identity is well known or proved to me, personally appeared before me this _____ day of _____ , 19_____ ,

at _____ , and signed this instrument.
　　　　　　　　(City and State)

**(OFFICIAL STAMP
OR SEAL)**
　　　　　　　　_____
　　　　　　　　(Signature and title of authorized certifying officer)

　　　　　　　　_____
　　　　　　　　(Address)

Figure C–3   **Form PD 1003**

Form PD 1003
Dept. of the Treasury
Bureau of the Public Debt
(Rev. Feb. 1976)

POWER OF ATTORNEY BY CORPORATION
OR UNINCORPORATED ASSOCIATION AUTHORIZING
DISPOSITION OF REGISTERED TRANSFERABLE SECURITIES

IMPORTANT. – Follow instructions on the reverse in completing this form.

KNOW ALL MEN BY THESE PRESENTS:

That_____ , { ☐ a corporation,
(Complete name of grantor)   { ☐ an unincorporated association,

hereby appoints _____ of _____ ,
(Name of grantee)   (Post office address)

its attorney in fact to assign, or to sell, or to otherwise dispose of

STRIKE OUT ITEM 1 OR 2 – SEE INSTRUCTION 2

1. the following-described registered transferable United States securities or securities or which the Department of the Treasury acts as transfer agency { ☐ owned by this organization in its own right }
☐ *(for corporation only)* held by this organization in any representative or fiduciary capacity }

with authority to appoint one or more substitutes for such purpose:

LOAN TITLE (Include interest rate, call and maturity dates)	DENOMINATION	SERIAL NUMBER	REGISTRATION (Exact inscription on each security)

(If space is insufficient, list additional securities on back. Any separate list must refer to this document expressly.)

2. any and all registered transferable securities or securities for which the Department of the Treasury acts as transfer agency now or hereafter owned by it, with authority to appoint one or more substitutes for such purpose.

Said organization hereby ratifies any and all action as authorized herein previously taken by its above-named attorney in fact.

_____
(Complete name of organization and fiduciary capacity, if any)

by_____
(Signature and title of officer)

and_____
(Additional signature and title, if necessary)

I CERTIFY that the above-named person(s) as described, whose identity (identities) is (are) well known or proved to me, personally appeared before me this_____ day of _____ , 19_____ ,

at_____ , and signed this instrument.
(City and State)

(OFFICIAL STAMP   _____
OR SEAL)   (Signature and title of authorized certifying officer)

_____
(Address)

Figure   C–4   **Form PD 1006**

Form PD 1006
Dept. of the Treasury
Bureau of the Public Debt
(Rev. Jan. 1976)

SPECIFIC POWER OF SUBSTITUTION
UNDER POWER OF ATTORNEY GRANTED TO AN
INDIVIDUAL TO DISPOSE OF REGISTERED SECURITIES

| IMPORTANT. – Follow instructions on back in completing this form. |

To: ☐ Federal Reserve Bank or Branch at _____
☐ Bureau of the Public Debt, Division of Securities Operations, Washington, D.C. 20226

The undersigned,_____ ,
(Name of attorney-in-fact)

of _____ ,
(Post office address)

by virtue of authority conferred by a power of attorney dated the_____ day of _____ , 19___ , executed by

_____ ,said power of attorney being in full force as of the date of this
(Name of grantor)

instrument, hereby substitutes and appoints_____ , of

_____ , to act in his place as such attorney to
(Post office address)

assign, or to sell, or to otherwise dispose of the following-described registered United States securities or securities for
which the Treasury Department acts as transfer agency :

LOAN TITLE (Include interest rate, call and maturity dates)	DENOMINATION	SERIAL NUMBER	REGISTRATION (Exact inscription on each security)

(If space is insufficient additional securities may be listed on the back.)

The undersigned hereby ratifies any and all action as authorized herein previously taken by virtue hereof.

Dated this_____ day of _____ , 19___ .

_____
(Signature)

I CERTIFY that the above-named person as described, whose identity is well known or proved to me, personally appeared

before me the day, month and year last above written, at _____ ,
(City)   (State)

and signed this instrument.

(SEAL)   _____
(Signature and title of certifying officer)

_____
(Address)

Figure C–5   **Form PD 1008**

Form PD 1008
Dept. of the Treasury
Bureau of the Public Debt
(Rev. Nov. 1975)

SPECIFIC POWER OF SUBSTITUTION
UNDER POWER OF ATTORNEY GRANTED TO
CORPORATION TO DISPOSE OF REGISTERED SECURITIES

IMPORTANT. – Follow instructions on back in completing this form.

KNOW ALL MEN BY THESE PRESENTS:

That _____ ,
(Exact corporate name)

a corporation organized under the laws of _____ and having its principal office at
(State)

_____ , by virtue of authority
(Post office address)

conferred by a power of attorney executed by _____ ,

of _____ , and dated the _____ day of _____ , 19 ___ ,

hereby substitutes and appoints _____ , of

_____ , to act in the place of said corporation as
(Post office address)

such attorney to assign, or to sell, or to otherwise dispose of the following-described registered United States securities
or securities for which the Treasury Department acts as transfer agency:

LOAN TITLE (Include interest rate, call and maturity dates)	DENOMINATION	SERIAL NUMBER	REGISTRATION (Exact inscription on each security)

(If space is insufficient additional securities may be listed on the back.)

Said corporation hereby ratifies any and all action as authorized herein previously taken by virtue hereof.

Dated this_____day of _____ , 19 _____ .

_____
(Name of corporation)

(SEAL)   By _____
(Signature and title of officer)

and _____
(Signature and title of officer)

I CERTIFY that the above-named person(s) as described, whose identity (or each of whose identities) is well known or

proved to me, personally appeared before me the day, month and year last above written, at _____ ,
(City)

_____ , and signed this instrument.
(State)

_____
(Signature and title of certifying officer)

(SEAL)

_____
(Address)

Figure C–6   **Form PD 1010**

Form PD 1010 (Rev. Oct. 1974)
Dept. of the Treasury
Bureau of the Public Debt

**RESOLUTION BY GOVERNING BODY OF AN ORGANIZATION
AUTHORIZING ASSIGNMENT AND DISPOSITION OF SPECIFIED
SECURITIES OWNED IN ITS OWN RIGHT OR IN A FIDUCIARY CAPACITY**

| IMPORTANT |
| FOLLOW INSTRUCTIONS ON THE REVERSE IN COMPLETING THIS FORM. |

To : ☐ Federal Reserve Bank or Branch at _____
☐ Bureau of the Public Debt, Division of Securities Operations, Washington, D. C. 20226

RESOLVED, That _____
_____(Titles, or names and titles, of officers)_____

_____

_____ { is hereby authorized   *(See Instruc-*
                                  { are hereby jointly and severally authorized   *tion 2.)*

to assign, or to sell, or to otherwise dispose of the following-described registered United States securities, or securities
for which the Department of the Treasury acts as transfer agency, in the total face amount of $ _____ ,

(Check appropriate   { ☐ owned by this organization in its own right
block.)   { ☐ held by this corporation in any representative or fiduciary capacity (**NOTE** : *Use ONLY when
                          a corporation is acting in such capacity; see Instruction 1.)*

with authority to appoint an attorney in fact with authority in turn to appoint one or more substitutes :

LOAN TITLE (Include interest rate, issue date, call and maturity dates)	DENOMINATION	SERIAL NUMBER	REGISTRATION (Exact inscription on each security)

(If space is insufficient, list additional securities on the back.)

IT IS FURTHER RESOLVED, That any and all action as authorized herein previously taken by the above-listed officers is hereby ratified. _____

I CERTIFY that the foregoing is a true copy of a resolution adopted at a meeting of the _____
_____ , the governing body (or the body duly authorized to act in these premises)

of _____ , { ☐ an unincorporated association,
_____(Complete name of organization)_____ { ☐ a corporation,

held on the _____ day of _____ , 19 ____ , at _____ .
I further certify that said meeting was duly called and held, and that the resolution was duly adopted and is in full force.

I FURTHER CERTIFY that _____ , and
_____(Name of officer and title)_____

_____ , was/were on said date, and is/are
_____(Name of officer and title)_____

presently, the duly qualified and acting incumbent(s) of the office(s) indicated. *(See Instruction 4.)*

Dated this _____ day of _____ , 19 ___ .

(SEAL)
IF ORGANIZATION HAS NO SEAL, SO STATE _____ ,
AND HAVE CERTIFICATE BELOW COMPLETED.

_____
(Signature and title of officer)

_____
(Additional signature and title, if necessary. See Instruction 3.)

Subscribed and certified to before me this _____ day of _____ , 19 ___ , at _____
                                                                                           (City)

_____ , by the above-named person(s) as described, whose identity and office
(County)   (State)
(or the identity and office of each of whom) is well known or proved to me.

(OFFICIAL STAMP
OR SEAL)

_____
(Signature and title of certifying officer)

_____
(Address)

My commission expires _____ .
_____(For notaries only)_____

Figure C–7   **Form PD 1014**

FORM PD 1014
Dept. of the Treasury
Bur. of the Public Debt
(Rev. June 1981)

CERTIFICATE OF INCUMBENCY OF OFFICERS
(Corporation or unincorporated association)

> **IMPORTANT. –** Follow instructions on reverse in filling out this form. Any person who makes a claim or statement on this form which he knows to be false, fictitious, or fraudulent may be fined $10,000 or imprisoned for 5 years, or both.
> **PRINT IN INK OR TYPE ALL INFORMATION**

To ☐ Federal Reserve Bank or Branch at _____
    ☐ Bureau of the Public Debt, Division of Securities Operations, Washington, D.C. 20226

The undersigned officer(s) of _____
(Exact name of organization)

☐ a corporation ☐ an unincorporated association, with principal office at _____
(Complete address)

_____ , hereby certify that the

persons named below were on _____ and are presently the duly qualified and acting incumbents of the
(Date)

offices indicated:

NAME OF OFFICER	OFFICER'S TITLE
_____	_____
_____	_____
_____	_____
_____	_____
_____	_____
_____	_____
_____	_____

Dated this _____ day of _____ , 19 ____ .

(SEAL OF ORGANIZATION)
IF NONE, HAVE FORM
BELOW COMPLETED.

_____
(Signature and title of officer)

_____
(Additional signature and title, if necessary. See Instruction 2.)

(THE FORM BELOW MUST BE COMPLETED IF THE ORGANIZATION HAS NO SEAL.)

Subscribed and sworn/certified to before me, this _____ day of _____ , 19 ____, at _____ ,
(City)

_____ , by the above-named person(s) as described, whose identity (or the
(County)   (State)

identity of each of whom) is well known or proved to me.

(OFFICIAL
STAMP OR SEAL)

_____
(Signature and title of certifying officer)

_____
(Address)

My commission expires _____ .
(For notaries only)

Figure   C–8   **Form PD 1071**

FORM PD 1071
Dept. of the Treasury
Bur. of the Public Debt
(Rev. Feb. 1978)

CERTIFICATE OF OWNERSHIP OF
UNITED STATES BEARER SECURITIES

	FOR FRB USE ONLY
IMPORTANT. – Follow the instructions on the reverse in filling out this form. Any person who makes a claim or statement on this form which he knows to be false, fictitious, or fraudulent may be fined $10,000 or imprisoned for five years, or both. **PRINT IN INK OR TYPE ALL INFORMATION**	CO NO. FRB OR BRANCH

I, _____ , am of age and reside
(Name in full)

at _____ .
(Complete address)

I CERTIFY that—

1. I am the lawful owner of the following-described bearer securities in the total face amount of $ _____ :

LOAN TITLES (Identify securities by interest rates, titles, call and maturity dates)	DENOMINATIONS (Face amounts)	SERIAL NUMBERS	NUMBER OF PIECES

2. I acquired the securities on or about _____ , from _____ ,
(Date)   (Name in full)

of _____ , without notice of
(Complete address)

any defect in title, by _____
(See Instruction 1)

_____

_____ .

3. I did not present the securities for payment at their face maturity dates or before they became overdue because

_____

_____

_____ .

4. As owner of said securities I warrant the title thereto and request payment thereof.

_____
(Signature of owner)

Subscribed and sworn/certified to before me this _____ day of _____ , 19 _____ ,

at _____ , by the above-named person
(City)   (County)   (State)

whose identity is well known or proved to me.

FOR FRB/DEPT. USE ONLY	
Approved By _____	
Date _____	
FRB/SECURITIES OPERATIONS	

(OFFICIAL SEAL
OR STAMP)

_____
(Signature and official title of certifying officer)

_____
(Address)

My commission expires _____ .
(For notaries only)

Figure   C–9   **Form PD 1461**

Form PD 1461
TREASURY DEPARTMENT
Bureau of the Public Debt
(Rev. 11/75)

APPLICATION FOR RECOGNITION AS VOLUNTARY GUARDIAN OF INCOMPETENT OWNER OF REGISTERED SECURITIES AND FOR DISPOSITION OF THE SECURITIES OR INTEREST THEREON

> **IMPORTANT. –** Follow attached instructions in filling out this form. Any person who makes a claim or statement on this form which he knows to be false, fictitious, or fraudulent may be fined $10,000 or imprisoned for 5 years, or both.
> **PRINT IN INK OR TYPE ALL INFORMATION**

To : Bureau of the Public Debt, Division of Securities Operations, Washington, D.C. 20226

I,_____, am of age and reside
(Name of applicant)

at_____ .
(Complete address)

I. I CERTIFY that_____ is an adult, _____ years
(Name of incompetent)

of age, that his social security account number is ☐☐–☐☐–☐☐☐ and that he resides

at_____ ;
(Complete address)

that he is incompetent to manage his own affairs, that no legal guardian or similar representative of his estate has been appointed and no application for such appointment is pending; and that the incompetent is the owner, wholly or in part, of the following-described securities :

TITLE OF SECURITY (Identify securities by interest rate, title, call and maturity dates)	DENOMINATION (Face value)	SERIAL NUMBER	REGISTRATION (Exact inscription on each security)

(If space is insufficient, use continuation sheet, sign it and refer to it above. Form PD 3500 may be amended and used for this purpose.)

II. I request that I be recognized as voluntary guardian of the incompetent, and in such capacity I hereby assign any transferable securities described for the purposes indicated, and I further request :

☐ (A) Reissue of the securities in the form "_____, an
(Name of incompetent)

incompetent (☐☐–☐☐–☐☐☐), under voluntary guardianship''.

☐ (B) Payment to me as voluntary guardian of checks covering interest now due or hereafter payable on the securities, or on any securities issued in exchange pursuant to a redemption-exchange or an advance refunding offer, or purchased upon reinvestment, registered as provided in (A) above. I hereby agree to use the proceeds of such interest checks solely for the purpose of paying expenses already incurred, or to be incurred, for the care and support of the incompetent or his legal dependents. I further agree to notify the Bureau of the Public Debt if the incompetent becomes competent, if he dies, or if a legal guardian or similar representative of his estate is appointed or otherwise legally qualifies.

☐ (C) (1) Payment of redeemable securities in the amount of $_____, or
(2) Exchange of presently unredeemable securities for coupon securities in the amount of $_____.
I further certify that the proceeds of payment or sale, as the case may be, of these securities are necessary to pay expenses already incurred, or to be incurred, for the care and support of the incompetent or his legal dependents, and I agree to so use the proceeds.

☐ (D) (1) Redemption of the securities for reinvestment of the proceeds in_____
(Specify type of securities and denominations desired)
_____ offered
pursuant to a redemption-exchange or an advance refunding offer, to be registered in the form shown in (A) above.
(2) Payment of presently redeemable securities, the proceeds of which are not now necessary, and reinvestment of
the proceeds in _____
(Specify type of securities and denominations desired)
_____, to be registered in the form shown in (A) above.
I agree to furnish any additional amount necessary to complete payment for the new securities or to use for the incompetent's benefit any excess over that needed to complete the transaction.

Figure   C–9 (*concluded*)

III. In support of the above requests, I hereby declare my answers to the questions and other information below are true and complete, to the best of my knowledge and belief.

    A. What is your relationship to the incompetent?_____.

    B. (1) Do you contribute to his care and support or that of his legal dependents?_____. To what extent?_____.

        (2) Do other persons so contribute?_____. *If so, complete the following:*

NAME	ADDRESS	RELATIONSHIP	EXTENT OF CONTRIBUTIONS

    C. Has he been declared mentally incompetent?_____. *If so, attach copy of court order or proceedings. If not, describe his disability.*_____

          (Attach opinion by attending physician on his professional stationery)

    D. Is he a patient in a hospital or other institution?_____

          (If so, furnish name and address and state whether public or private)

    E. (1) What amount is required monthly for his support? $_____.

        (2) What are the outstanding expenses already incurred for the care and support of the incompetent or his legal dependent? *List the amounts and purposes for which incurred.*_____

        (3) What is his own total monthly income? $_____. *List the amounts and sources of this income.*_____

        (4) Has he a bank account or cash on hand?_____

          (Specify amounts, locations, etc.)

        (5) Does he own, in addition to the securities described on this application, any other United States securities including savings bonds?_____. *(If so, describe the additional holdings on a separate sheet and attach it to this application.)*

                              _____

                              (Signature of applicant)

I (we) hereby consent to the action(s) requested in this application.

_____   _____
       (Signature)   (Signature)

_____   _____
       (Signature)   (Signature)

I CERTIFY that_____ and _____,
whose identities are well known or proved to me, personally appeared before me this_____ day of_____,
19_____, at_____, and signed the foregoing instrument.
              (City and State)

        (OFFICIAL STAMP   _____
          OR SEAL)   (Signature and title of authorized certifying officer)

                                _____
                                 (Address)

I CERTIFY that_____ and _____,
whose identities are well known or proved to me, personally appeared before me this_____ day of_____,
19_____, at_____, and signed the foregoing instrument.
              (City and State)

        (OFFICIAL STAMP   _____
          OR SEAL)   (Signature and title of authorized certifying officer)

                                _____
                                 (Address)

I CERTIFY that_____ and _____,
whose identities are well known or proved to me, personally appeared before me this_____ day of_____,
19_____, at_____, and signed the foregoing instrument.
              (City and State)

        (OFFICIAL STAMP   _____
          OR SEAL)   (Signature and title of authorized certifying officer)

                                _____
                                 (Address)

Figure C–10   Form PD 1646

Form PD 1646
Dept. of the Treasury
Bureau of the Public Debt
(Rev. Nov. 1975)

APPLICATION FOR DISPOSITION
UNITED STATES REGISTERED SECURITIES AND RELATED CHECKS
WITHOUT ADMINISTRATION OF DECEASED OWNER'S ESTATE

> **IMPORTANT. –** Follow attached instructions in filling out this form. Any person who makes a claim or statement on this form which he knows to be false, fictitious, or fraudulent may be fined $10,000 or imprisoned for 5 years, or both.
> **PRINT IN INK OR TYPE ALL INFORMATION**

To: Bureau of the Public Debt, Division of Securities Operations, Washington, D.C. 20226

We, the undersigned, certify that the following statements and information furnished are true and correct to the best of our knowledge and belief:

1._____died at_____
        (Name of decedent)   (Place of death)

on the_____day of_____ , 19_____ , at the age of_____ years; his last legal residence was in the state

of_____ ; and no legal representative of his estate has been appointed by any court and no application for such appointment is pending (see Instruction 1).

2. Decedent { ☐ left / ☐ did not leave } a will. (See Instruction 2.)

3. The gross value of the decedent's personal estate, including his entire or partial interest in securities or checks described

herein, was $_____ . (See Instruction 3.)

4. (a) The names of all persons who rendered services during the last illness, death and burial (or cremation) of decedent, with their charges, are as follows:

NAMES OF UNDERTAKERS, PHYSICIANS, HOSPITALS, SPECIAL NURSES, ETC.	NATURE OF SERVICES	TOTAL AMOUNT OF BILL	AMOUNT PAID	WITH WHOSE FUNDS PAID

(b) All other unsecured debts owed by the decedent at the time of his death { ☐ have / ☐ have not } been paid in full.

5. Except for creditors listed in Item 4 (a), following are all of the persons who had any interest in the personal estate of decedent at the time of his death, including unpaid creditors and legatees, if any, and all other persons required by Instruction 5 to be listed:

NAME	AGE	RELATIONSHIP OR BASIS OF INTEREST	STREET ADDRESS OR RURAL ROUTE	CITY OR TOWN	STATE

6. The persons listed in Item 5 who are under legal disability are (see Instruction 6):

NAME (If none under disability, insert "None")	NATURE OF DISABILITY (Minority, incompetency, etc.)	NAME, ADDRESS AND CAPACITY OF LEGAL REPRESENTATIVE (If none, give name and relationship of person managing his affairs)

Figure C–10 (*concluded*)

7. We request that the following-described securities which the decedent owned or had an interest in be disposed of as indicated in favor of the person or persons we agree are entitled as designated, the securities or checks in payment to be delivered to them at their addresses as given above or to a bank for their account if they so request, and we hereby assign the securities for that purpose (see Instruction 7):

(a) DESCRIPTION OF SECURITIES AND/OR SERIAL NUMBERS OF CHECKS (INCLUDE FACE AMOUNTS)	(b) DISPOSITION DESIRED	(c) PERSONS ENTITLED AND THEIR TAXPAYER IDENTIFYING NUMBERS	(d) EXTENT ENTITLED TO

8. Signatures of applicants (see Instruction 8):

_____   _____   _____

_____   _____   _____

_____

(All signatures must be certified by an authorized officer)

9. Certifications (see Instruction 9):

I CERTIFY that_____
(Names of applicants)

whose identities are well known or proved to me, personally appeared before me this_____ day of_____ , 19_____,

at_____ and signed this application, each acknowledging the same
(City and State)

to be his or her free act and deed.

(OFFICIAL STAMP OR SEAL)   _____
(Signature and official designation of certifying officer)

_____
(Address)

I CERTIFY that_____
(Names of applicants)

whose identities are well known or proved to me, personally appeared before me this_____ day of_____ , 19_____,

at_____ and signed this application, each acknowledging the same
(City and State)

to be his or her free act and deed.

(OFFICIAL STAMP OR SEAL)   _____
(Signature and official designation of certifying officer)

_____
(Address)

(Form PD 2778 may be attached to provide space for additional certifications, if required.)

Figure   C–11   **Form PD 1782**

FORM PD 1782
Dept. of the Treasury
Bureau of the Public Debt
(Rev. June 1982)

OMB
Control Number
1535-0010
(Nov., 1982)

ESTATE OF _____

APPLICATION FOR REDEMPTION AT PAR OF UNITED STATES TREASURY BONDS
ELIGIBLE FOR PAYMENT OF FEDERAL ESTATE TAX

IMPORTANT. — Follow the attached instructions in filling out this form. Any person who makes a claim or statement on this form or attachments which he knows to be false, fictitious, or fraudulent may be fined $10,000 or imprisoned for 5 years, or both. **PRINT IN INK OR TYPE ALL INFORMATION**

FOR FRB OR DEPT. USE ONLY

E _____

Tax due date: _____

Bonds rec'd: _____
(Date)

Effective Redemption: _____
(Date)

By : _____
(FRB or Departmental Office)

To: ☐ Federal Reserve Bank or Branch at _____
    ☐ Bureau of the Public Debt, Division of Securities Operations,
    Washington, D. C. 20226

1. The undersigned herewith submits, and assigns for redemption at par and accrued inter-

est on _____ , the following-described Treasury bonds in the total face amount of $ _____
(Date—See Detailed Instructions, Sec. 1)

for credit on the Federal estate tax due on the estate of _____ ,

deceased, whose State of last legal residence was _____ ;

BOND DESCRIPTION		DENOMI-NATION	TYPE	SERIAL NUMBERS	EXACT INSCRIPTION ON BONDS OR THE NUMBERS ON COUPONS ATTACHED	DATE ACQUIRED	SOURCE OF FUNDS
%	MATURITY YEAR						
Bond(s)							
Bond(s)							
Bond(s)							
Bond(s)							
Bond(s)							
Bond(s)							

(If space is insufficient, continue on a separate sheet, sign it, and refer to it above.)

and in support thereof certifies that all of the above-described bonds were purchased by the decedent himself during his lifetime,

except bonds bearing serial Nos. _____ which were purchased

for him by _____ _____ as _____ .
(Name)   (Capacity)

Complete the following if applicable:
☐ The above-described bonds were held in a book-entry account at the Federal Reserve Bank or Branch at_____

_____ at the time of the decedent's death and
        a. ☐ were thereafter withdrawn from book-entry and were converted to definitive form.
        b. ☐ are being redeemed directly from book-entry without conversion to definitive form.

2. The undersigned hereby certifies that the said bonds were owned by the above-named decedent at the time of his death and:
    ☐ a. Thereupon constituted part of his estate, or

    ☐ b. Were held by _____ , as nominee, for the benefit of the owner, or
        (Name of Nominee)
    ☐ c. Were otherwise held as shown on Schedule J, C, P or T attached to this application
so as to render them eligible, under applicable Treasury regulations, for redemption at par, plus accrued interest from the last preceding interest date to the date of redemption, for credit on said decedent's Federal estate tax.

Figure C–11 (*concluded*)

3. The undersigned further certifies as follows:

    a. Decedent's date of death was _____ .

    b. Decedent's social security number was ☐☐☐ – ☐☐ – ☐☐☐☐

    c. The Employer Identification Number, if any, assigned to the decedent's estate is ☐☐ – ☐☐☐☐☐☐☐

    d. The decedent's estate ☐ is ☐ is not being administered.
       <u>Complete the following, if applicable</u>:

       ☐ Letters testamentary or of administration have been issued to:
          (1) Name of representative and capacity (show whether administrator, executor, personal representative, etc.)

          _____

          _____

          (2) On (date on which letters granted) _____

          (3) By (name and location of court) _____

          _____

          (4) With case or index number _____

4. The undersigned further certifies that:

    a. Form 706 (Estate Tax Return) for the decedent's estate ☐ has been, ☐ will be sent to _____
    _____ (location of IRS Center).

    b. The total tax liability (including interest, penalties and deficiency assessments) is: $ __ _____

    c. Assessed deficiencies amount to _____ $ __ _____

    d. Total prior payments in cash _____ $ _____

                   in bonds _____ $ _____

    e. Balance of unpaid tax amounts to _____ $ _____

5. <u>Complete the following, if applicable</u>:

    ☐ The above-described bonds are being submitted in substitution of amount(s) previously paid on account of the above-described tax, and, in support of this request for substitution, it is certified that:

    a. Two years ☐ have ☐ have not elapsed since date tax was paid.

    b. The decedent's estate ☐ is ☐ is not still open.

    c. In consideration of the substitution, the undersigned waives claim to interest on the overpayment resulting from such action.

Indicate name and telephone number of person who
may be contacted for further information if necessary _____

(Complete below in accordance with General Instructions, Item 3)

(Signature)	(Date)	(Signature)	(Date)
(Print or type name and exact capacity)		(Print or type name and exact capacity)	
(Mailing address, including ZIP code)		(Mailing address, including ZIP code)	

Notice of bond credit will be mailed to the above name and address.

FOR DEPARTMENT USE ONLY

CD# _____ dtd _____ .   TO: Director, Internal Revenue Service Center,
Symbol 20-09- _____   P.O. Box _____ , _____

Loan Title	Principal	+Accrued Interest	Total	−Deducted Interest	+Matured Interest	Total
___	___	___	___	___	___	___
___	___	___	___	___	___	___
___	___	___	___	___	___	___

TOTAL CREDIT $ _____

Figure   C–12   **Form PD 1832**

FORM PD 1832
Dept. of the Treasury
Bur. of the Public Debt
(Rev. Mar. 1977)

SPECIAL FORM OF DETACHED ASSIGNMENT FOR
UNITED STATES REGISTERED SECURITIES

FOR VALUE RECEIVED I assign to _____

(Name)

_____

(Taxpayer identifying number and address of assignee)

the following-described registered securities of which I am (we are) the owner(s) or the duly authorized representative of the owner:

TITLE OF LOAN and/or ISSUE _____

(Include interest rate, series, issue date and call and maturity dates)

DENOMINATION	SERIAL NUMBERS	REGISTRATION (Exact inscription on each security)

and hereby authorize discharge of registration thereof on the books of the Department of the Treasury.

_____

(Signature by or on behalf of owner)

_____

(Additional signature, if required)

I CERTIFY that the above-named person(s) as described, whose identity (or the identity of each of whom) is well known

or proved to me, personally appeared before me this _____ day of _____, 19_____,

at _____ , and signed the above assignment.

(City and State)

(SEAL)

_____

(Signature and title of certifying officer)

_____

(Address)

(See other side for list of officers authorized to certify assignments)

Figure C–13   **Form PD 2446**

Certificate of Incumbency
for Fiduciaries

> **IMPORTANT.** – Follow the instructions on the back in filling out this form. Any person who makes a claim or statement on this form which he knows to be false, fictitious, or fraudulent may be fined $10,000 or imprisoned for 5 years, or both.
> **PRINT IN INK OR TYPE ALL INFORMATION**

TO: Federal Reserve Bank or Branch at_____
        Bureau of the Public Debt, Washington, D.C. 20226
        Bureau of the Public Debt, 200 Third Street, Parkersburg, West Virginia 26101

I HEREBY CERTIFY THAT

_____
Complete title of trust, including names of grantors and beneficiaries and date of execution, or statutory reference. See Instruction 2.)

the records of which are, by due authorization, kept

☐ by me as_____ of the _____.
                 (Official title)   (Name of organization, board, trustees or other body)

☐ by the_____, of which
                          (Name of organization, board, trustees or other body)

I am _____.
              (Official title)

I FURTHER CERTIFY that the authority governing the trust provides for _____
                                                                        (Number and titles of fiduciaries)
and that the names of the several present incumbents and the respective periods of time for which they were elected, or otherwise duly qualified to act, are as follows (if period for which qualified is indefinite, insert the words "no limit" in the last column):

NAME OF INCUMBENTS	PERIODS FOR WHICH QUALIFIED	
	TO (INSERT DATE)	FROM (INSERT DATE)

Dated this_____ day of _____, 19_____

(SEAL)   _____
See below if no seal   (Signature and capacity)

                                _____
                                (Additional signature and capacity, if necessary. See Instruction 3)

(THIS JURAT FORM MUST BE COMPLETED IF THE CUSTODIAN OR TRUSTEES HAVE NO SEAL)

Subscribed and certified/sworn to before me the day, month and year last written above, at_____,

_____, by the above-named person(s) as described, whose identity (or the
      (County)   (State)
identity of each of whom) is well known or proved to me.

                                _____
                                (Signature and title of certifying officer)

                                _____
                                (Address)

My commission expires _____
                         (For notaries only)

FORM PD 2446 · Dept. of the Treasury, Bur. of the Public Debt, (Rev. May 1980)

Figure   C–14   **Form PD 2481**

Form PD 2481
TREASURY DEPARTMENT
Bureau of the Public Debt
(Rev. Apr. 1975)

APPLICATION FOR RECOGNITION AS NATURAL GUARDIAN OF MINOR NOT UNDER LEGAL GUARDIANSHIP AND FOR DISPOSITION OF MINOR'S INTEREST IN REGISTERED SECURITIES

> **IMPORTANT.** - Follow the attached instructions in filling out this form. Any person who makes a claim or statement on this form which he knows to be false, fictitious or fraudulent may be fined $10,000 or imprisoned for 5 years, or both.
> **PRINT IN INK OR TYPE ALL INFORMATION**

To: Bureau of the Public Debt, Division of Securities Operations, Washington, D.C. 20226

I. I, _____ , am of full legal age and reside
(Name of applicant)

at _____ . I certify that _____
(Complete address)   (Name of minor)

was born on the _____ day of _____ , 19____ ; that his social security account number

is ☐☐☐–☐☐–☐☐☐☐ ; that no legal guardian or similar representative of his estate has been appointed and no application for such appointment is pending; and that he is the owner, wholly or in part, of the following-described registered securities:

TITLE OF SECURITY (Identify by interest rate, title, call and maturity dates)	DENOMINATION (Face amount)	SERIAL NUMBER	REGISTRATION (Exact inscription on each security)

(If space is insufficient, use continuation sheet, attach it to the form, and sign the attachment.)

II. With respect to the securities described, I request that I be recognized as natural guardian of the minor, and in such capacity I further request disposition of the securities as indicated below, hereby assigning the securities for that purpose:

☐ (a) Reissue of the securities to show or substitute my name as natural guardian in the registration.

☐ (b) Exchange of the securities for coupon securities.

☐ (c) Redemption of the securities for reinvestment of the proceeds in securities offered in redemption-exchange or pursuant to an advance refunding offer.

☐ (d) Payment of called or matured securities.

III. In support of the above requests, I hereby declare that my answers to the following questions are true and complete, to the best of my knowledge and belief:

(a) What is your relationship to the minor? _____

(b) If you are a parent and the other parent has not consented to this application, give the reason for his (her) non-

consent. _____

_____

(c) If you are not a parent, complete the following:

(i) Why has neither parent applied? _____

_____

Figure C–14 (*concluded*)

(ii) Do you furnish the minor's chief support?_____

(iii) What are the names and addresses of other persons regularly contributing to the minor's support and the extent of their contributions?_____

_____

(iv) Does the minor reside with you?_____. *If not, give the name and address of the person with whom he resides.* _____

_____

IV. In consideration of my recognition as natural guardian of the minor, I hereby agree that I will promptly notify the Treasury Department (a) if his disability of minority is removed under the laws of the State of his residence, (b) if a legal guardian or similar representative is appointed for his estate, (c) if I no longer furnish his chief support or regularly contribute to his support (when support is the basis for recognition), or (d) if he dies.

I CONSENT:
_____
(Signature(s) of parent(s) or other applicant)

_____
(Signature of minor's other parent when required by Instruction 1)

_____
(Signature and address of contributor)

_____
(Signature and address of contributor)

I CERTIFY that the above-named person(s) whose identity (or the identity of each of whom) is well known or proved to me, personally appeared before me at _____ ____ ____ _____ _____ , on this_____ day
(City or County and State)

of _____ ____ ____ , 19__ ___, and signed the above application, (each) acknowledging the same to be his free act and deed.

(OFFICIAL STAMP
OR SEAL)   _____
(Signature and title of authorized certifying officer)

_____
(Address)

I CERTIFY that the above-named person(s) whose identity (or the identity of each of whom) is well known or proved to me, personally appeared before me at _____ , on this _____day
(City or County and State)

of _____ , 19_____, and signed the above application, (each) acknowledging the same to be his free act and deed.

(OFFICIAL STAMP
OR SEAL)   _____
(Signature and title of authorized certifying officer)

_____
(Address)

I CERTIFY that the above-named person(s) whose identity (or the identity of each of whom) is well known or proved to me, personally appeared before me at _____ , on this_____ day
(City or County and State)

of_____ , 19_____, and signed the above application, (each) acknowledging the same to be his free act and deed.

(OFFICIAL STAMP
OR SEAL)   _____
(Signature and title of authorized certifying officer)

_____
(Address)

Figure C–15   **Form PD 3905**

FORM PD 3905
Dept. of the Treasury
Bur. of the Public Debt
(Rev. Oct. 1978)

REQUEST FOR SECURITIES TRANSACTION

NOTE. – To protect against loss, coupon securities should be forwarded by registered mail, insured.

To ☐ Federal Reserve Bank or Branch at _____

☐ Bureau of the Public Debt, Division of Securities Operation, Washington, D.C. 20226

Pursuant to the provisions of Treasury Department Circular No. 300, current revision, the undersigned presents

_____ and requests that they be :
(Insert loan title of securities)

CHECK ONLY ONE BOX ☐ Redeemed   ☐ Exchanged for Coupon Securities   ☐ Exchanged for Registered Securities

☐ Exchanged for an equal face amount of the same issue in the denominations indicated below

☐ Transferred on the books of the Department and that new Registered Securities be issued

SECURITIES PRESENTED			DENOMI-NATION	SECURITIES TO BE ISSUED IN FOLLOWING DENOMINATIONS		
SERIAL NUMBERS	AMOUNT	NUMBER OF PIECES		NUMBER OF PIECES	AMOUNT	SERIAL NUMBERS (To be assigned by Department or Federal Reserve Bank)
	$		$ 500		$	
			1,000			
			5,000			
			10,000			
			15,000			
			100,000			
			500,000			
			1,000,000			
	$		◀ TOTALS ▶		$	

1. IF **REGISTERED** SECURITIES PRESENTED, GIVE EXACT INSCRIPTION(S) IF **COUPON** SECURITIES PRESENTED GIVE NUMBERS OF COUPONS ATTACHED THERETO

2. IF REGISTERED SECURITIES TO BE ISSUED, GIVE REGISTRATION, TAX PAYER IDENTIFYING NUMBER AND ADDRESS, INCLUDING ZIP CODE, FOR MAILING SECURITIES AND INTEREST CHECKS

3. IF SECURITIES TO BE REDEEMED, GIVE NAME AND TAXPAYER IDENTIFYING NUMBER OF PAYEE, AND ADDRESS, INCLUDING ZIP CODE, FOR DELIVERY OF REDEMPTION PROCEEDS

4. IF COUPON SECURITIES TO BE ISSUED, GIVE MAILING ADDRESS, INCLUDING ZIP CODE, FOR THEIR DELIVERY

5. IT IS UNDERSTOOD THAT **REGISTERED** SECURITIES WILL BE DELIVERED BY REGISTERED MAIL AT THE RISK OF BUT WITHOUT EXPENSE TO THE OWNER, AND THAT **COUPON** SECURITIES WILL BE DELIVERED BY REGISTERED MAIL INSURED, AT THE RISK AND EXPENSE OF THE OWNER, UNLESS OTHER ARRANGEMENTS ARE MADE.

Name *(Print or type)* _____

Signature _____   Date _____

Address _____
(Complete only if **not** shown in block 2, 3 or 4)

Figure   C–16   **Form PD 4633-1**

FORM PD 4633-1
Dept. of the Treasury
Bur. of the Public Debt
(Rev. Jan. 1980)

BPD NO.
(FOR OFFICIAL USE ONLY)

REQUEST FOR REINVESTMENT OF
BOOK ENTRY TREASURY BILLS

SEND TO: BUREAU OF THE PUBLIC DEBT   TELEPHONE: (202) 287-4113
DEPT. X   TELEPHONE FOR THE DEAF: (202) 287-4097
WASHINGTON, D.C. 20226

This form can only be used to request the reinvestment of a book-entry bill account maintained by the Treasury. A reinvestment represents an investment of the proceeds of a maturing security into a newly issued security. This form must be submitted each time you wish to reinvest your account. A request for continuous reinvestment will not be accepted.

This form **cannot** be used to:
- (a)   Change an address.
- (b)   Add or delete a second named depositor.
- (c)   Cancel a previous request for reinvestment.
- (d)   Submit any other request other than to reinvest an account currently scheduled for redemption. (Use Form PD 4633 to request such changes.)

This form **must be received** by this office not later than:
- (a)   Ten (10) **business** days before maturity for bills issued prior to January 15, 1980.
- (b)   Twenty (20) **business** days before maturity for bills issued after January 15, 1980. (**NOTE:** Do not count Saturdays, Sundays or Federal holidays.)

Before you check which type of bill you want issued at reinvestment, please note that
- (a)   **Only** one type of bill may be selected when requesting reinvestment.
- (b)   26 week and 13 week bills are interchangeable.
- (c)   52 week bills maturing on or before October 14, 1980 may be reinvested in 52 week bills **only**.
- (d)   52 week bills maturing on or after November 6, 1980 may be reinvested in 52 week, 26 week or 13 week bills.
- (e)   Your account number must be shown.

I hereby request that the proceeds of maturing Treasury bills as identified by the following account number be reinvested at maturity on a noncompetitive basis for Treasury bills then being offered for the number of weeks indicated.

(Account No. as shown on Statement of Account)

CHECK ONE BOX ONLY:

(2) ☐ 52 week bill

(6) ☐ 26 week bill

(3) ☐ 13 week bill

Print name and mailing address below:

Social Security Number or
Employer Identification Number

Telephone no. and area code during the hours
of 8:30 a.m. to 5:00 p.m. Eastern Time

Signature and Date

(This form does not require certification)

Appendix **D**

*Comparison of Selected
Interest Rates for the Period
1977–1982*

This appendix compares seven selected interest rates over the six year period from 1977 to 1982. The following rates are presented on a weekly basis:

- Weekly average prime rate.
- 3-month Treasury bill market yield.
- 6-month Treasury bill auction rate.
- 1-year Treasury bill market yield.
- 3 to 5 year Treasury note rate.
- Long term Treasury bond (20–30 years) rate.
- Municipal bond yield—bond buyer's average index of 20 municipal bonds.

The source for all data is the Federal Reserve Bank of St. Louis.

1977 WEEK ENDING FRIDAY	WEEKLY AVERAGE PRIME RATE	3 MO T-BILL MARKET YIELD	6 MO T-BILL AUCTION RATE	1 YR T-BILL MARKET YIELD	3 TO 5 YR T-NOTE RATE	LONG TERM T-BOND RATE	MUNI BOND YIELD
01-07	6.25%	4.49%	4.76%	R	6.12%	7.14%	5.78%
01-14	6.25	4.58	4.93	A	6.48	7.35	5.89
01-21	6.25	4.65	5.08	T	6.57	7.40	5.90
01-28	6.25	4.72	5.18	E	6.71	7.49	5.92
02-04	6.25	4.71	5.24	S	6.78	7.52	5.93
02-11	6.25	4.62	5.11		6.64	7.49	5.86
02-18	6.25	4.63	5.08		6.60	7.50	5.83
02-25	6.25	4.71	5.22	N	6.76	7.59	5.92
03-04	6.25	4.66	5.23	O	6.76	7.60	5.92
03-11	6.25	4.63	5.22	T	6.77	7.60	5.92
03-18	6.25	4.59	5.18		6.71	7.56	5.90
03-25	6.25	4.57	5.17		6.68	7.55	5.88
04-01	6.25	4.57	5.15	A	6.70	7.56	5.85
04-08	6.25	4.58	5.14	V	6.70	7.55	5.79
04-15	6.25	4.55	5.03	A	6.52	7.48	5.76
04-22	6.25	4.51	5.04	I	6.49	7.45	5.73
04-29	6.25	4.51	5.18	L	6.61	7.51	5.68
05-06	6.25	4.75	5.28	A	6.72	7.57	5.76
05-13	6.25	4.96	5.46	B	6.78	7.61	5.82
05-20	6.50	5.05	5.52	L	6.79	7.58	5.76
05-27	6.50	5.06	5.45	E	6.77	7.53	5.71
06-03	6.75	5.03	5.42		6.71	7.52	5.72
06-10	6.75	5.06	5.43		6.68	7.48	5.65
06-17	6.75	5.01	5.40	F	6.56	7.41	5.55
06-24	6.75	5.01	5.41	R	6.54	7.41	5.61
07-01	6.75	4.97	5.39	O	6.49	7.38	5.56
07-08	6.75	5.12	5.46	M	6.60	7.43	5.63
07-15	6.75	5.16	5.16		6.62	7.43	5.64
07-22	6.75	5.21	5.60		6.69	7.46	5.62
07-29	6.75	5.27	5.70	F	6.77	7.49	5.62
08-05	6.75	5.35	5.83	E	6.86	7.53	5.63
08-12	6.75	5.47	5.94	D	6.90	7.54	5.63
08-19	6.75	5.56	6.07		6.97	7.52	5.63
08-26	7.00	5.53	6.02		6.89	7.45	5.58
09-02	7.00	5.56	5.98	B	6.84	7.40	5.54
09-09	7.00	5.65	6.04	A	6.86	7.41	5.48
09-16	7.00	5.86	6.14	N	6.93	7.45	5.51
09-23	7.25	5.90	6.15	K	6.93	7.47	5.50
09-30	7.25	5.89	6.21		6.98	7.49	5.51
10-07	7.25	6.09	6.38		7.05	7.53	5.60
10-14	7.50	6.32	6.61	O	7.21	7.61	5.70
10-21	7.50	6.17	6.59	F	7.30	7.62	5.67
10-28	7.50	6.09	6.49		7.32	7.64	5.59
11-04	7.50	6.20	6.60		7.36	7.71	5.55
11-11	7.50	6.15	6.55	S	7.30	7.71	5.51
11-18	7.50	6.07	6.49	T	7.24	7.67	5.45
11-25	7.50	6.06	6.48		7.25	7.65	5.45
12-02	7.50	6.04	6.49	L	7.29	7.66	5.47
12-09	7.50	6.07	6.52	O	7.36	7.72	5.54
12-16	7.50	6.03	6.50	U	7.38	7.75	5.55
12-23	7.50	6.03	6.53	I	7.43	7.81	5.62
12-30	7.50	6.16	6.57	S	7.51	7.87	5.66

1978 WEEK ENDING FRIDAY	WEEKLY AVERAGE PRIME RATE	3 MO T-BILL MARKET YIELD	6 MO T-BILL AUCTION RATE	1 YR T-BILL MARKET YIELD	3 TO 5 YR T-NOTE RATE	LONG TERM T-BOND RATE	MUNI BOND YIELD
01-06	7.75%	6.20%	6.42%	6.57%	7.52%	7.91%	5.64%
01-13	8.00	6.60	6.85	6.94	7.78	8.05	5.75
01-20	8.00	6.48	6.76	6.84	7.75	8.04	5.74
01-27	8.00	6.44	6.71	6.82	7.74	8.05	5.70
02-03	8.00	6.42	6.72	6.80	7.68	8.05	5.63
02-10	8.00	6.44	6.74	6.84	7.71	8.08	5.59
02-17	8.00	6.48	6.75	6.90	7.81	8.12	5.61
02-24	8.00	6.45	6.76	6.88	7.83	8.12	5.65
03-03	8.00	6.39	6.71	6.84	7.78	8.11	5.63
03-10	8.00	6.29	6.68	6.81	7.77	8.09	5.58
03-17	8.00	6.27	6.62	6.80	7.72	8.06	5.58
03-24	8.00	6.22	6.55	6.77	7.71	8.06	5.59
03-31	8.00	6.34	6.67	6.89	7.83	8.16	5.69
04-07	8.00	6.37	6.72	6.94	7.87	8.21	5.76
04-14	8.00	6.29	6.74	6.91	7.87	8.23	5.74
04-21	8.00	6.22	6.56	6.93	7.87	8.20	5.79
04-28	8.00	6.26	6.78	7.06	7.98	8.27	5.89
05-05	8.00	6.38	6.94	7.16	8.02	8.31	5.98
05-12	8.25	6.37	6.99	7.25	8.09	8.38	5.99
05-19	8.25	6.32	7.01	7.32	8.10	8.36	5.98
05-26	8.25	6.51	7.14	7.38	8.16	8.41	6.18
06-02	8.50	6.62	7.16	7.37	8.19	8.43	6.19
06-09	8.50	6.62	7.10	7.36	8.18	8.39	6.18
06-16	8.50	6.65	7.12	7.46	8.22	8.40	6.16
06-23	8.75	6.79	7.23	7.64	8.39	8.48	6.26
06-30	8.75	6.93	7.40	7.72	8.50	8.56	6.29
07-07	9.00	7.05	7.45	7.75	8.52	8.60	6.31
07-14	9.00	7.16	7.52	7.82	8.56	8.64	6.32
07-21	9.00	7.05	7.50	7.82	8.55	8.62	6.26
07-28	9.00	6.83	7.43	7.78	8.53	8.58	6.24
08-04	9.00	6.80	7.36	7.65	8.36	8.43	6.12
08-11	9.00	6.79	7.17	7.58	8.22	8.34	6.03
08-18	9.00	7.12	7.26	7.78	8.34	8.44	6.10
08-25	9.00	7.25	7.47	7.79	8.33	8.35	6.11
09-01	9.00	7.50	7.55	7.86	8.36	8.34	6.16
09-08	9.25	7.60	7.74	7.86	8.33	8.31	6.13
09-15	9.25	7.70	7.79	7.95	8.32	8.28	6.02
09-22	9.50	8.02	7.98	8.08	8.40	8.40	6.12
09-29	9.50	7.96	8.28	8.16	8.48	8.51	6.09
10-06	9.75	8.14	8.38	8.23	8.48	8.55	6.07
10-13	9.75	7.98	8.42	8.28	8.47	8.53	6.10
10-20	10.00	7.89	8.56	8.46	8.56	8.59	6.14
10-27	10.00	7.70	8.61	8.53	8.69	8.64	6.21
11-03	10.50	8.73	8.98	9.17	9.05	8.72	6.22
11-10	10.75	8.79	9.42	9.32	9.04	8.73	6.17
11-17	10.75	8.14	9.29	9.08	8.93	8.65	6.11
11-24	11.00	8.63	9.40	9.12	8.87	8.66	6.16
12-01	11.50	8.98	9.33	9.29	9.01	8.71	6.29
12-08	11.50	8.93	9.22	9.32	9.02	8.75	6.29
12-15	11.50	8.93	9.26	9.28	9.12	8.80	6.45
12-22	11.50	9.28	9.52	9.61	9.41	8.94	6.67
12-29	11.75	9.25	9.50	9.65	9.48	8.94	6.61

1979 WEEK ENDING FRIDAY	WEEKLY AVERAGE PRIME RATE	3 MO T-BILL MARKET YIELD	6 MO T-BILL AUCTION RATE	1 YR T-BILL MARKET YIELD	3 TO 5 YR T-NOTE RATE	LONG TERM T-BOND RATE	MUNI BOND YIELD
01-05	11.75%	9.34%	9.55%	9.61%	9.46%	8.96%	6.58%
01-12	11.75	9.30	9.44	9.61	9.46	8.97	6.50
01-19	11.75	9.44	9.53	9.61	9.43	8.97	6.48
01-26	11.75	9.34	9.48	9.46	9.27	8.89	6.30
02-02	11.75	9.28	9.38	9.31	9.02	8.81	6.22
02-09	11.75	9.24	9.31	9.34	9.07	8.90	6.31
02-16	11.75	9.28	9.34	9.35	9.16	8.96	6.33
02-23	11.75	9.41	9.37	9.49	9.25	9.00	6.38
03-02	11.75	9.44	9.50	9.50	9.32	9.03	6.42
03-09	11.75	9.44	9.42	9.40	9.24	8.98	6.35
03-16	11.75	9.51	9.46	9.43	9.24	8.99	6.30
03-23	11.75	9.54	9.48	9.37	9.24	8.99	6.29
03-30	11.75	9.46	9.44	9.29	9.23	8.97	6.28
04-06	11.75	9.53	9.50	9.26	9.24	8.97	6.25
04-13	11.75	9.70	9.57	9.37	9.34	9.02	6.33
04-20	11.75	9.41	9.63	9.22	9.32	9.03	6.30
04-27	11.75	9.23	9.30	9.27	9.35	9.09	6.26
05-04	11.75	9.58	9.57	9.40	9.42	9.17	6.27
05-11	11.75	9.63	9.62	9.39	9.42	9.20	6.30
05-18	11.75	9.60	9.46	9.26	9.32	9.13	6.30
05-25	11.75	9.64	9.60	9.14	9.14	9.03	6.21
06-01	11.75	9.55	9.41	9.05	9.08	8.98	6.16
06-08	11.75	9.36	9.43	8.94	8.97	8.90	6.09
06-15	11.75	8.97	9.05	8.74	8.85	8.81	6.11
06-22	11.50	8.96	8.87	8.84	8.93	8.85	6.18
06-29	11.50	8.83	8.90	8.64	8.78	8.76	6.12
07-06	11.50	9.10	8.87	8.70	8.71	8.74	6.08
07-13	11.50	9.28	9.16	8.79	8.82	8.82	6.11
07-20	11.50	9.31	9.26	8.93	8.91	8.80	6.15
07-27	11.50	9.28	9.47	9.00	9.00	8.90	6.19
08-03	11.75	9.23	9.30	8.93	8.98	8.88	6.14
08-10	11.75	9.40	9.32	8.95	8.95	8.85	6.13
08-17	11.75	9.52	9.48	9.15	9.02	8.87	6.16
08-24	12.00	9.55	9.50	9.28	9.12	8.90	6.23
08-31	12.25	9.74	9.65	9.41	9.30	8.98	6.36
09-07	12.25	10.20	9.78	9.84	9.52	9.12	6.47
09-14	12.75	10.45	10.29	9.96	9.51	9.12	6.49
09-21	13.00	10.26	10.32	9.90	9.59	9.13	6.57
09-28	13.25	10.14	10.11	9.87	9.61	9.18	6.56
10-05	13.50	10.43	10.33	10.07	9.72	9.31	6.64
10-12	14.50	11.62	10.66	11.30	10.48	9.77	7.12
10-19	14.50	11.91	11.72	11.40	10.79	9.99	7.18
10-26	15.00	12.60	12.65	11.94	11.57	10.36	7.38
11-02	15.00	12.07	12.19	11.65	11.43	10.36	7.26
11-09	15.25	12.25	12.09	11.66	11.36	10.44	7.27
11-16	15.50	11.90	11.95	11.12	10.97	10.34	7.31
11-23	15.75	11.77	12.04	11.25	11.00	10.31	7.38
11-30	15.75	11.26	11.02	10.74	10.42	9.97	7.26
12-07	15.50	11.75	11.77	10.86	10.33	9.97	7.17
12-14	15.25	12.34	11.77	11.10	10.49	10.14	7.26
12-21	15.25	12.06	12.00	10.85	10.45	10.00	7.22
12-28	15.25	11.99	11.85	10.86	10.51	10.13	7.23

1980 WEEK ENDING FRIDAY	WEEKLY AVERAGE PRIME RATE	3 MO T-BILL MARKET YIELD	6 MO T-BILL AUCTION RATE	1 YR T-BILL MARKET YIELD	3 TO 5 YR T-NOTE RATE	LONG TERM T-BOND RATE	MUNI BOND YIELD
01-04	15.25%	12.10%	11.88%	10.97%	10.52%	10.21%	7.32%
01-11	15.25	11.72	11.86	10.78	10.54	10.27	7.30
01-18	15.25	11.91	11.78	10.83	10.64	10.42	7.28
01-25	15.25	12.17	11.89	11.05	10.87	10.73	7.33
02-01	15.25	12.15	11.85	11.23	11.15	10.61	7.52
02-08	15.25	12.05	11.99	11.51	11.68	11.51	7.71
02-15	15.25	12.36	12.26	11.91	11.99	11.76	7.75
02-22	15.39	13.38	13.01	13.12	13.22	12.53	8.46
02-29	16.39	13.78	13.63	13.53	13.76	12.49	8.72
03-07	16.86	15.37	14.79	13.94	13.65	12.41	8.94
03-14	17.68	15.32	14.96	13.92	13.22	12.11	9.08
03-21	18.46	14.76	14.95	13.89	13.21	12.06	9.29
03-28	19.00	15.55	15.70	14.39	13.83	12.47	9.44
04-04	19.43	14.78	14.80	13.90	13.29	12.20	9.44
04-11	20.00	14.30	14.23	13.11	12.57	11.61	9.07
04-18	20.00	13.57	13.55	11.97	11.67	10.95	7.89
04-25	19.57	12.18	11.89	10.86	11.08	10.74	8.11
05-02	19.50	10.47	10.79	9.99	10.63	10.51	7.96
05-09	18.36	9.14	9.50	9.00	9.94	9.94	7.11
05-16	17.50	8.53	8.87	8.72	9.94	10.20	7.44
05-23	16.64	8.15	8.92	8.34	9.89	10.22	7.72
05-30	14.71	7.70	7.75	8.03	9.79	10.13	7.73
06-06	14.00	7.51	8.17	7.19	9.58	10.08	7.67
06-13	13.14	6.44	6.94	7.23	9.08	9.64	7.53
06-20	12.43	6.76	6.66	7.30	8.90	9.45	7.55
06-27	12.00	7.42	7.11	7.65	9.23	9.74	7.76
07-04	12.00	7.92	8.10	7.86	9.47	10.05	7.88
07-11	11.79	8.08	8.11	7.91	9.46	10.13	7.95
07-18	11.50	7.98	8.11	7.93	9.44	10.16	8.03
07-25	11.43	7.93	7.91	7.94	9.46	10.17	8.19
08-01	11.00	8.44	8.28	8.43	9.92	10.51	8.59
08-08	11.00	8.58	8.87	8.61	10.12	10.65	8.61
08-15	11.00	8.60	8.89	8.94	10.47	10.86	8.53
08-22	11.00	9.41	9.77	9.85	11.21	11.02	8.68
08-29	11.25	10.01	10.25	10.28	11.69	11.26	8.85
09-05	11.50	9.78	10.25	9.84	11.23	11.03	8.78
09-12	11.70	10.09	10.23	10.15	11.31	11.14	8.82
09-19	12.21	10.26	10.88	10.58	11.68	11.37	8.98
09-26	12.46	10.45	10.82	10.94	12.01	11.66	9.16
10-03	13.00	11.39	11.72	11.14	11.80	11.71	9.22
10-10	13.50	11.24	11.14	10.87	11.46	11.35	9.01
10-17	13.50	11.07	11.28	10.85	11.55	11.31	8.81
10-24	13.93	11.66	11.41	11.36	11.89	11.64	9.06
10-31	14.07	12.51	12.28	12.16	12.62	12.19	9.45
11-07	14.50	13.28	13.27	12.47	12.94	12.41	9.64
11-14	15.50	13.29	13.23	12.21	12.59	12.28	9.50
11-21	16.89	13.98	13.92	12.74	12.77	12.23	9.50
11-28	17.00	14.31	14.03	13.22	13.06	12.26	9.61
12-05	17.96	14.98	14.55	13.43	13.40	12.39	9.84
12-12	19.07	16.76	15.07	13.75	13.68	12.74	10.42
12-19	20.29	16.21	15.42	13.71	13.69	12.63	10.56
12-26	21.43	14.62	14.03	12.40	12.50	11.79	9.90

1981 WEEK ENDING FRIDAY	WEEKLY AVERAGE PRIME RATE	3 MO T-BILL MARKET YIELD	6 MO T-BILL AUCTION RATE	1 YR T-BILL MARKET YIELD	3 TO 5 YR T-NOTE RATE	LONG TERM T-BOND RATE	MUNI BOND YIELD
01-02	21.50%	14.31%	13.41%	12.38%	12.54%	11.92%	9.76%
01-09	20.64	14.31	13.18	12.26	12.53	11.81	9.49
01-16	20.07	15.19	14.23	12.51	12.69	12.02	9.57
01-23	20.00	15.65	14.47	13.03	13.01	12.21	9.68
01-30	20.00	15.01	14.12	12.68	12.89	12.22	9.91
02-06	19.86	14.90	13.74	12.84	13.13	12.45	9.90
02-13	19.50	15.51	14.43	13.31	13.59	12.88	9 99
02-20	19.50	14.68	14.76	12.98	13.32	12.64	10.22
02-27	19.29	14.19	13.61	12.89	13.63	12.78	10.27
03-06	18.86	14.44	14.13	13.07	13.76	12.88	10.40
03-13	18.36	13.79	13.43	12.46	13.30	12.51	10.34
03-20	17.86	12.63	12.10	11.59	12.98	12.20	9.81
03-27	17.36	12.91	12.27	12.09	13.55	12.74	10.09
04-03	17.36	12.60	12.08	11.66	13.46	12.68	10.21
04-10	17.00	3.67	13.78	12.53	13.84	13.02	10.45
04-17	17.21	13.66	13.65	12.80	14.01	13.11	10.70
04-24	17.21	13.74	13.62	13.05	14.14	13.12	10.80
05-01	17.57	14.52	14.04	13.41	14.36	13.37	10.94
05-08	18.43	16.44	15.10	14.40	14.94	13.78	10.90
05-15	19.21	16.75	15.53	14.68	14.88	13.60	10.83
05-22	19.71	16.61	15.03	14.42	14.64	13.27	10.73
05-29	20.43	15.61	15.66	13.67	14.09	13.10	10.64
06-05	20.36	15.69	14.49	13.53	14.06	12.93	10.59
06-12	20.00	14.79	14.00	13.15	13.83	12.73	10.63
06-19	20.00	14.31	13.36	13.03	13.81	12.62	10.73
06-26	20.00	14.39	13.94	13.20	14.05	12.92	10.74
07-03	20.00	14.34	13.62	13.30	14.28	13.22	10.85
07-10	20.00	14.82	14.08	13.58	14.48	13.28	10.97
07-17	20.50	14.56	14.23	13.56	14.53	13.29	11.09
07-24	20.50	15.50	15.32	14.40	15.17	13.74	11.34
07-31	20.50	15.70	14.79	14.25	15.13	13.76	11.44
08-07	20.50	15.43	15.57	14.63	15.45	14.06	11.63
08-14	20.50	15.25	15.12	14.43	15.13	13.17	11.94
08-21	20.50	15.63	15.64	14.70	15.51	13.89	12.49
08-28	20.50	15.71	15.85	14.99	16.04	14.45	12.97
09-04	20.50	15.59	15.65	15.05	16.13	14.64	13.10
09-11	20.50	15.14	15.80	14.80	16.07	14.63	13.21
09-18	20.36	14.35	14.66	14.21	15.70	14.29	12.79
09-25	19.86	14.29	14.13	14.15	15.73	14.49	12.57
10-02	19.50	14.37	14.93	14.54	16.11	15.05	12.93
10-09	19.29	13.81	14.22	13.71	15.39	14.42	12.73
10-16	19.71	13.41	13.50	13.42	15.14	14.34	12.53
10-23	18.00	13.37	13.80	13.60	15.45	14.61	12.99
10-30	18.00	13.14	13.62	13.36	15.36	14.72	12.99
11-06	17.79	12.21	12.72	12.35	14.36	13.81	12.44
11-13	17.29	10.98	11.61	11.29	13.43	13.16	11.43
11-20	16.79	10.31	10.97	10.78	13.12	12.76	11.71
11-27	16.36	10.23	10.92	10.63	12.81	12.71	11.98
12-04	15.93	10.39	10.70	10.85	13.03	12.78	12.18
12-11	15.75	10.47	10.77	11.13	13.47	13.21	12.89
12-18	15.75	10.94	11.60	11.53	13.44	13.19	13.00
12-25	15.75	11.14	11.84	12.16	14.03	13.54	13.17

1982 WEEK ENDING FRIDAY	WEEKLY AVERAGE PRIME RATE	3 MO T-BILL MARKET YIELD	6 MO T-BILL AUCTION RATE	1 YR T-BILL MARKET YIELD	3 TO 5 YR T-NOTE RATE	LONG TERM T BOND RATE	MUNI BOND YIELD
01-01	15.7 %	11.35%	12.45%	12.23%	14.04%	13.69%	13.30%
01-08	15.75	11.59	12.28	12.34	14.46	14.07	13.36
01-15	15.75	12.07	12.81	12.84	14.79	14.35	13.44
01-22	15.75	12.66	13.10	13.11	14.81	14.27	13.16
01-29	15.75	12.79	13.53	12.78	14.52	14.01	13.15
02-05	15.96	13.68	13.85	13.19	14.73	14.28	13.13
02-12	16.50	14.12	13.93	13.43	14.91	14.50	13.09
02-19	16.57	14.06	14.36	13.37	14.58	14.01	12.96
02-26	16.86	12.31	12.70	12.56	14.02	13.54	12.70
03-05	16.50	12.26	12.79	12.27	13.76	13.29	12.53
03-12	16.50	12.47	12.06	12.30	13.82	13.37	12.53
03-19	16.50	12.89	12.96	12.58	14.04	13.39	12.90
03-26	16.50	12.72	12.67	12.50	14.03	13.31	13.04
04-02	16.50	13.34	13.24	12.79	14.40	13.60	13.13
04-09	16.50	13.10	12.80	12.69	14.25	13.50	12.99
04-16	16.50	12.77	12.90	12.59	14.00	13.18	12.54
04-23	16.50	12.39	12.72	12.38	13.85	13.07	12.29
04-30	16.50	12.42	12.64	12.30	13.87	13.12	11.97
05-07	16.50	12.54	12.78	12.29	13.87	13.10	12.04
05-14	16.50	12.38	12.24	12.11	13.69	12.96	12.04
05-21	16.50	11.90	12.19	11.83	13.72	13.04	11.96
05-28	16.50	11.54	11.68	11.71	13.74	13.10	11.99
06-04	16.50	12.09	11.59	12.09	13.98	13.49	12.13
06-11	16.50	12.06	12.12	12.20	14.04	13.51	12.49
06-18	16.50	12.46	12.50	12.68	14.48	13.83	12.63
06-25	16.50	12.88	13.03	13.00	14.90	14.03	12.62
07-02	16.50	12.81	13.42	12.86	14.73	13.85	12.58
07-09	16.50	12.23	12.98	12.50	14.48	13.68	12.47
07-16	16.50	11.71	11.97	12.06	14.10	13.40	12.36
07-23	16.36	10.64	11.44	11.29	13.66	13.11	12.01
07-30	16.00	10.51	11.38	11.50	13.89	13.30	11.97
08-06	15.29	9.80	10.67	11.13	13.62	13.08	11.87
08-13	15.00	9.70	10.94	11.06	13.59	13.02	11.86
08-20	14.71	7.86	9.82	9.71	12.53	12.17	10.82
08-27	13.79	7.50	8.99	9.68	12.38	12.04	10.38
09-03	13.50	8.31	9.75	10.12	12.54	12.16	10.74
09-10	13.50	8.34	9.61	10.09	12.43	12.03	10.73
09-17	13.50	8.03	9.70	10.12	12.47	12.02	10.74
09-24	13.50	7.53	9.44	9.77	12.11	11.68	10.58
10-01	13.50	7.52	9.20	9.51	11.74	11.54	10.48
10-08	13.50	7.93	9.23	9.24	11.29	11.28	9.75
10-15	12.85	7.48	7.73	8.19	10.46	10.50	9.25
10-22	12.00	7.54	7.76	8.28	10.50	10.57	9.69
10-29	12.00	7.93	8.47	8.58	10.73	10.74	10.69
11-05	12.00	7.78	8.23	8.36	10.34	10.31	9.96
11-12	12.00	8.07	8.40	8.47	10.44	10.39	9.92
11-19	12.00	8.31	8.54	8.49	10.51	10.49	10.20
11-26	11.79	7.94	8.11	8.35	10.21	10.50	10.20
12-03	11.50	8.14	8.51	8.53	10.31	10.69	10.23
12-10	11.50	7.96	8.25	8.36	10.26	10.59	10.13
12-17	11.50	7.80	8.21	8.15	10.23	10.64	10.05
12-24	11.50	7.91	8.10	8.14	10.22	10.62	9.84
12-31	11.50	8.01	8.05	8.11	10.15	10.52	9.56

Appendix E

Regulations Governing
Book-Entry Treasury Bills

Title 31—Money and Finance: Treasury
CHAPTER II—FISCAL SERVICE, DEPARTMENT OF THE TREASURY
SUBCHAPTER B—BUREAU OF THE PUBLIC DEBT

PART 350—REGULATIONS GOVERNING BOOK-ENTRY TREASURY BILLS

Adoption of Regulations

On November 1, 1976, a notice of proposed rule making was published in the FEDERAL REGISTER (41 FR 47959) with respect to regulations which are to govern the issuance of, and transactions in, all 52-week, 26-week and 13-week Treasury bills and, any other Treasury bills which, after specified dates, are to be issued, with a limited exception, only in book-entry form.

The notice explained that the elimination of securities in the form of engraved certificates would provide substantial benefits to investors, the financial community, and the Treasury by protecting against losses due to theft, mishandling and counterfeiting; by reducing costs of issuing, storing and delivering securities in physical form; and, by moderating the burden of the paperwork created by the growing volume of public debt transactions.

Under the proposed regulations, book-entry Treasury bills would be maintained through accounts either at Federal Reserve Banks or at the Department of the Treasury. Definitive Treasury bills, in the $100,000 denomination only, would be available until December 31, 1978, to investors who establish that they are legally required to hold securities in physical form. By their terms, the regulations would not apply to Treasury bills issued prior to the dates on which they would be available only in book-entry form.

Interested parties were given an opportunity to submit comments on the proposed regulations until November 24, 1976. It is noted that in a series of public meetings and special briefings held during the past several months in various parts of the country, the Department of the Treasury also undertook directly to acquaint investors, financial institutions, securities dealers, etc., about the new mandatory book-entry system, and to solicit their reactions.

Following consideration of the comments submitted in response to the notice, and after reviewing the suggestions otherwise received as a result of its public information program, the Department of the Treasury has modified, where appropriate, the proposed regulations. Aside from editorial and other minor changes, the principal differences between the final regulations and those previously proposed are as follows:

1. Proposed § 350.6(a) (2), relating to the identification of accounts held at or through member banks of the Federal Reserve System, was modified to replace the phrase reading "provided identification of each customer account is possible by name, address, taxpayer identifying number, and includes appropriate loan transaction data" with a provision that permits more flexibility in the manner in which accounts may be maintained, and provides specific information as to the data that should be included.

2. Former § 350.7(c), which related to the issuance of confirmations of transactions involving bills in the Treasury book-entry system, was redesignated as Sec. 350.9, and reworded to indicate that its provisions would apply to all transactions affecting bills maintained in a Treasury account. As a result, the proposed § 350.9 was renumbered as § 350.10, and all subsequent sections were successively redesignated.

3. Proposed § 350.8, was modified to provide that book-entry Treasury bills maintained by or through member banks could be transferred through the Federal Reserve Bank communication system to an account maintained at the Treasury, provided such transfer occurred no later than one month before the maturity date of the bills, and was otherwise acceptable under the subpart.

Accordingly, the proposed regulations governing book-entry Treasury bills, as modified, are hereby adopted and added as Part 350 to 31 CFR, and designated as Department of the Treasury Circular, Public Debt Series No. 26–76.

Dated: December 2, 1976.

DAVID MOSSO,
Fiscal Assistant Secretary.

Subpart A—Applicability and Effect—Definitions

Sec.
350.0 Applicability and effect.
350.1 Definition of terms in this part.

Subpart B—Book-Entry Treasury Bills—Federal Reserve Banks

350.2 Authority of Reserve Banks.
350.3 Scope and effect of book-entry Treasury bill accounts maintained by Reserve Bank under this subpart.
350.4 Transfer of pledge.
350.5 Reserve Bank discharged by acting on instructions—delivery of Treasury securities.
350.6 Book-entry Treasury bill accounts.

Subpart C—Book-Entry Treasury Bills—Department of the Treasury

350.7 Establishing a book-entry Treasury bill account.
350.8 Confirmation of transaction.
350.9 Transfer.
350.10 Attorney-in-fact.
350.11 Succeeding fiduciaries, partners, officers—succeeding corporations, unincorporated association, partnerships.
350.12 Termination of trust, guardianship estate, life tenancy—dissolution of corporation, partnership, unincorporated association.
350.13 Death of individual (natural person in own right).
350.14 Reinvestment or payment at maturity.
350.15 Conclusive presumptions.
350.16 Transactions in regular course—notices not effective—unacceptable notices.

Subpart D—Definitive Treasury Bills

350.17 Definitive Treasury bills—available where holding of definitive securities required by law—termination date December 31, 1978.
350.18 Sanctions for abuse of definitive Treasury bill privilege.

AUTHORITY: R.S. 3706; 40 Stat. 288, 502, 844, 1309; 42 Stat. 321; 46 Stat. 20; 48 Stat. 343; 49 Stat. 20; 50 Stat. 481; 52 Stat. 447; 53 Stat. 1359; 56 Stat. 189; 73 Stat. 622; and 85 Stat. 5. 74 (31 U.S.C. 738a, 739, 752, 752a, 753, 754, 754a, and 754b); 5 U.S.C. 301.

Subpart A—Applicability and Effect—Definitions

§ 350.0 Applicability and effect.

(a) *Applicability.* The regulations in this part govern the issuance of, and transactions in, the following Treasury bills:

(1) 52-week Treasury bills issued after December 1, 1976;

(2) 26-week Treasury bills issued after June 1, 1977;

(3) 13-week Treasury bills issued on or after September 1, 1977; and

(4) Any other Treasury bills issued after September 1, 1977, including, but not limited to, tax anticipation Treasury bills.

(b) *Effect.* The Treasury bills described in paragraph (a) shall, after the date specified therefor, be issued only in book-entry form, except as provided in Subpart D.

§ 350.1 Definition of terms in this part.

In this part, unless the context otherwise requires or indicates:

(a) "Treasury bill" means an obligation of the United States issued under Section 5 of the Second Liberty Bond Act, as amended (31 U.S.C. 754).

(b) "Book-entry Treasury bill" means any Treasury bill issued on or after the dates specified in § 350.0(a) in the form of an entry on the records of a Reserve Bank or the records of the Department of the Treasury. (See Department of the Treasury Circular, Public Debt Series No. 27–76, descriptive of the issue and sale of book-entry Treasury bills.) (31 CFR, Part 349)

(c) "Definitive Treasury bill", as used in Subpart D, means a Treasury bill of the $100,000 denomination issued in the form of an engraved certificate.

(d) "Certified request" or "certified statement", as used in Subpart C, means a request or statement signed by or on behalf of a depositor and certified by an officer authorized to certify assignments of Treasury securities under Department of the Treasury Circular No. 300, current revision, the general regulations governing U.S. securities (31 CFR, Part 306).

(e) "Bureau" means Bureau of the Public Debt, Washington, D.C. 20226.

(f) "Depositor", as used in Subpart C, means the individual, fiduciary or other entity in whose name (including, where appropriate, the title of an officer) an account is established and maintained on the books of the Treasury.

(g) "Fiduciary", as used in Subpart C, means an executor, administrator, trustee; a legal guardian, committee, conservator or similar representative appointed by a court for the estate of a minor or incompetent; a custodian under a statute authorizing gifts to minors; a natural guardian of a minor; a voluntary guardian; or a life tenant under a will.

(h) "Member bank" means any national bank, or State bank or other bank or trust company, which is a member of a Reserve Bank.

(i) "Natural guardian", as used in Subpart C, means either parent of a minor or other person acting on the minor's behalf.

(j) "Pledge" includes a pledge of, or any other security interest in, book-entry Treasury bills as collateral for loans or advances, or to secure deposits of public moneys or the performance of an obligation.

(k) "Reserve Bank" means a Federal Reserve Bank and its branches, acting as Fiscal Agent of the United States and, where indicated, acting in its individual capacity.

(l) "Taxpayer identifying number" means the appropriate identifying number as required on tax returns and other documents submitted to the Internal Revenue Service, i.e., an individual's social security number or an employer identification number. A social security account number is composed of nine digits separated by two hyphens, for example, 123–45–6789; an employer identification number is composed of nine digits separated by one hyphen, for example, 12–3456789. The hyphens are an essential part of the numbers and must be included.

(m) "Treasury" means Department of the Treasury.

(n) "Voluntary guardian", as used in Subpart C, means the person who is acting for an individual who is incapacitated by reason of age, infirmity, or mental disability.

Subpart B—Book-Entry Treasury Bills— Federal Reserve Banks

§ 350.2 Authority of Reserve Banks.

Each Reserve Bank is hereby authorized, in accordance with this subpart, to (a) issue book-entry Treasury bills by means of entries on its records, which shall include the name of the Bank's depositor, the latter's employer identification number, where appropriate, and the amount and maturity date of the bills, including the CUSIP number of each loan; (b) issue a confirmation of transaction in the form of an advice (serially numbered or otherwise), which specifies the amount, maturity date and CUSIP number of the bills, as well as the date of the transaction; and (c) otherwise service and maintain book-entry Treasury bills.

§ 350.3 Scope and effect of book-entry Treasury bill accounts maintained by Reserve Bank under this subpart.

(a) *Scope and effect of accounts maintained by Reserve Bank.* Except as provided in Subpart D, each Reserve Bank, as Fiscal Agent of the United States, is authorized to maintain book-entry Treasury bills held in accounts in its individual capacity, under terms and conditions which indicate that the Reserve Bank will continue to maintain such deposit accounts in its individual capacity, notwithstanding application of the book-entry procedure to such bills. This paragraph is applicable, but not limited to, book-entry Treasury bills maintained:

(1) As collateral pledged to a Reserve Bank (in its individual capacity) for advances by it;

(2) For a member bank for its sole account;

(3) For a member bank held for the account of its customers (see § 350.6 of this subpart);

(4) In connection with deposits in a member bank of funds of States, municipalities, or other political subdivisions;

(5) In connection with the performance of an obligation or duty under Federal, State, municipal, or local law, or judgments or decrees of courts; or

(6) The maintenance by a Reserve Bank of book-entry Treasury bills under this paragraph shall not derogate from or adversely affect the relationships that would otherwise exist between a Reserve Bank in its individual capacity and the entities for which accounts are maintained. The Reserve Bank is authorized to take all action necessary in respect of book-entry Treasury bills to enable such Reserve Bank in its individual capacity to perform its obligations as depositary with respect to such bills.

(b) *Use as collateral under Treasury circulars.* Each Reserve Bank, as Fiscal Agent of the United States, shall hold in book-entry form Treasury bills pledged as collateral to the United States under current revisions of Department of the Treasury Circulars No. 92 and No. 176 (31 CFR, Parts 203 and 202).

§ 350.4 Transfer or pledge.

(a) *Reserve Bank records.* A transfer or a pledge of book-entry Treasury bills to a Reserve Bank (in its individual capacity or as Fiscal Agent of the United States), or to the United States, or to any transferee or pledgee eligible to maintain an appropriate book-entry account in its name with a Reserve Bank under this subpart, is effected and perfected, notwithstanding any provision of law to the contrary, by a Reserve Bank making an appropriate entry in its records of the Treasury bills transferred or pledged. The making of such an entry in the records of a Reserve Bank shall (1) have the same effect as the delivery of Treasury bills in bearer definitive form; (2) have the effect of a taking of delivery by the transferee or pledgee; (3) constitute the transferee or pledgee a holder; and (4) if a pledge, effect a perfected security interest therein in favor of the pledgee. A transfer or pledge of Treasury bills effected under this paragraph shall have priority over any transfer, pledge, or other interest, theretofore or thereafter effected or perfected under paragraph (b) of this section or in any other manner.

(b) *Member banks and others.* A transfer or a pledge of book-entry Treasury bills, or any interest therein, maintained by a Reserve Bank (in its individual capacity or as Fiscal Agent of the United States) in a book-entry account under this subpart, including book-entry Treasury bills in accounts at the Reserve Bank maintained under Sec. 350.3(a)(3) of this subpart by member banks for the account of their customers, is effected, and a pledge is perfected, by any means that would be effective under applicable law to effect a transfer or to effect and perfect a pledge of the Treasury bills, or any interest therein, if the Treasury bills were maintained by the Reserve Bank in bearer definitive form. For purposes of transfer or pledge hereunder, book-entry Treasury bills maintained by a Reserve Bank shall, notwithstanding any provision of law to the contrary, be deemed to be maintained in bearer definitive form. A Reserve Bank maintaining book-entry Treasury bills either in its individual capacity or as Fiscal Agent of the United States is not a bailee for purposes of notification of pledges of those bills under this paragraph or a third person in possession for purposes of acknowledgment of transfers thereof under this paragraph. A Reserve Bank will not accept notice or advice of a transfer or pledge effected or perfected under this paragraph, and any such notice or advice shall have no effect. A Reserve Bank may continue to deal with its depositor in accordance with the provisions of this subpart, notwithstanding any transfer or pledge effected or perfected under this paragraph.

(c) *Filing and recording unnecessary.* No filing or recording with a public recording office or officer shall be necessary or effective with respect to any transfer or pledge of book-entry Treasury bills or any interest therein.

(d) *Transfer by Reserve Banks.* A transfer of book-entry Treasury bills within a Reserve Bank shall be made in accordance with procedures established by the Reserve Bank not inconsistent with this subpart. The transfer of book-entry Treasury bills by a Reserve Bank may be made through a telegraphic transfer procedure.

(e) *Timeliness of requests.* All requests for transfer or any authorized transaction must be received prior to the maturity of the bills.

§ 350.5 Reserve Bank discharged by action on instructions—delivery of Treasury securities.

A Reserve Bank which has received book-entry Treasury bills and effected pledges, made entries regarding them, or transferred or delivered them according to the instructions of its depositor is not liable for conversion or for participation in breach of fiduciary duty even though the depositor had no right to dispose of or take other action in respect of the securities. A Reserve Bank shall be fully discharged of its obligations under this subpart by the transfer or delivery of book-entry Treasury bills upon the order of its depositor.

§ 350.6 Book-entry Treasury bill accounts.

(a) *Scope and effect of book-entry Treasury bill accounts.—(1) Classes of accounts.* Reserve Banks are authorized to maintain book-entry Treasury bills for member banks for bills the member banks hold for their own account, or hold for the account of their customers, and as otherwise specified in § 350.3. Purchasers of book-entry Treasury bills, on original issue or otherwise, may have such bills maintained at member banks, or in accounts maintained at entities providing securities safekeeping services for customers (*e.g.*, nonmember banks or thrift institutions, or securities dealers) which have related accounts at member banks.

(2) *Identification of accounts.* Book-entry accounts may be established in such form or forms as customarily permitted by the entity (*e.g.*, member bank, or other banking or thrift institution, or a securities dealer) maintaining them, except that each account should include data to permit both customer identification by name, address and taxpayer identifying number, as well as a determination of the Treasury bills being held in such account by amount, maturity date and CUSIP number, and of transactions relating thereto.

(3) *Pledges and transfers.* Where book-entry Treasury bills are maintained on the books of an entity for account of the pledgor or transferor thereof, such entity shall, for purposes of perfecting a pledge of such Treasury bills or effecting their delivery to a purchaser under applicable provisions of law, be the bailee to which notification of the pledge of the bills may be given or the third person in possession from which acknowledgment of the holding of the bills for the purchaser may be obtained.

(b) *Servicing book-entry Treasury bills—payment of book-entry Treasury bills at maturity.* Book-entry Treasury bills governed by this part may be transferred between accounts prior to maturity through a wire transfer arrangement maintained by Reserve Banks. At maturity, the bills shall be redeemed and charged by a Reserve Bank in the account of the United States Treasury as of the date of maturity, and the redemption proceeds shall be disposed of in acocrdance with the instructions from the member bank or other Reserve Bank depositor for whose account the Treasury bills shall have been maintained.

Subpart C—Book-Entry Treasury Bills— Department of the Treasury

§ 350.7   Establishing a book-entry Treasury bill account.

(a) *General.* Treasury bills may be held as book-entries in accounts maintained by the Treasury. Such accounts may be established, either upon the original issue of book-entry Treasury bills or upon the subsequent transfer of such bills to the Treasury, but no later than one month prior to their maturity date. Each account shall consist of an entry showing the amount, maturity date and CUSIP number of the bills, the name of the individual, fiduciary or other entity (including, where appropriate, the title of an officer) for whom the account is held, the address, and the taxpayer identifying

number. The records shall also include appropriate transaction data.

(b) *Recordation.*—(1) *Individuals.* Accounts for book-entry Treasury bills may be held in the names of individuals in one of two forms: single name, i.e., "John A. Doe (123–45–6789) (address)"; or two names, i.e., "John A. Doe (123–45–6789) (address) or (Mrs.) Mary B. Doe (987–65–4321). No other form of recordation in two names, whether individuals or others, will be permitted, except in the case of co-fiduciaries.

(2) *Others.* Accounts for book-entry Treasury bills may be held in the names of fiduciaries and other entities in the forms indicated by the following examples:

John A. Smith and First National Bank, executors of the will of James B. Smith, deceased (12–3456789) (address).

May A. Queen, trustee under agreement with Thomas J. King, dated June 1, 1971 (12-3456789) (address).

Smith Manufacturing Company, Inc., James C. Brown, Treasurer (12–3456789) (address).

Grey and White (12–3456789), John D. Grey, General Partner (address).

J. Francis Doe, Secretary-Treasurer of Local 100, Brotherhood of Locomotive Engineers, an unincorporated association (12-3456789) (address).

John R. Greene, as natural guardian of Maxine S. Greene (123–45–6789) (address).

John A. Jones, as voluntary guardian of Henry M. Jones (123–45–6789) (address).

§ 350.8   Transfer.

Book-entry Treasury bills maintained under this subpart may not be transferred from one account maintained by the Treasury to another such account, except in cases of lawful succession, as provided in this subpart. They may be withdrawn from an account maintained by the Treasury hereunder and transferred through the Federal Reserve Bank communication system to an account maintained by or through a member bank under Subpart B, which transfer shall be made in the name or names appearing in the account recorded on the books of the Treasury. Such withdrawal may be effected by a certified request therefor by, or on behalf of, the depositor, provided the request therefor is received no earlier than ten business days after the issue date or the date the securities are transferred to the Treasury, whichever is later. The request must: (a) identify the book-entry account by the name of the depositor and title, if any, the address, and the taxpayer identifying number; (b) specify by amount, maturity date and CUSIP number the book-entry Treasury bills to be withdrawn and transferred; and (c) specify the name of the member bank to or through which the transfer is to be effected and, where appropriate, the name of the institution or entity which is to maintain the book-entry account. In the case of book-entry Treasury bills held in the names of two individuals, a certified request by either will be accepted, but the transfer shall be made in the names of both. A transfer after original issue of book-entry Treasury bills

from an account maintained by or through a member bank to one maintained by the Treasury may be made through the Federal Reserve Bank communication system, provided the account is to be held in a form authorized by this subpart, and provided the transfer is made no later than one month prior to the maturity date of the bills.

§ 350.9   Confirmation of transaction.

The Treasury will issue to each depositor following any transaction affecting book-entry Treasury bills maintained for such depositor under this subpart a confirmation thereof in the form of an advice (serially numbered or otherwise) which shall describe the amount, maturity date and CUSIP number of the bills, and include pertinent transaction data.

§ 350.10   Attorney-in-fact.

A request by an attorney-in-fact for any transaction in book-entry Treasury bills after their original issue will be recognized in accordance with this subpart if supported by an adequate power of attorney. The original power or a photocopy showing the grantor's autograph signature, properly certified, must be submitted to the Bureau. A request for transfer for the apparent benefit of the attorney-in-fact will not be recognized unless expressly authorized.

§ 350.11   Succeeding fiduciaries, partners, officers—succeeding corporations, unincorporated associations, partnerships.

(a) *Death of fiduciary, partner or officer.* In case of the death, removal or disqualification of a fiduciary, partner or officer of an organization in whose name book-entry Treasury bills have been recorded, the successor or other authorized person will be recognized as the depositor under this subpart. Proof of death, resignation, removal or disqualification, as the case may be, and evidence that the successor or such other person is fully authorized to act must be submitted to the Bureau. Proof of death shall be in the form of a death certificate or photocopy thereof showing the official seal. Evidence of authority should be in the form of a certified statement by: (1) the surviving fiduciary or fiduciaries, if any, stating that application for the appointment of a successor has not been-made. is not contemplated and is not necessary under the terms of the trust instrument or otherwise, (2) a surviving partner or partners that the partnership is being continued in the same, or another name, which must be identified, or (3) the secretary or other authorized officer of the corporation or unincorporated association as to the name and title of the successor officer. If there is more than one surviving fiduciary, a request for transfer of the bills must be signed by all, unless evidence is submitted to the Bureau that one is authorized to act for the other or others. If there is more than one surviving partner, evidence should be submitted to the Bureau as to which survivor is authorized to act in behalf of the partnership; otherwise, the signatures of all surviving partners will be required for transfer of the bills.

(b) *Succeeding corporations, unincorporated associations or partnerships.* If a corporation has been succeeded by another corporation, or if an unincorporated association or partnership has been succeeded by a corporation, and such succession is by operation of law or otherwise, as the result of merger, consolidation, reincorporation, conversion or reorganization, or if a lawful succession has occured in any manner whereby the business or activities of the original organization are continued without substantial change, an authorized officer or partner, as the case may be, of the successor organization will be recognized as the depositor under this subpart upon submission to the Bureau of satisfactory evidence of such succession.

§ 350.12 **Termination of trust, guardianship estate, life tenancy—dissolution of corporation, partnership, unincorporated association.**

(a) *Termination of trust, life tenancy or guardianship estate.*—(1) *Trust or life estate.* Upon the termination of a trust or life estate, the beneficiary or remainderman will be recognized as the depositor under this subpart. The trustee will be required to submit to the Bureau a certified statement concerning the termination of the trust and the respective shares, if there is more than one beneficiary. In the case of a life estate, proof of death in the form of a death certificate or photocopy thereof showing the official seal will be required, together with a certified statement identifying the remainderman, and, if there is more than one, specifying the respective shares.

(2) *Guardianship.* A former minor or incompetent will be recognized as the depositor under this subpart upon submission to the Bureau of a certified statement, or other evidence showing, in the case of a minor, attainment of majority or other removal of the legal disability, and, in the case of an incompetent, his restoration to competency.

(b) *Dissolution of corporations, unincorporated associations and partnerships.* The person or persons (other than creditors) entitled to the assets upon dissolution of a corporation, unincorporated association or partnership will be recognized under this subpart upon proof of dissolution. If there is more than one person entitled and the book-entry Treasury bills have not matured, no change in the book-entry account will be made pending transfer or redemption at maturity.

§ 350.13 **Death of individual (natural person in own right).**

Upon the death of an individual in whose name an account is held and who was not acting as a fiduciary or in any other representative capacity, the following person(s), in the order shown below, will be recognized under this subpart as entitled to the book-entry Treasury bills:

(a) The surviving joint designee of an account in the names of two individuals, if any;

(b) Executor or administrator;

(c) Widow or widower;

(d) Child or children of the decedent and descendants of deceased children by representation;

(e) Parents of the decedent or the survivor of them;

(f) Surviving brothers or sisters;

(g) Descendants of deceased brothers or sisters;

(h) Other next-of-kin as determined by the laws of the domicile at the time of death.

(i) Any person or persons entitled in the above order of preference may request payment or other disposition to any person or persons related to the decedent by blood or marriage, but no payment will be made prior to maturity of the bills. The provisions of this section are for the convenience of the Treasury and do not purport to determine ownership of the bills or of their redemption proceeds.

§ 350.14 **Reinvestment or payment at maturity.**

(a) *Request for reinvestment.* Upon the request of the depositor, book-entry Treasury bills held therein will be reinvested at maturity, i.e., their proceeds at maturity will be applied to the purchase of new Treasury bills at the average price (in three decimals) of accepted competitive bids for such Treasury bills then being offered. The request for a reinvestment may be made on the tender form at the time of purchase; subsequent requests for reinvestment will be accepted if received by the Bureau no later than ten business days prior to the maturity of the bills. The difference between the par value of the maturing bills and the issue price of the new bills will be remitted to the subscriber in the form of a Treasury check. Requests for the revocation of the reinvestment of bills will also be accepted if received no later than ten business days prior to the maturity date.

(b) *Reinvestment in cases of delay.* Where a delay occurs in the submission or receipt of evidence to support a request for transfer, payment or other authorized transaction of book-entry Treasury bills, and such delay is likely to extend beyond the maturity dates of the bills, upon request or prior notice, the bills will be redeemed, at maturity or thereafter, and their proceeds reinvested in new book-entry Treasury bills. The bills purchased upon such reinvestment shall be those having the shortest term to maturity then being offered, and will be issued at the average price (in three decimals) of the accepted competitive bids therefor. The discount representing the difference between the par value of the maturing or matured bills and the issue price of the new bills will be remitted in the form of a Treasury check.

(c) *Payment.* If reinvestment is not effected pursuant to this section, book-entry Treasury bills will be paid as of maturity in regular course.

§ 350.15 **Conclusive presumptions.**

For the purposes of this subpart and not withstanding any State law or any regula~~†   ~~ny notice to the contrary,

it shall be conclusively presumed (a) that any depositor in whose name, or name and title, book-entry Treasury bills are recorded, is a competent adult, (b) that recordation in two names, as prescribed in Sec. 350.7(b) (i) of this subpart, is intended, if there is an attempt to create some other form of recordation in two names, (c) that recordation in the names of the first two is intended, if there is an attempt to name more than two individuals, and (d) that the first name is the depositor in any case (not authorized and not otherwise provided for in this subpart) wherein an attempt is made to have book-entry Treasury bills recorded in two or more names, e.g., two officers of an organization or two partners.

§ 350.16 **Transactions in regular course—notices not effective—unacceptable notices.**

(a) *Transactions in regular course—notices not effective.* Transfers of book-entry Treasury bills, payment thereof or reinvestment at maturity or any other transaction therein will be conducted in the regular course of business in accordance with this subpart, notwithstanding notice of the appointment of an attorney-in-fact, or a legal guardian or similar representative, or notice of successorship, the termination of an estate, the dissolution of an entity, or the death of an individual, unless the requisite request, proof, and the evidence necessary to establish entitlement under this subpart is received by the Bureau no later than ten business days prior to the maturity date of the bills.

(b) *Unacceptable notices.* The Treasury will not under any conditions accept notices of pending judicial proceedings, or of judgments in favor of creditors or others, or of any claims whatsoever, for the purpose of suspending or modifying any book-entry account or any transaction in book-entry Treasury bills.

Subpart D—Definitive Treasury Bills

§ 350.17 **Definitive Treasury bills—available where holding of definitive securities required by law—termination date December 31, 1978.**

(a) *General.* Each Reserve Bank is authorized to issue definitive Treasury bills, in the $100,000 denomination only, upon original issue or otherwise (1) to any entity described in paragraph (b), and (2) for the account of any such entity described in paragraph (b), to a securities dealer or broker or any financial institution which in the regular course of its business purchases securities therefor.

(b) *Eligible entities.* Entities eligible to have definitive Treasury bills are those required by or pursuant to Federal, State. municipal or local law to hold or to pledge securities in definitive form, which may include, but are not limited to: a State, municipality, city, township, county or any other political subdivision, public corporation or other public body, an insurance company, and a fiduciary so required to hold securities in definitive form.

(c) *Conversion of book-entry Treasury bills.* Each Reserve Bank is hereby authorized to effect. upon the order of its depositor, conversions from and to book-entry Treasury bills of definitive bills issued pursuant to this subpart.

(d) *Evidence of eligibility.* In order to obtain a definitive Treasury bill on original issue or thereafter (1) an authorized officer on behalf of the entity must furnish to the Reserve Bank a statement that it is required by, or pursuant to, law to hold or pledge securities in definitive form; or (2) a financial institution, dealer, or broker purchasing definitive Treasury bills hereunder for the account of any such entity must submit to the Reserve Bank a statement that the entity has declared that it is required by or pursuant to law to hold or pledge securities in definitive form.

(e) *Redemption requirements.* Where a definitive Treasury bill issued pursuant to this subpart is presented for payment at or after maturity, it must be accompanied by a statement (1) by an authorized officer of the entity making the presentation that such entity is eligible under this subpart to hold definitive securities, or (2) by the institution making the presentation identifying the entity to whose account the redemption proceeds of the bill have been, or are to be credited, and affirming that such entity had declared that it is eligible under this subpart to hold definitive securities.

(f) *Termination date.* The provisions of this subpart will apply only to definitive Treasury bills issued to, or for the account of, eligible entities prior to December 31, 1978.

§ 350.18 **Sanctions for abuse of definitive Treasury bill privilege.**

The Secretary of the Treasury reserves the right to disqualify any eligible entity described in paragraph (b) of Sec. 350.17 from purchasing or holding definitive Treasury bills if he determines that such entity has disposed of such definitive Treasury bills solely for the purpose of accommodating another party, including a bank, broker, dealer, or other financial institution, or a customer of such institution.

[FR Doc.76–35799 Filed 12–3–76;10:23 am]

Appendix **F**

*Regulations on the Issue and
Sale of Book-Entry Treasury Bills
and Definitive Treasury Bills*

Title 31—Money and Finance: Treasury
CHAPTER II—FISCAL SERVICE, DEPARTMENT OF THE TREASURY
SUBCHAPTER B—BUREAU OF THE PUBLIC DEBT
PART 349—ISSUE AND SALE OF BOOK-ENTRY TREASURY BILLS AND OF DEFINITIVE TREASURY BILLS TO ELIGIBLE ENTITIES

The regulations in Department of the Treasury Circular, Public Debt Series No. 27–76, set forth below, are descriptive of the issue and sale of the 52-week, 26-week and 13-week Treasury bills, and other Treasury bills, which, after specified dates, will be available, with a limited exception, only in book-entry form. The regulations governing such book-entry Treasury bills, following a notice of proposed rule making, have been finally adopted and are being published simultaneously herewith.

Treasury bills issued in book-entry form prior to the dates when they will be available only in such form are maintained under, and will continue to be subject to, the regulations set out in Subpart 0 of Department of the Treasury Circular No. 300, current revision (31 CFR, Part 306). That subpart prescribes an optional book-entry procedure, and the sale and issue of Treasury bills to which it, in part, applies are generally provided for in Department of the Treasury Circular No. 418, Second Revision, dated October 5, 1976 (31 CFR, Part 309). The Treasury bills held under Subpart 0 will continue to be convertible to definitive bills at the request of the party for whose account they are maintained.

As the fiscal policy of the United States is involved in the issue and sale of Treasury securities, it is found unnecessary to issue these regulations with notice and public procedure thereof under 5 U.S.C. 553(b), or subject to the effective date limitation of 5 U.S.C. 553(d).

Dated: December 2, 1976.

DAVID MOSSO,
Fiscal Assistant Secretary.

Chapter II of Title 31 of the Code of Federal Regulations is amended by adding Part 349 as set forth below.

Sec.
349.0   Authority for issue and sale.
349.1   Description of Treasury bills—general—book entry—definitive.
349.2   Regulations.
349.3   Public notice of offering.
349.4   Amount of tender; price.
349.5   Form of tenders.
349.6   Tenders for customers and for own account.
349.7   Deposits with tenders submitted to Federal Reserve Banks.
349.8   Payment with tenders submitted to Treasury.
349.9   Submission of tenders.
349.10 Reservation of right.
349.11 Acceptance of tenders.
349.12 Payment of accepted tenders.
349.13 Acceptance of book-entry Treasury bills for various purposes.
349.14 Taxation.
349.15 Relief on account of loss.
349.16 Functions of Federal Reserve Banks.
349.17 Reservation as to terms of circular.

AUTHORITY: 80 Stat. 379; sec. 8, 50 Stat. 481, as amended; sec. 5, 40 Stat. 290, as amended; 5 U.S.C. 301; 31 U.S.C. 738a, 754, 754b.

§ 349.0   Authority for issue and sale.

The Secretary of the Treasury is authorized under the Second Liberty Bond Act, as amended, to issue Treasury bills of the United States on an interest-bearing basis, on a discount basis, or on a combination interest-bearing and discount basis, at such price or prices and with interest computed in such manner and payable at such time or times as he may prescribe, but not exceeding one year from the date of issue; and to fix the form, terms, and conditions thereof, and to offer them for sale on a competitive or other basis, under such regulations and upon such terms and conditions as he may prescribe.

§ 349.1   Description of Treasury bills—general—book-entry—definitive.

(a) *General.* Treasury bills are obligations of the United States, issued at a discount, promising to pay a specified amount on a specified date. They are issued only by Federal Reserve Banks and Branches, acting as Fiscal Agents of the United States, and by the Bureau of the Public Debt, Washington, D.C. 20226, pursuant to tenders accepted by the Department of the Treasury.

(b) *Book-entry Treasury bills.* Book-entry Treasury bills under this part are bills issued only in the form of entries on either the records of a Federal Reserve Bank or of the Department of the Treasury, as follows:

(1) 52-week Treasury bills issued after December 1, 1976;

(2) 26-week Treasury bills issued after June 1, 1977;

(3) 13-week Treasury bills issued on or after September 1, 1977; and

(4) Any other Treasury bills issued after September 1, 1977, including, but not limited to, tax anticipation Treasury bills.

(c) *Definitive Treasury bills for eligible entities.* Treasury bills in the form of engraved certificates will be issued on or after the dates specified in paragraph (b) of this section, and for the series shown, in the denomination of $100,000 only, and only until December 31, 1978, solely to entities required by or pursuant to, Federal, State, municipal, or other local law to hold securities in definitive form. Such entities may include, but are not limited to a State, municipality, city, township, county or any other political subdivision, public corporation or other public body, an insurance company, and a fiduciary so required to hold physical securities.

§ 349.2   Regulations.

The Treasury bills, the issue and sale of which are herein provided, shall be subject to the book-entry Treasury bill regulations set forth in Department of the Treasury Circular, Public Debt Series No. 26–76 (31 CFR, Part 350), and, to the extent applicable, to Department of the Treasury Circular No. 300, current revision (31 CFR, Part 306), the general regulations governing United States securities. Copies of the circulars may be obtained from a Federal Reserve Bank or Branch, or the Bureau of the Public Debt.

§ 349.3   Public notice of offering.

When Treasury bills are offered, tenders therefor will be invited, on a competitive and noncompetitive basis, through public notice given by the Secretary of the Treasury in the name of "The Department of the Treasury". In such notice, there will be set forth the amount of Treasury bills for which tenders are being invited, the date of issue, the CUSIP number, the date or dates when such bills will become due and payable, the date and closing hour for the receipt of tenders at the Federal Reserve Banks and Branches, and the Department of the Treasury, and the date on which payment for tenders must be made or completed.

§ 349.4   Amount of tender; price.

Tenders in response to the public notice must be for a minimum of $10,000, and tenders over that amount must be in multiples of $5,000. Definitive Treasury bills will be available, as set forth in § 349.1(c), only in the $100,000 denomination and only for the account of eligible investors. In the case of competitive tenders, the price or prices offered by the bidder for the amount or amounts applied for must be expressed on the basis of 100, with not more than three decimals, e.g., 99.925. Fractions may not be used. Noncompetitive tenders will be accepted at the average price of the competitive tenders accepted.

§ 349.5   Form of tenders.

Tenders may be submitted on printed forms and forwarded in special envelopes available from any Federal Reserve Bank or Branch. If a special envelope is not available, the inscription "Tender for Treasury Bills" should be placed on the envelope used. The instructions on the forms with respect to the submission of tenders should be observed. Tenders for book-entry Treasury bills to be maintained on the accounts of the Department of the Treasury should be submitted on special forms available for that purpose.

§ 349.6   Tenders for customers and for own account.

Banking institutions and dealers who make primary markets in Government securities and report daily to the Federal Reserve Bank of New York their positions with respect to Government securities and borrowings thereon may submit tenders for the accounts of customers, provided the names of the customers are set forth in such tenders. Others will not be permitted to submit tenders except for their own account.

§ 349.7   Deposits with tenders submitted to Federal Reserve Banks.

Tenders submitted to Federal Reserve Banks and Branches by incorporated

Source: *Federal Register* 41:235. Department of the Treasury—Fiscal Service, Bureau of the Public Debt. Department circular, public debt series no. 27–76 (December 6, 1976). Used with permission.

banks and trust companies, and responsible and recognized dealers in investment securities, will be received without deposit. Tenders from all others must be accompanied by a payment of such percent of the face amount of the Treasury bills applied for as prescribed in the public notice, except that such deposit will not be required if the tenders are accompanied by an express guaranty of payment in full by an incorporated bank or trust company. Forfeiture of the deposit may be declared by the Secretary of the Treasury, if payment is not completed, in the case of accepted tenders, on the prescribed date.

§ 349.8 Payment with tenders submitted to Treasury.

Tenders for Treasury bills to be issued and maintained on book-entry accounts of the Treasury must be accompanied by full payment of the face amount of the bills applied for. A cash adjustment will be made for the difference between the par payment submitted and the actual issue price of the bills.

§ 349.9 Submission of tenders.

Tenders must be received on or before the time fixed for closing, as set forth in the public notice, at Federal Reserve Banks and Branches, and at the Bureau of the Public Debt, Washington, D.C. 20226. Tenders not timely received will be disregarded.

§ 349.10 Reservation of right.

The Secretary of the Treasury expressly reserves the right on any occasion to accept noncompetitive tenders entered in accordance with specific offerings, to reject any or all tenders or parts of tenders, and to award less than the amount applied for; and any action he may take in any such respect or respects shall be final.

§ 349.11 Acceptance of tenders.

The Department of the Treasury will determine from the tenders received the amount and price range of the accepted bids. Those at the highest prices offered will be accepted in full down to the amount required, and if the same price appears in two or more tenders and it is necessary to accept only a part of the amount offered at such price, the amount accepted at such price will be prorated in accordance with the respective amounts applied for. Public announcement of the acceptance will then be made. Those submitting tenders will be advised of the acceptance or rejection thereof by the Federal Reserve Banks or by the Treasury, depending on where such tenders were received.

§ 349.12 Payment of accepted tenders.

Settlement for accepted tenders submitted to a Federal Reserve Bank must be made or completed at such Bank in cash or other immediately available funds on or before the date specified, except that the public notice inviting tenders may provide: (a) That any qualified depositary may make such settlement by credit, on behalf of itself and its customers, up to any amount for which it shall be qualified in excess of existing deposits, when so notified by the Federal Reserve Bank of its District, or (b) that such settlement may be made in maturing Treasury bills accepted in exchange. Whenever settlement in maturing Treasury bills is authorized, a cash adjustment will be made for the difference between the par value of the maturing bills and the issue price of the new ones.

§ 349.13 Acceptance of book-entry Treasury bills for various purposes.

(a) *Acceptable as security for public deposits.* Book entry Treasury bills will be acceptable at maturity value to secure deposits of public monies.

(b) *Acceptable in payment of taxes where authorized.* The public notice inviting tenders for book-entry Treasury bills may provide that such bills will be acceptable at maturity value, whether at or before maturity, under such rules and regulations as may be prescribed, in payment of income taxes payable under the provisions of the Internal Revenue Code.

(c) *Discounting by Federal Reserve Bank of notes secured by Treasury bills.* Notes secured by book-entry Treasury bills are eligible for discount or rediscount at Federal Reserve Banks as provided under the provisions of section 13 of the Federal Reserve Act, as are notes secured by bonds and notes of the United States.

(d) *Acceptable in connection with foreign obligations held by United States.* Treasury bills will be acceptable at maturity, but not before, in payment of interest or of principal on account of obligations of foreign governments held by the United States.

§ 349.14 Taxation.

The income derived from Treasury bills, issued pursuant to this part, whether interest or gain from the sale or other disposition of the bills, shall not have any exemption, as such, and loss from the sale or other disposition of Treasury bills shall not have any special treatment, as such, under the Internal Revenue Code, or laws amendatory or supplementary thereto. The bills shall be subject to estate, inheritance, gift or other excise taxes, whether Federal or State, but shall be exempt from all taxation now or hereafter imposed on the principal or interest thereof by any State, or any of the possessions of the United States, or by any local taxing authority. For purposes of taxation, the amount of discount at which Treasury bills are originally sold by the United States shall be considered to be interest.

§ 349.15 Relief on account of loss.

Relief on account of the loss of any Treasury bills issued pursuant to this part may be given only under the authority of, and subject to the conditions set forth in section 8 of the Act of July 8, 1937 (50 Stat. 481), as amended (31 U.S.C. 738a), and the regulations issued pursuant thereto, as set forth in Department of the Treasury Circular No. 300 (31 CFR, Part 306), insofar as applicable.

§ 349.16 Functions of Federal Reserve Banks.

Federal Reserve Banks and Branches, as Fiscal Agents of the United States, are authorized to perform all such acts as may be necessary to carry out the provisions of this circular and of any public notice or notices issued in connection with any offering of Treasury bills.

§ 349.17 Reservation as to terms of circular.

The Secretary of the Treasury reserves the right further to amend, supplement, revise or withdraw all or any of the provisions of this circular at any time, or from time to time.

[FR Doc.76–36000 Filed 12–3–76; 10:23 am]

Appendix **G**

*General Regulations
Governing U.S. Securities*

Title 31—Money and Finance: Treasury

CHAPTER II—FISCAL SERVICE, DEPARTMENT OF THE TREASURY

SUBCHAPTER B—BUREAU OF THE PUBLIC DEBT

PART 306—GENERAL REGULATIONS GOVERNING U.S. SECURITIES

The regulations in 31 CFR Part 306 have been revised and amended for the purpose of facilitating the functioning of transactions in marketable U.S. securities.

Notice and public procedures are unnecessary and are dispensed with as the revision is largely declaratory of the revisions and amendments heretofore published in the FEDERAL REGISTER and fiscal policy of the United States is involved. The changes were effected under authority of R.S. 3706; 40 Stat. 288, 502, 844, 1309; 42 Stat. 321; 46 Stat. 20; 48 Stat. 343; 49 Stat. 20; 50 Stat. 481; 52 Stat. 447; 53 Stat. 1359; 56 Stat. 189; 73 Stat. 622; and 85 Stat. 5, 74 (31 U.S.C. 738a, 739, 752, 752a, 753, 754, 754a, and 754b); 5 U.S.C. 301.

Dated: March 9, 1973.

[SEAL]   JOHN K. CARLOCK,
Fiscal Assistant Secretary.

Department of the Treasury Circular No. 300, Third Revision, dated December 23, 1964 (31 CFR Part 306), as amended, is hereby further amended and issued as the Fourth Revision.

AUTHORITY: R.S. 3706; 40 Stat. 288, 502, 844, 1309; 42 Stat. 321; 46 Stat. 20; 48 Stat. 343; 49 Stat. 20; 50 Stat. 481; 52 Stat. 477; 53 Stat. 1359; 56 Stat. 189; 73 Stat. 622; and 85 Stat. 5, 74 (31 U.S.C. 738a, 739, 752, 752a, 753, 754, 754a, and 754b); 5 U.S.C. 301.

Subpart A—General Information

§ 306.0   Applicability of regulations.

These regulations apply to all U.S. transferable and nontransferable securities,[1] other than U.S. Savings Bonds and U.S. Savings Notes, to the extent specified in these regulations, the offering circulars or special regulations governing such securities.

§ 306.1   Official agencies.

(a) *Subscriptions—tenders—bids.* Securities subject to these regulations are issued from time to time pursuant to public offerings by the Secretary of the Treasury, through the Federal Reserve banks, fiscal agents of the United States, and the Treasurer of the United States. Only the Federal Reserve banks and branches and the Department of the Treasury are authorized to act as official agencies, and subscriptions or tenders for Treasury securities, and bids, to the extent provided in the regulations governing the sale of Treasury securities through competitive bidding, may be made direct to them. However, tenders for Treasury bills are not received at the Department.

(b) *Transactions after issue.* The Bureau of the Public Debt of the Department of the Treasury is charged with matters relating to transactions in securities. Correspondence concerning transactions in securities and requests for appropriate forms may be addressed to (1) the Federal Reserve bank or branch of the district in which the correspondent is located, or (2) the Bureau of the Public Debt, Division of Securities Operations, Washington, D.C. 20226, or (3) the Office of the Treasurer of the

---

[1] These regulations may also be applied to securities issued by certain agencies of the United States and certain Government and Government-sponsored corporations.

Source: *Federal Register* 38:50. Department of the Treasury—Fiscal Service, Bureau of the Public Debt. Department circular no. 300, 4th revision (March 9, 1973). Used with permission.

United States, Securities Division, Washington, D.C. 20222, except where specific instructions are otherwise given in these regulations. The addresses of the Federal Reserve banks and branches are:

Federal Reserve Bank of Boston, Boston, Mass. 02106.

Federal Reserve Bank of New York, New York, N.Y. 10045.

    Buffalo Branch, Buffalo, N.Y. 14240.

Federal Reserve Bank of Philadelphia, Philadelphia, Pa. 19101.

Federal Reserve Bank of Cleveland, Cleveland, Ohio 44101.

    Cincinnati Branch, Cincinnati, Ohio 45201.

    Pittsburgh Branch, Pittsburgh, Pa. 15230.

Federal Reserve Bank of Richmond, Richmond, Va. 23261.

    Baltimore Branch, Baltimore, Md. 21203.

    Charlotte Branch, Charlotte, N.C. 28201.

Federal Reserve Bank of Atlanta, Atlanta, Ga. 30303.

    Birmingham Branch, Birmingham, Ala. 35202.

    Jacksonville Branch, Jacksonville, Fla. 32203.

    Nashville Branch, Nashville, Tenn. 37203.

    New Orleans Branch, New Orleans, La. 70160.

    Miami Office, Miami, Fla. 33152.

Federal Reserve Bank of Chicago, Chicago, Ill. 60609.

    Detroit Branch, Detroit, Mich. 48231.

Federal Reserve Bank of St. Louis, St. Louis, Mo. 63166.

    Little Rock Branch, Little Rock, Ark. 72203.

    Louisville Branch, Louisville, Ky. 40201.

    Memphis Branch, Memphis, Tenn. 38101.

Federal Reserve Bank of Minneapolis, Minneapolis, Minn. 55480.

    Helena Branch, Helena, Mont. 59601.

Federal Reserve Bank of Kansas City, Kansas City, Mo. 64198.

    Denver Branch, Denver, Colo. 80217.

    Oklahoma City Branch, Oklahoma City, Okla. 73125.

    Omaha Branch, Omaha, Nebr. 68102.

Federal Reserve Bank of Dallas, Dallas, Tex. 75222.

    El Paso Branch, El Paso, Tex. 79999.

    Houston Branch, Houston, Tex. 77001.

    San Antonio Branch, San Antonio, Tex. 78295.

Federal Reserve Bank of San Francisco, San Francisco, Calif. 94120.

    Los Angeles Branch, Los Angeles, Calif. 90051.

    Portland Branch, Portland, Oreg. 97208.

    Salt Lake City Branch, Salt Lake City, Utah 84110.

    Seattle Branch, Seattle, Wash. 98124.

§ 306.2 Definitions of words and terms as used in these regulations.

(a) "Advance refunding offer" is an offer to a holder of a security, usually a year or more in advance of its call or maturity date, to exchange it for another security.

(b) A "bearer" security is payable on its face at maturity or call for redemption before maturity in accordance with its terms to "bearer." The ownership is not recorded. Title to such a security may pass by delivery without endorsement and without notice. A "coupon" security is a bearer security with interest coupons attached.

(c) "Bureau" refers to the Bureau of the Public Debt, Division of Securities Operations, Washington, D.C. 20226.

(d) "Call date" or "date of call" is the date fixed in the official notice of call published in the FEDERAL REGISTER as the date on which the obligor will make payment of the security before maturity in accordance with its terms.

(e) "Court" means one which has jurisdiction over the parties and the subject matter.

(f) "Department" refers to the Department of the Treasury.

(g) "Face maturity date" is the payment date specified in the text of a security.

(h) "Incompetent" refers to a person under any legal disability except minority.

(i) "Joint owner" and "joint ownership" refer to any permitted form of ownership by two or more persons.

(j) "Nontransferable securities" are those issued only in registered form which according to their terms are payable only to the registered owners or recognized successors in title to the extent and in the manner provided in the offering circulars or special applicable regulations.

(k) "Payment" and "redemption," unless otherwise indicated by the context, are used interchangeably for payment at maturity or payment before maturity pursuant to a call for redemption in accordance with the terms of the securities.

(l) "Prerefunding offer" is an offer to a holder of a security, usually within the year preceding its call or maturity date, to exchange it for another security.

(m) "Redemption-exchange" is any authorized redemption of securities for the purpose of applying the proceeds in payment for other securities offered in exchange.

(n) A "registered" security refers to a security the ownership of which is registered on the books of the Department. It is payable at maturity or call for redemption before maturity in accordance with its terms to the person in whose name it is inscribed, or his assignee.

(o) "Securities assigned in blank" or "securities so assigned as to become in effect payable to bearer" refers to registered securities which are assigned by the owner or his authorized representative without designating the assignee. Registered securities assigned simply to "The Secretary of the Treasury" or in the case of Treasury Bonds, Investment Series B—1975–80, to "The Secretary of the Treasury for exchange for the current Series EA or EO Treasury notes" are considered to be so assigned as to become in effect payable to bearer.

(p) "Taxpayer identifying number" means the appropriate identifying number as required on tax returns and other documents submitted to the Internal Revenue Service, i.e., an individual's social security account number or an employer identification number. A social security account number is composed of nine digits separated by two hyphens, for example, 123–45–6789; an employer identification number is composed of nine digits separated by one hyphen, for example, 12–3456789. The hyphens are an essential part of the numbers and must be included.

(q) "Transferable securities," which may be in either registered or bearer form, refers to securities which may be sold on the market and transfer of title accomplished by assignment and delivery if in registered form, or by delivery only if in bearer form.

(r) "Treasurer's Office" refers to the Office of the Treasurer of the United States, Securities Division, Washington, D.C. 20222.

(s) "Treasury securities," "Treasury bonds," "Treasury notes," "Treasury certificates of indebtedness," and "Treasury bills," or simply "securities," "bonds," "notes," "certificates," and "bills," unless otherwise indicated by the context, refer only to transferable securities.

§ 306.3 Transportation charges and risks in the shipment of securities.

The following rules will govern transportation to, from, and between the Department and the Federal Reserve banks and branches of securities issued on or presented for authorized transactions:

(a) The securities may be presented or received by the owners or their agents in person.

(b) Securities issued on original issue, unless delivered in person, will be delivered by registered mail or by other means at the risk and expense of the United States.

(c) The United States will assume the risk and expense of any transportation of securities which may be necessary between the Federal Reserve banks and branches and the Treasury.

(d) Securities submitted for any transaction after original issue, if not presented in person, must be forwarded at the owner's risk and expense.

(e) Bearer securities issued on transactions other than original issue will be delivered by registered mail, covered by insurance, at the owner's risk and expense, unless called for in person by the owner or his agent. Registered securities issued on such transactions will be delivered by registered mail at the risk of, but without expense to, the registered owner. Should delivery by other means be desired, advance arrangements should be made with the official agency to which the original securities were presented.

Subpart B—Registration

§ 306.10 General.

The registration used must express the actual ownership of a security and may not include any restriction on the authority of the owner to dispose of it in any manner, except as otherwise specifically provided in these regulations. The Treasury Department reserves the right to treat the registration as conclusive of ownership. Requests for registration should be clear, accurate, and complete, conform with one of the forms set forth in this subpart, and include appropriate taxpayer identifying numbers.[1] The registration of all bonds owned by the same person, organization, or fiduciary should be uniform with respect to the name of the owner and, in the case of a fiduciary, the description of the fiduciary capacity. Individual owners should be designated by the names by which they are ordinarily known or under which they do business, preferably including at least one full given name. The name of an individual may be preceded by any applicable title, as, for example, "Mrs.," "Miss," "Ms.," "Dr.," or "Rev.," or followed by a designation such as "M.D.," "D.D.," "Sr." or "Jr." Any other similar suffix should be included when ordinarily used or when necessary to distinguish the owner from a member of his family. A married woman's own given name, not that of her husband, must be used, for example, "Mrs. Mary A. Jones," not "Mrs. Frank B. Jones." The address should include, where appropriate, the number and street, route, or any other local feature and the Zip Code.

§ 306.11   Forms of registration for transferable securities.

The forms of registration described below are authorized for transferable securities:

(a) *Natural persons in their own right.* In the names of natural persons who are not under any legal disability, in their own right, substantially as follows:

(1) *One person.* In the name of one individual. Examples:

John A. Doe (123-45-6789).
Mrs. Mary C. Doe (123-45-6789).
Miss Elizabeth Jane Doe (123-45-6789).

An individual who is sole proprietor of a business conducted under a trade name may include a reference to the trade name. Examples:

John A. Doe, doing business as Doe's Home Appliance Store (12-3456789).
or
John A. Doe (123-45-6789), doing business as Doe's Home Appliance Store.

(2) *Two or more persons—general.* Securities will not be registered in the name of one person payable on death to another, or in any form which purports to authorize transfer by less than all the persons named in the registration (or all the survivors).[2] Securities will not be

registered in the forms "John A. Doe and Mrs. Mary C. Doe, or either of them" or "William C. Doe or Henry J. Doe, or either of them" and securities so assigned will be treated as though the words "or either of them" do not appear in the assignments. The taxpayer identifying number of any of the joint owners may be shown on securities registered in joint ownership form.

(i) *With right of survivorship.* In the names of two or more individuals with right of survivorship. Examples:

John A. Doe (123-45-6789) or Mrs. Mary C. Doe or the survivor.
John A. Doe (123-45-6789) or Mrs. Mary C. Doe or Miss Mary Ann Doe or the survivors or survivor.
John A. Doe (123-45-6789) or Mrs. Mary C. Doe.
John A. Doe (123-45-6789) and Mrs. Mary C. Doe.
John A. Doe (123-45-6789) and Mrs. Mary C. Doe as joint tenants with right of survivorship and not as tenants in common.

Limited to husband and wife:

John A. Doe (123-45-6789) and Mrs Mary C. Doe, as tenants by the entireties.

(ii) *Without right of survivorship.* In the names of two or more individuals in such manner as to preclude the right of survivorship. Examples:

John A. Doe (123-45-6789) and William B. Doe as tenants in common.
John A. Jones as natural guardian of Henry B. Jones, a minor, and Robert C. Jones (123-45-6789), without right of survivorship.

Limited to husband and wife:

Charles H. Brown (123-45-6789) and Ann R. Brown, as partners in community.

(b) *Minors and incompetents*—(1) *Natural guardians of minors.* A security may be registered in the name of a natural guardian of a minor for whose estate no legal guardian or similar representative has legally qualified. Example:

John R. Jones as natural guardian of Henry M. Jones, a minor (123-45-6789).

Either parent with whom the minor resides, or if he does not reside with either parent, the person who furnishes his chief support, will be recognized as his natural guardian and will be considered a fiduciary. Registration in the name of a minor in his own right as owner or as joint owner is not authorized. Securities so registered, upon qualification of the natural guardian, will be treated as though registered in the name of the natural guardian in that capacity.

(2) *Custodian under statute authorizing gifts to minors.* A security may be purchased as a gift to a minor under a gifts to minors statute in effect in the State in which either the donor or the minor resides. The security should be registered as provided in the statute, with an identifying reference to the statute if the registration does not clearly identify it. Examples:

William C. Jones, as custodian for John A. Smith, a minor (123-45-6789), under the California Uniform Gifts to Minors Act.

Robert C. Smith, as custodian for Henry L. Brown, a minor (123-45-6789), under the laws of Georgia; Ch. 48-3, Code of Ga. Anno.

(3) *Incompetents not under guardianship.* Registration in the form "John A. Brown, an incompetent (123-45-6789), under voluntary guardianship," is permitted only on reissue after a voluntary guardian has qualified for the purpose of collecting interest. (See §§ 306.37(c)(2) and 306.57(c)(2).) Otherwise, registration in the name of an incompetent not under legal guardianship is not authorized.

(c) *Executors, administrators, guardians, and similar representatives or fiduciaries.* A security may be registered in the names of legally qualified executors, administrators, guardians, conservators, or similar representatives or fiduciaries of a single estate. The names and capacities of all the representatives or fiduciaries, as shown in their letters of appointment, must be included in the registration and must be followed by an adequate identifying reference to the estate. Examples:

John Smith, executor of will (or administrator of estate) of Henry J. Jones, deceased (12-3456789).
William C. Jones, guardian (or conservator, etc.) of estate of James D. Brown, a minor (or an incompetent) (123-45-6789).

(d) *Life tenant under will.* A security may be registered in the name of a life tenant followed by an adequate identifying reference to the will. Example:

Anne B. Smith, life tenant under the will of Adam A. Smith, deceased (12-3456789).

The life tenant will be considered a fiduciary.

(e) *Private trust estates.* A security may be registered in the name and title of the trustee or trustees of a single duly constituted private trust, followed by an adequate identifying reference to the authority governing the trust. Examples:

John Jones and Blank Trust Co., Albany, N.Y., trustees under will of Sarah Jones, deceased (12-3456789).
John Doe and Richard Roe, trustees under agreement with Henry Jones dated February 9, 1970 (12-3456789).

The names of all trustees, in the form used in the trust instrument, must be included in the registration, except as follows:

(1) If there are several trustees designated as a board or authorized to act as a unit, their names should be omitted and the words "Board of Trustees" substituted for the word "trustees." Example:

Board of Trustees of Blank Co. Retirement Fund, under collective bargaining agreement dated June 30, 1970 (12-3456789).

(2) If the trustees do not constitute a board or otherwise act as a unit, and are either too numerous to be designated in the inscription by names and title, or serve for limited terms, some or all of the names may be omitted. Examples:

John Smith, Henry Jones, et al., trustees under will of Henry J. Smith, deceased (12-3456789).

---

[1] Taxpayer identifying numbers are not required for foreign governments, nonresident aliens not engaged in trade or business within the United States, international organizations and foreign corporations not engaged in trade or business and not having an office or place of business or a financial or paying agent within the United States, and other persons or organizations as may be exempted from furnishing such numbers under regulations of the Internal Revenue Service.

[2] *Warning.* Difference Between Transferable Treasury Securities Registered in the Names of Two or More Persons and United States Savings Bonds in Coownership Form. The effect of registering Treasury securities to which these regulations apply in the names of two or more persons differs decidedly from registration of savings bonds in coownership form. Savings bonds are virtually redeemable on demand at the option of either coowner on his signature alone. Transferable Treasury securities are redeemable only at maturity or upon prior call by the Secretary of the Treasury.

Trustees under will of Henry J. Smith, deceased (12–3456789).

Trustees of Retirement Fund of Industrial Manufacturing Co., under directors' resolution of June 30, 1950 (12–3456789).

(f) *Private organizations (corporations, unincorporated associations and partnerships).* A security may be registered in the name of any private corporation, unincorporated association, or partnership, including a nominee, which for purposes of these regulations is treated as the owner. The full legal name of the organization, as set forth in its charter, articles of incorporation, constitution, partnership agreement, or other authority from which its powers are derived, must be included in the registration and may be followed, if desired, by a reference to a particular account or fund, other than a trust fund, in accordance with the rules and examples given below:

(1) *A corporation.* The name of a business, fraternal, religious, or other private corporation must be followed by descriptive words indicating the corporate status unless the term "corporation" or the abbreviation "Inc." is part of the name or the name is that of a corporation or association organized under Federal law, such as a national bank or Federal savings and loan association. Examples:

Smith Manufacturing Co., a corporation (12–3456789).

The Standard Manufacturing Corp. (12–3456789).

Jones & Brown, Inc.—Depreciation Acct. (12–3456789).

First National Bank of Albemarle (12–3456789).

Abco & Co., Inc., a nominee corporation (12–3456789).

(2) *An unincorporated association.* The name of a lodge, club, labor union, veterans' organization, religious society, or similar self-governing organization which is not incorporated (whether or not it is chartered by or affiliated with a parent organization which is incorporated) must be followed by the words "an unincorporated association." Examples:

American Legion Post No. ——, Department of the D.C., an unincorporated association (12–3456789).

Local Union No. 100, Brotherhood of Locomotive Engineers, an unincorporated association (12–3456789).

Securities should not be registered in the name of an unincorporated association if the legal title to its property in general, or the legal title to the funds with which the securities are to be purchased, is held by trustees. In such a case the securities should be registered in the title of the trustees in accordance with paragraph (e) of this section. The term "unincorporated association" should not be used to describe a trust fund, a partnership or a business conducted under a trade name.

(3) *A partnership.* The name of a partnership must be followed by the words "a partnership." Examples:

Smith & Brown, a partnership (12–3456789).

Acme Novelty Co., a limited partnership (12–3456789).

Abco & Co., a nominee partnership (12–3456789).

(g) *States, public bodies, and corporations and public officers.* A security may be registered in the name of a State or county, city, town, village, school district, or other political entity, public body or corporation established by law (including a board, commission, administration, authority or agency) which is the owner or official custodian of public funds, other than trust funds, or in the full legal title of the public officer having custody. Examples:

State of Maine.
Town of Rye, N.Y.
Maryland State Highway Administration.
Treasurer, City of Springfield, Ill.
Treasurer of Rhode Island—State Forestry Fund.

(h) *States, public officers, corporations or bodies as trustees.* A security may be registered in the title of a public officer or in the name of a State or county or a public corporation or public body acting as trustee under express authority of law. An appropriate reference to the statute creating the trust may be included in the registration. Examples:

Insurance Commissioner of Pennsylvania, trustee for benefit of policyholders of Blank Insurance Co. (12–3456789), under Sec. ——, Pa. Stats.

Rhode Island Investment Commission, trustee of General Sinking Fund under Ch. 35, Gen. Laws of R.I.

State of Colorado in trust for Colorado Surplus Property Agency.

§ 306.12 Errors in registration.

If an erroneously inscribed security is received, it should not be altered in any respect, but the Bureau, a Federal Reserve bank or branch, or the Treasurer's Office should be furnished full particulars concerning the error and asked to furnish instructions.

§ 306.13 Nontransferable securities.

Upon authorized reissue, Treasury Bonds, Investment Series B—1975–80, may be registered in the forms set forth in § 306.11.

Subpart C—Transfers, Exchanges and Reissues

§ 306.15 Transfers and exchanges of securities—closed periods.

(a) *General.* The transfer of registered securities should be made by assignment in accordance with Subpart F of this part. Transferable registered securities are eligible for denominational exchange and exchange for bearer securities. Bearer securities are eligible for denominational exchange, and when so provided in the offering circular, are eligible for exchange for registered securities. Specific instructions for issuance and delivery of the new securities, signed by the owner or his authorized representative, must accompany the securities presented. (Form PD 3905 or PD 1827, as appropriate, may be used.) Denominational exchanges, exchanges of Treasury Bonds, Investment Series B—1975–80, for the current series of EA or EO 1½ percent 5-year Treasury notes, and optional redemption of bonds at par as provided in § 306.28 may be made at any time. Securities presented for transfer or for exchange for bearer securities of the same issue must be received by the Bureau not less than 1 full month before the date on which the securities mature or become redeemable pursuant to a call for redemption before maturity. Any security so presented which is received too late to comply with this provision will be accepted for payment only.

(b) *Closing of transfer books.* The transfer books are closed for 1 full month preceding interest payment dates and call or maturity dates. If the date set for closing of the transfer books falls on Saturday, Sunday, or a legal holiday, the books will be closed as of the close of business on the last business day preceding that date. The books are reopened on the first business day following the date on which interest falls due. Registered securities which have not matured or been called, submitted for transfer, reissue, or exchange for coupon securities, and coupon securities which have not matured or been called, submitted for exchange for registered securities, which are received during the period the books for that loan are closed, will be processed on or after the date such books are reopened. If registered securities are received for transfer or exchange for bearer securities, or coupon securities are received for exchange for registered securities, during the time the books are closed for payment of final interest at maturity or call, unless otherwise provided in the offering circular or notice of call, the following action will be taken:

(1) Payment of final interest will be made to the registered owner of record on the date the books were closed.

(2) Payment of principal will be made to (i) the assignee under a proper assignment of the securities, or (ii) if the securities have been assigned for exchange for bearer securities, to the registered owner of record on the date the books were closed.

§ 306.16 Exchanges of registered securities.

No assignments will be required for (a) authorized denominational exchanges of registered securities for like securities in the same names and forms of registration and (b) redemption-exchanges, or prerefundings, or advance refundings in the same names and forms as appear in the registration or assignments of the securities surrendered.

§ 306.17 Exchanges of registered securities for coupon securities.

Registered securities submitted for exchange for coupon securities should be assigned to "The Secretary of the Treasury for exchange for coupon securities to be delivered to (inserting the name and address of the person to whom delivery of the coupon securities is to be made)." Assignments to "The Secretary of the Treasury for exchange for coupon securities," or assignments in blank will also be accepted. The coupon securities issued upon exchange will have all unmatured coupons attached.

§ 306.18 Exchanges of coupon securities for registered securities.

Coupon securities presented for exchange for registered securities should have all matured interest coupons detached. All unmatured coupons should be attached, except that if presented when the transfer books are closed (in which case the exchange will be effected on or after the date on which the books are reopened), the next maturing coupons should be detached and held for collection in ordinary course when due. If any coupons which should be attached are missing, the securities must be accompanied by a remittance in an amount equal to the face amount of the missing coupons. The new registered securities will bear interest from the interest payment date next preceding the date on which the exchange is made.

§ 306.19 Denominational exchanges of coupon securities.

All matured interest coupons and all unmatured coupons likely to mature before an exchange can be completed should be detached from securities presented for denominational exchange. All unmatured coupons should be attached. If any are missing, the securities must be accompanied by a remittance in an amount equal to the face amount of the missing coupons. The new coupon securities will have all unmatured coupons attached.

§ 306.20 Reissue of registered transferable securities.

Assignments are not required for reissue of registered transferable securities in the name(s) of (a) the surviving joint owner(s) of securities registered in the names of or assigned to two or more persons, unless the registration or assignment includes words which preclude the right of survivorship, (b) a succeeding fiduciary or other lawful successor, (c) a remainderman, upon termination of a life estate, (d) an individual, corporation or unincorporated association whose name has been legally changed, (e) a corporation or unincorporated association which is the lawful successor to another corporation or unincorporated association, and (f) a successor in title to a public officer or body. Evidence of survivorship, succession, or change of name, as appropriate, must be furnished. The appropriate taxpayer identifying number also must be furnished if the registration of the securities submitted does not include such number for the person or organization to be named on the reissued securities.

§ 306.21 Reissue of nontransferable securities.

Treasury Bonds, Investment Series B–1975–80, may be reissued only in the names of (a) lawful successors in title, (b) the legal representatives or distributees of a deceased owner's estate, or the distributees of a trust estate, and (c) State supervisory authorities in pursuance of any pledge required of the owner under State law, or upon termination of the pledge in the names of the pledgors or their successors. Bonds presented for reissue must be accompanied by evidence of entitlement.

§ 306.22 Exchange of Treasury Bonds, Investment Series B–1975–80.

Bonds of this series presented for exchange for 1½ percent 5-year Treasury notes must bear duly executed assignments to "The Secretary of the Treasury for exchange for the current series of EA or EO Treasury notes to be delivered to (inserting the name and address of the person to whom the notes are to be delivered)." The notes will bear the April 1 or October 1 date next preceding the date the bonds, duly assigned with supporting evidence, if necessary, are received by the Bureau or a Federal Reserve Bank or Branch. Interest accrued at the rate of 2¾ percent on the bonds surrendered from the next preceding interest payment date to the date of exchange will be credited, and interest at the rate of 1½ percent on the notes for the same period will be charged and the difference will be paid to the owner.

Subpart D—Redemption or Payment

§ 306.25 Presentation and surrender.

(a) *General.* Securities, whether in registered or bearer form, are payable in regular course of business at maturity unless called for redemption before maturity in accordance with their terms, in which case they will be payable in regular course of business on the date of call. The Secretary of the Treasury may provide for the exchange of maturing or called securities, or in advance of call or maturity, may afford owners the opportunity of exchanging a security for another security pursuant to a prerefunding or an advance refunding offer. Registered securities should be presented and surrendered for redemption to the Bureau, a Federal Reserve bank or branch, or the Treasurer's Office, and bearer securities to a Federal Reserve bank or branch or the Treasurer's Office.[4] No assignments or evidence in support of assignments will be required by or on behalf of the registered owner or assignee for redemption for his or its account, or for redemption-exchange, or exchange pursuant to a prerefunding or an advance refunding offer, if the new securities are to be registered in exactly the same names and forms as appear in the registrations or assignments of the securities surrendered. To the extent appropriate, these rules also apply to securities registered in the titles of public officers who are official custodians of public funds.

(b) *"Overdue" securities.* If a bearer security or a registered security assigned in blank, or to bearer, or so assigned as to become in effect payable to bearer, is presented and surrendered for redemption after it has become overdue, the Secretary of the Treasury will ordinarily require satisfactory proof of ownership. (Form PD 1071 may be used.) A security

---

[4] See § 306.28 for presentation and surrender of bonds eligible for use in payment of Federal estate taxes.

shall be considered to be overdue after the lapse of the following periods of time from its face maturity:

(1) One month for securities issued for a term of 1 year or less.

(2) Three months for securities issued for a term of more than 1 year but not in excess of 7 years.

(3) Six months for securities issued for a term of more than 7 years.

§ 306.26 Redemption of registered securities at maturity, upon prior call, or for prerefunding or advance refunding.

Registered securities presented and surrendered for redemption at maturity or pursuant to a call for redemption before maturity need not be assigned, unless the owner desires that payment be made to some other person, in which case assignments should be made to "The Secretary of the Treasury for redemption for the account of (inserting name and address of person to whom payment is to be made)." Specific instructions for the issuance and delivery of the redemption check, signed by the owner or his authorized representative, must accompany the securities, unless included in the assignment. (Form PD 3905 may be used.) Payment of the principal will be made either (a) by check drawn on the Treasurer of the United States to the order of the person entitled and mailed in accordance with the instructions received, or (b) upon appropriate request, by crediting the amount in a member bank's account with the Federal Reserve Bank of its District. Securities presented for prerefunding or advance refunding should be assigned as provided in the prerefunding or advance refunding offer.

§ 306.27 Redemption of bearer securities at maturity, upon prior call, or for advance refunding or prerefunding.

All interest coupons due and payable on or before the date of maturity or date fixed in the call for redemption before maturity should be detached from coupon securities presented for redemption and should be collected separately in regular course. All coupons bearing dates subsequent to the date fixed in a call for redemption, or offer of prerefunding or advance refunding, should be left attached to the securities. If any such coupons are missing, the full face amount thereof will be deducted from the payment to be made upon redemption or the prerefunding or advance refunding adjustment unless satisfactory evidence of their destruction is submitted. Any amounts so deducted will be held in the Department to provide for adjustments or refunds in the event it should be determined that the missing coupons were subsequently presented or their destruction is later satisfactorily established. In the absence of other instructions, payment of bearer securities will be made by check drawn to the order of the person presenting and surrendering the securities and mailed to him at his address, as given in the advice accompanying the securities. (Form PD 3905 may be used.) A Federal Reserve bank, upon appropriate request, may make payment to a member bank from which bearer securities are received by crediting the amount of the proceeds of redemption to the member bank's account.

§ 306.28   Optional redemption of Treasury bonds at par (before maturity or call redemption date) and application of the proceeds in payment of Federal estate taxes.

(a) *General.* Treasury bonds to be redeemed at par for the purpose of applying the entire amount of principal and accrued interest to payment of the Federal estate tax on a decedent's estate [5] must be presented and surrendered to a Federal Reserve bank or to the Bureau. They should be accompanied by Form PD 1782, fully completed and duly executed in accordance with the instructions on the form, and evidence as described therein. Redemption will be made at par plus accrued interest from the last preceding interest payment date to the date of redemption, except that if registered bonds are received by a Federal Reserve bank or branch or the Bureau within 1 month preceding an interest payment date for redemption before that date, a deduction will be made for interest from the date of redemption to the interest payment date, and a check for the full 6 months' interest will be paid in due course. The proceeds of redemption will be deposited to the credit of the Internal Revenue Service Center designated in Form PD 1782, and the representative of the estate will be notified of the deposit. A formal receipt may be obtained upon request addressed to the Center.

(b) *Conditions.* The bonds presented for redemption under this section must have (1) been owned by the decedent at the time of his death and (2) thereupon constituted part of his estate, as determined by the following rules in the case of joint ownership, partnership, and trust holdings:

(i) *Joint ownerships.* Bonds held by the decedent at the time of his death in joint ownership with another person or persons will be deemed to have met the above conditions either (a) to the extent to which the bonds actually became the property of the decedent's estate, or (b) in an amount not to exceed the amount of the Federal estate tax which the surviving joint owner or owners is required to pay on account of such bonds and other jointly held property.[6]

(ii) *Partnerships.* Bonds held at the time of the decedent's death by a partnership in which he had an interest will be deemed to have met the above conditions to the extent of his fractional share of the bonds so held proportionate to his interest in the assets of the partnership.

(iii) *Trusts.* Bonds held in trust at the time of the decedent's death will be deemed to have met the above conditions in an amount not to exceed the amount of the Federal estate tax (a) if the trust actually terminated in favor of the decedent's estate, or (b) if the trustee is required to pay the decedent's Federal estate tax under the terms of the trust instrument or otherwise, or (c) to the extent the debts of the decedent's estate, including costs of administration, State inheritance and Federal estate taxes, exceed the assets of his estate without regard to the trust estate.

(c) *Transactions after owner's death.* No transactions involving changes of ownership may be conducted after an owner's death without affecting the eligibility of the bonds for redemption at par for application of the proceeds to payment of the Federal estate tax. Transactions involving no changes of ownership which may be conducted without affecting eligibility are (1) exchange of bonds for those of lower denominations where the bonds exceed the amount of the tax and are not in the lowest authorized denominations, (2) exchange of registered bonds for coupon bonds, (3) exchange of coupon bonds for bonds registered in the names of the representatives of the estate, (4) transfer of bonds from the owner or his nominee to the names of the representatives of the owner's estate, and (5) purchases by or for the account of an owner prior to his death, held in book-entry form, and thereafter converted to definitive bonds. However, any such transactions must be explained on Form PD 1782 or in a supplemental statement.

Subpart E—Interest

§ 306.35   Computation of interest.

The interest on Treasury securities accrues and is payable on a semiannual basis unless otherwise provided in the circular offering them for sale or exchange. If the period of accrual is an exact 6 months, the interest accrual is an exact one-half year's interest without regard to the number of days in the period. If the period of accrual is less than an exact 6 months, the accrued interest is computed by determining the daily rate of accrual on the basis of the exact number of days in the full interest period and multiplying the daily rate by the exact number of days in the fractional period for which interest has actually accrued. A full interest period does not include the day as of which the securities were issued or the day on which

the last preceding interest became due, but does include the day on which the next succeeding interest payment is due. A fractional part of an interest period does not include the day as of which the securities were issued or the day on which the last preceding interest payment became due, but does include the day as of which the transaction terminating the accrual of interest is effected. The 29th of February in a leap year is included whenever it falls within either a full interest period or a fractional part thereof.[7]

§ 306.36   Termination of interest.

Securities will cease to bear interest on the date of their maturity unless they have been called for redemption before maturity in accordance with their terms, or are presented and surrendered for redemption-exchange or exchange pursuant to an advance refunding or prerefunding offer, in which case they will cease to bear interest on the date of call, or the exchange date, as the case may be.

§ 306.37   Interest on registered securities.

(a) *Method of payment.* The interest on registered securities is payable by checks drawn on the Treasurer of the United States to the order of the registered owners, except as otherwise provided herein. Interest checks are prepared by the Department in advance of the interest payment date and are ordinarily mailed in time to reach the addressees on that date. Interest on a registered security which has not matured or been called and which is presented for any transaction during the period the books for that loan are closed will be paid by check drawn to the order of the registered owner of record. Upon receipt of notice of the death or incompetency of an individual named as registered owner, a change in the name or in the status of a partnership, corporation, or unincorporated association, the removal, resignation, succession, or death of a fiduciary or trustee, delivery of interest checks will be withheld pending receipt and approval of evidence showing who is entitled to receive the interest checks. If the inscriptions on securities do not clearly identify the owners, delivery of interest checks will be withheld pending reissue of the securities in the correct registration. The final installment of interest, unless otherwise provided in the offering circular or notice of call, will be paid by check drawn to the order of the registered owner of record and mailed in advance of the interest payment date in time to reach the addressee on or about that date. Interest on securities presented for prerefunding or advance refunding will be adjusted as provided in the prerefunding or advance refunding offer.

---

[5] Certain issues of Treasury bonds are redeemable at par and accrued interest upon the death of the owner, at the option of the representative of, or if none, the persons entitled to, his estate, for the purpose of having the entire proceeds applied in payment of the Federal estate tax on the decedent's estate, in accordance with the terms of the offering circulars cited on the face of the bonds. A current list of eligible issues may be obtained from any Federal Reserve bank or branch, the Bureau of the Public Debt, or the Treasurer's Office.

[6] Substantially the same rule applies to community property except that upon the death of either spouse bonds which constitute part of the community estate are deemed to meet the required conditions to the extent of one-half of each loan and issue of bonds.

[7] The appendix to this subpart contains a complete explanation of the method of computing interest on a semiannual basis on Treasury bonds, notes, and certificates of indebtedness, and an outline of the method of computing the discount rates on Treasury bills. Also included are tables of computation of interest on semiannual and annual basis.

(b) *Change of address*. To assure timely delivery of interest checks, owners should promptly notify the Bureau of any change of address. (Form PD 345 may be used.) The notification must be signed by the registered owner or a joint owner or an authorized representative, and should show the owner's taxpayer identifying number, the old and new addresses, the serial number and denomination of each security, the titles of the securities (for example: 4¼ percent Treasury Bonds of 1987–92, dated August 15, 1962), and the registration of each security. Notifications by attorneys in fact, trustees, or by the legal representatives of the estates of deceased, incompetent, or minor owners should be supported by proof of their authority, unless, in the case of trustees or legal representatives, they are named in the registration.

(c) *Collection of interest checks*—(1) *General*. Interest checks may be collected in accordance with the regulations governing the endorsement and payment of Government warrants and checks, which are contained in the current revision of Department Circular No. 21 (Part 360 of this chapter).

(2) *By voluntary guardians of incompetents*. Interest checks drawn to the order of a person who has become incompetent and for whose estate no legal guardian or similar representative has been appointed should be returned to the Bureau with a full explanation of the circumstances. For collection of interest, the Department will recognize the relative responsible for the incompetent's care and support or some other person as voluntary guardian for the incompetent. (Application may be made on Form PD 1461.)

(d) *Nonreceipt, loss, theft, or destruction of interest checks*. If an interest check is not received within a reasonable period after an interest payment date, the Bureau should be notified. Should a check be lost, stolen, or destroyed after receipt, the Office of the Treasurer of the United States, Check Claims Division, Washington, D.C. 20227, should be notified. Notification should include the name and address of the owner, his taxpayer identifying number, and the serial number, denomination, and title of the security upon which the interest was payable. If the check is subsequently received or recovered, the latter office should also be advised.

§ 306.38   **Interest on bearer securities.**

Unless the offering circular and notice of call provide otherwise, interest on coupon securities is payable in regular course of business upon presentation and surrender of the interest coupons as they mature. Such coupons are payable at any Federal Reserve bank or branch, or the Treasurer's Office.[*] Interest on Treasury bills, and any other bearer securities which may be sold and issued on a discount basis and which are payable at

---

[*] Banking institutions will usually cash the coupons without charge as an accommodation to their customers.

par at maturity, is represented by the difference between the purchase price and the par value, and no coupons are attached.

Subpart F—Assignments of Registered Securities—General

§ 306.40   **Execution of assignments or special endorsements.**

(a) *Execution of assignments*. The assignment of a registered security should be executed by the owner or his authorized representative in the presence of an officer authorized to certify assignments. All assignments must be made on the backs of the securities, unless otherwise authorized by the Bureau, a Federal Reserve bank or branch, or the Treasurer of the United States. An assignment by mark (X) must be witnessed not only by a certifying officer but also by at least one other person, who should add an endorsement substantially as follows: "Witness to signature by mark," followed by his signature and address.

(b) *Special endorsement in lieu of assignments*. A security may be presented without assignment for any authorized transaction by a financial institution which is (1) a member of the Federal Reserve System, (2) a member of the Federal Home Loan Bank System, or (3) insured by the Federal Deposit Insurance Corporation, provided full instructions are furnished as to the transaction desired and the security bears the endorsement, under the official seal of the institution, as follows:

Presented in accordance with instructions of the owner(s).
Absence of assignment guaranteed.

```
----------------------------
     (Name of financial
        institution)
By ------------------------
    (Signature and title of
           officer)
----------------------------
          (Date)
```

This form of endorsement of a security will be an unconditional guarantee to the Department of the Treasury that the institution is acting as attorney in fact for the registered owner, or his assignee, under proper authorization and that the officer is duly authorized to act.

§ 306.41   **Form of assignment.**

Registered securities may be assigned in blank, to bearer, to a specified transferee, to the Secretary of the Treasury for exchange for coupon securities, or to the Secretary of the Treasury for redemption or for exchange for other securities offered at maturity, upon call or pursuant to an advance refunding or prerefunding offer. Assignments to "The Secretary of the Treasury," "The Secretary of the Treasury for transfer," or "The Secretary of the Treasury for exchange" will not be accepted unless supplemented by specific instructions by or in behalf of the owner.

§ 306.42   **Alterations and erasures.**

If an alteration or erasure has been made in an assignment, the assignor should appear before an authorized cer-

tifying officer and execute a new assignment to the same assignee. If the new assignment is to other than the assignee whose name has been altered or erased, a disclaimer from the first-named assignee should be obtained. Otherwise, an affidavit of explanation by the person responsible for the alteration or erasure should be submitted for consideration.

§ 306.43   **Voidance of assignments.**

An assignment of a security to or for the account of another person, not completed by delivery, may be voided by a disclaimer of interest from that person. This disclaimer should be executed in the presence of an officer authorized to certify assignments of securities. Unless otherwise authorized by the Bureau, a Federal Reserve bank or branch, or the Treasurer of the United States, the disclaimer must be written, typed, or stamped on the back of the security in substantially the following form:

The undersigned as assignee of this security hereby disclaims any interest herein.

```
----------------------------
         (Signature)
```

I certify that the above-named person as described, whose identity is well known or proved to me, personally appeared before me the -------- day of ----------------------
```
         (Month and year)
```
at ------------------------------ and
```
           (Place)
```
signed the above disclaimer of interest.

(SEAL) ----------------------------
```
    (Signature and official designation
          of certifying officer)
```

In the absence of a disclaimer, an affidavit or affidavits should be submitted for consideration explaining why a disclaimer cannot be obtained, reciting all other material facts and circumstances relating to the transaction, including whether or not the security was delivered to the person named as assignee and whether or not the affiants know of any basis for the assignee claiming any right, title, or interest in the security. After an assignment has been voided, in order to dispose of the security, an assignment by or on behalf of the owner will be required.

§ 306.44   **Discrepancies in names.**

The Department will ordinarily require an explanation of discrepancies in the names which appear in inscriptions, assignments, supporting evidence or in the signatures to any assignments. (Form PD 385 may be used for this purpose.) However, where the variations in the name of the registered owner, as inscribed on securities of the same or different issues, are such that both may properly represent the same person, for example, "J. T. Smith" and "John T. Smith," no proof of identity will be required if the assignments are signed exactly as the securities are inscribed and are duly certified by the same certifying officer.

§ 306.45   **Officers authorized to certify assignments.**

(a) *Officers authorized generally*. The following persons are authorized to act as certifying officers for the purpose of certifying assignments of, or forms with respect to, securities:

(1) Officers and employees of banks and trust companies incorporated in the United States, its territories or possessions, or the Commonwealth of Puerto Rico, Federal Savings and Loan Associations, or other organizations which are members of the Federal Home Loan Bank System, who have been authorized to: (i) Generally bind their respective institutions by their acts, (ii) unqualifiedly guarantee signatures to assignments of securities, or (iii) expressly certify assignments of securities.

(2) Officers of Federal Reserve banks and branches.

(3) Officers of Federal Land Banks, Federal Intermediate Credit Banks and Banks for Cooperatives, the Central Bank for Cooperatives, and Federal Home Loan Banks.

(4) U.S. Attorneys, Collectors of Customs, and Regional Commissioners, District Directors, and Service Center Directors, Internal Revenue Service.

(5) Judges and Clerks of U.S. Courts.

(b) *Authorized officers in foreign countries.* The following are authorized to certify assignments in foreign countries:

(1) U.S. diplomatic or consular representatives.

(2) Managers, assistant managers and other officers of foreign branches of banks or trust companies incorporated in the United States, its territories or possessions, or the Commonwealth of Puerto Rico.

(3) Notaries public and other officers authorized to administer oaths. The official position and authority of any such officer must be certified by a U.S. diplomatic or consular representative under seal of his office.

(c) *Officers having limited authority.* The following are authorized to certify assignments to the extent set forth in connection with each class of officers:

(1) Postmasters, acting postmasters, assistant postmasters, inspectors in charge, chief and assistant chief accountants, and superintendents of stations of any post office, notaries public and justices of the peace in the United States, its territories and possessions, the Commonwealth of Puerto Rico and the Canal Zone, but only for assignment of securities for redemption for the account of the assignor, or for redemption exchange, or pursuant to an advance refunding or prerefunding offer for other securities to be registered in his name, or in his name with a joint owner. The signature of any post office official, other than a postmaster, must be in the following form: "John A. Doe, Postmaster, by Richard B. Roe, Superintendent of Station."

(2) Commissioned officers and warrant officers of the Armed Forces of the United States for assignment of securities of any class for any authorized transaction, but only with respect to assignments executed by: (i) Armed Forces personnel and civilian field employees, and (ii) members of the families of such personnel or civilian employees.

(d) *Special provisions for certifying assignments.* The Commissioner of the Public Debt, the Chief of the Division of Securities Operations, any Federal Reserve bank or branch, or the Treasurer of the United States, is authorized to make special provisions for any case or class of cases.

§ 306.46   Duties and responsibilities of certifying officer.

A certifying officer must require execution of an assignment, or a form with respect to securities, in his presence after he has established the identity of the assignor and before he certifies the signature. He must then complete the certification. An employee who is not an officer should insert "Authorized signature" in the space provided for the title. However, an assignment of a security need not be executed in the presence of the certifying officer if he unqualifiedly guarantees the signature thereto, in which case he must place his endorsement on the security, following the signature, in the form "Signature guaranteed, First National Bank of Jonesville, Jonesville, N.H., by A. B. Doe, President," and add the date. The certifying officer and, if he is an officer or employee of an organization, the organization will be held responsible for any loss the United States may suffer as the result of his fault or negligence.

§ 306.47   Evidence of certifying officer's authority.

The authority of an individual to act as a certifying officer is established by affixing to a certification of an assignment, or a form with respect to securities, or an unqualified guarantee of a signature to an assignment, either: (a) The official seal of the organization, or (b) a legible imprint of the issuing agent's dating stamp, if the organization is an authorized issuing agent for U.S. Savings Bonds of Series E. Use of such stamp shall result in the same responsibility on the part of the organization as if its official seal were used. A certification which does not bear a seal or issuing agent's dating stamp will not be accepted. Any post office official must use the official stamp of his office. A commissioned or warrant officer of any of the Armed Forces of the United States should indicate his rank and state that the person executing the assignment is one of the class whose signature he is authorized to certify. A judge or clerk of court must use the seal of the court. Any other certifying officer must use his official seal or stamp, if any, but, if he has neither, his official position and a specimen of his signature must be certified by some other authorized officer under official seal or stamp or otherwise proved to the satisfaction of the Department.

§ 306.48   Interested persons not to act as certifying officer or witness.

Neither the assignor, the assignee, nor any person having an interest in a security may act as a certifying officer, or as a witness to an assignment by mark. However, a bank officer may certify an assignment to the bank, or an assignment executed by another officer in its behalf.

§ 306.49   Nontransferable securities.

The provisions of this subpart, so far as applicable, govern transactions in Treasury Bonds, Investment Series B–1975–80.

Subpart G—Assignments by or in Behalf of Individuals

§ 306.55   Signatures, minor errors and change of name.

The owner's signature to an assignment should be in the form in which the security is inscribed or assigned, unless such inscription or assignment is incorrect or the name has since been changed. In case of a change of name, the signature to the assignment should show both names and the manner in which the change was made, for example, "John Young, changed by order of court from Hans Jung." Evidence of the change will be required. However, no evidence is required to support an assignment if the change resulted from marriage and the signature, which must be duly certified by an authorized officer, is written to show that fact, for example, "Mrs. Mary J. Brown, changed by marriage from Miss Mary Jones."

§ 306.56   Assignment of securities registered in the names of or assigned to two or more persons.

(a) *Transfer or exchange.* Securities registered in the names of or assigned to two or more persons may be transferred or exchanged for coupon bonds during the lives of all the joint owners only upon assignments by all or on their behalf by authorized representatives. Upon proof of the death of one, the Department will accept an assignment by or in behalf of the survivor or survivors, unless the form of registration or assignment includes words which precludes the right of survivorship.[*] In the latter case, in addition to assignment by or in behalf of the survivor or survivors, an assignment in behalf of the decedent's estate will be required.

(b) *Advance refunding or prerefunding offers.* No assignments are required for exchange of securities registered in the names of or assigned to two or more persons if the securities to be received in the exchange are to be registered in the same names and form. If bearer securities or securities in a different form are to be issued, all persons named must assign, except that in case of death paragraph (a) of this section shall apply.

(c) *Redemption or redemption-exchange.* (1) *Alternative registration or assignment.* Securities registered in the names of or assigned to two or more persons in the alternative, for example, "John B. Smith or Mrs. Mary J. Smith" or "John B. Smith or Mrs. Mary J. Smith or the survivor," may be assigned by one of them at maturity or upon call, for redemption or redemption-exchange, for his own account or otherwise, whether

---

[*] See § 306.11(a)(2) for forms of registration expressing or precluding survivorship.

or not the other joint owner or owners are deceased.

(2) *Joint registration or assignment.* Securities registered in the names of or assigned to two or more persons jointly, for example, "John B. Smith and Mrs. Mary J. Smith," or "John B. Smith and Mrs. Mary J. Smith as tenants in common," or "John B. Smith and Mary J. Smith as partners in community," may be assigned by one of them during the lives of all only for redemption at maturity or upon call, and then only for redemption for the account of all. No assignments are required for redemption-exchange for securities to be registered in the same names and forms as appear in the registration or assignment of the securities surrendered. Upon proof of the death of a joint owner, the survivor or survivors may assign securities so registered or assigned for redemption or redemption-exchange for any account, except that, if words which preclude the right of survivorship* appear in the registration or assignment, assignment in behalf of the decedent's estate also will be required.

§ 306.57   Minors and incompetents.

(a) *Assignments by natural guardian of securities registered in name of minor.* Securities registered in the name of a minor for whose estate no legal guardian or similar representative has qualified may be assigned by the natural guardian upon qualification. (Form PD 2481 may be used for this purpose.)

(b) *Assignments of securities registered in name of natural guardian of minor.* Securities registered in the name of a natural guardian of a minor may be assigned by the natural guardian for any authorized transaction except one for the apparent benefit of the natural guardian. If the natural guardian in whose name the securities are registered is deceased or is no longer qualified to act as natural guardian, the securities may be assigned by the person then acting as natural guardian. The assignment by the new natural guardian should be supported by proof of the death or disqualification of the former natural guardian and by evidence of his own status as natural guardian. (Form PD 2481 may be used for this purpose.) No assignment by a natural guardian will be accepted after receipt of notice of the minor's attainment of majority, removal of his disability of minority, disqualification of the natural guardian to act as such, qualification of a legal guardian or similar representaitve, or the death of the minor.

(c) *Assignments by voluntary guardians of incompetents.* Registered securities belonging to an incompetent for whose estate no legal guardian or similar representative is legally qualified may be assigned by the relative responsible for his care and support or some other person as voluntary guardian:

(1) For redemption or exchange for bearer securities, if the proceeds of the securities are needed to pay expenses al-

* See § 306.11 (a) (2) for forms of registration expressing or precluding survivorship.

ready incurred, or to be incurred during any 90-day period, for the care and support of the incompetent or his legal dependents.

(2) For redemption-exchange, if the securities are matured or have been called, or pursuant to an advance refunding or prerefunding offer, for reinvestment in other securities to be registered in the form "A, an incompetent (123–45–6789) under voluntary guardianship."

An application on Form PD 1461 by the person seeking authority to act as voluntary guardian will be required.

(d) *Assignments by legal guardians of minors or incompetents.* Securities registered in the name and title of the legal guardian or similar representative of the estate of a minor or incompetent may be assigned by the representative for any authorized transaction without proof of his qualification. Assignments by a representative of any other securities belonging to a minor or incompetent must be supported by properly certified evidence of qualification. The evidence must be dated not more than 1 year before the date of the assignments and must contain a statement showing the appointment is in full force unless (1) it shows the appointment was made not more than 1 year before the date of the assignment, or (2) the representative or a corepresentative is a corporation. An assignment by the representative will not be accepted after receipt of notice of termination of the guardianship, except for transfer to the former ward.

§ 306.58   Nontransferable securities.

The provisions of this subpart, so far as applicable, govern transactions in Treasury Bonds, Investment Series B–1975–80.

Subpart H—Assignments in Behalf of Estates of Deceased Owners

§ 306.65   Special provisions applicable to small amounts of securities, interest checks or redemption checks.

Entitlement to, or the authority to dispose of, a small amount of securities and checks issued in payment thereof or in payment of interest thereon, belonging to the estate of a decedent, may be established through the use of certain short forms, according to the aggregate amount of securities and checks involved (excluding checks representing interest on the securities), as indicated by the following table:

Amount	Circumstances	Form	To be executed by—
$100	No administration.	PD 2216	Person who paid burial expenses.
500	Estate being administered.	PD 2488	Executor or administrator.
500	Estate settled.	PD 2488-1	Former executor or administrator, attorneys or other qualified person.

§ 306.66   Estates—administration.

(a) *Temporary or special administrators.* Temporary or special administra-

tors may assign securities for any authorized transaction within the scope of their authority. The assignments must be supported by:

(1) *Temporary administrators.* A certificate, under court seal, showing the appointment in full force within thirty days preceding the date of receipt of the securities.

(2) *Special administrators.* A certificate, under court seal, showing the appointment in full force within 6 months preceding the date of receipt of the securities.

Authority for assignments for transactions not within the scope of appointment must be established by a duly certified copy of a special order of court.

(b) *In course of administration.* A security belonging to the estate of a decedent which is being administered by a duly qualified executor or general administrator will be accepted for any authorized transaction upon assignment by such representative. (See § 306.77.) Unless the security is registered in the name of and shows the capacity of the representative, the assignment must be supported by a certificate or a copy of the letters of appointment, certified under court seal. The certificate or certification, if required, must be dated not more than 6 months before the date of the assignment and must contain a statement that the appointment is in full force, unless (1) it shows the appointment was made not more than 1 year before the date of the assignment, or (2) the representative or a corepresentative is a corporation, or (3) redemption is being made for application of the proceeds in payment of Federal estate taxes as provided by § 306.28.

(c) *After settlement through court proceedings.* Securities belonging to the estate of a decedent which has been settled in court will be accepted for any authorized transaction upon assignments by the person or persons entitled, as determined by the court. The assignments should be supported by a copy, certified under court seal, of the decree of distribution, the representative's final account as approved by the court, or other pertinent court records.

§ 306.67   Estates not administered.

(a) *Special provisions under State laws.* If, under State law, a person has been recognized or appointed to receive or distribute the assets of a decedent's estate without regular administration, his assignment of securities belonging to the estate will be accepted provided he submits appropriate evidence of his authority.

(b) *Agreement of persons entitled.* When it appears that no legal representative of a decedent's estate has been or is to be appointed, securities belonging to the estate may be duly disposed of pursuant to an agreement and assignment by all persons entitled to share in the decedent's personal estate. (Form PD 1646 may be used.) However, all debts of the decedent and his estate must be paid or provided for and the interests of any minors or incompetents must be protected.

§ 306.68   Nontransferable securities.

The provisions of this subpart, so far as applicable, govern transactions in Treasury Bonds, Investment Series B–1975–80.

Subpart I—Assignments by or in Behalf of Trustees and Similar Fiduciaries

§ 306.75   Individual fiduciaries.

(a) *General.* Securities registered in, or assigned to, the names and titles of individual fiduciaries will be accepted for any authorized transaction upon assignment by the designated fiduciaries without proof of their qualification. If the fiduciaries in whose names the securities are registered, or to whom they have been assigned, have been succeeded by other fiduciaries, evidence of successorship must be furnished. If the appointment of a successor is not required under the terms of the trust instrument or otherwise and is not contemplated, assignments by the surviving or remaining fiduciary or fiduciaries must be supported by appropriate proof. This requires (1) proof of the death, resignation, removal or disqualification of the former fiduciary and (2) evidence that the surviving or remaining fiduciary or fiduciaries are fully qualified to administer the fiduciary estate, which may be in the form of a certificate by them showing the appointment of a successor has not been applied for, is not contemplated and is not necessary under the terms of the trust instrument or otherwise. Assignments of securities registered in the titles, without the names of the fiduciaries, for example, "Trustees of the George E. White Memorial Scholarship Fund under deed of trust dated 11/10/40, executed by John W. White," must be supported by proof that the assignors are the qualified and acting trustees of the designated trust estate, unless they are empowered to act as a unit in which case the provisions of § 306.76 shall apply. (Form PD 2446 may be used to furnish proof of incumbency of fiduciaries.) Assignments by fiduciaries of securities not registered or assigned in such manner as to show that they belong to the estate for which the assignors are acting must also be supported by evidence that the estate is entitled to the securities.

(b) *Life tenants.* Upon termination of a life estate by reason of the death of the life tenant in whose name a security is registered, or to whom it has been assigned, the security will be accepted for any authorized transaction upon assignment by the remainderman, supported by evidence of entitlement.

§ 306.76   Fiduciaries acting as a unit.

Securities registered in the name of or assigned to a board, committee or other body authorized to act as a unit for any public or private trust estate may be assigned for any authorized transaction by anyone authorized to act in behalf of such body. Except as otherwise provided in this section, the assignments must be supported by a copy of a resolution adopted by the body, properly certified under its seal, or, if none, sworn to by a member of the body having access to its records. (Form PD 2495 may be used.) If the person assigning is designated in the resolution by title only, his incumbency must be duly certified by another member of the body. (Form PD 2446 may be used.) If the fiduciaries of any trust estate are empowered to act as a unit, although not designated as a board, committee or other body, securities registered in their names or assigned to them as such, or in their titles without their names, may be assigned by anyone authorized by the group to act in its behalf. Such assignments may be supported by a sworn copy of a resolution adopted by the group in accordance with the terms of the trust instrument, and proof of their authority to act as a unit may be required. As an alternative, assignments by all the fiduciaries, supported by proof of their incumbency, if not named on the securities, will be accepted.

§ 306.77   Corepresentatives and fiduciaries.

If there are two or more executors, administrators, guardians or similar representatives, or trustees of an estate, all must unite in the assignment of any securities belonging to the estate. However, when a statute, a decree of court, or the instrument under which the representatives or fiduciaries are acting provides otherwise, assignments in accordance with their authority will be accepted. If the securities have matured or been called and are submitted for redemption for the account of all, or for redemption-exchange or pursuant to an advance refunding or prerefunding offer, and the securities offered in exchange are to be registered in the names of all, no assignment is required.

§ 306.78   Nontransferable securities.

The provisions of this subpart, so far as applicable, govern assignments of Treasury Bonds, Investment Series B–1975–80.

Subpart J—Assignments in Behalf of Private or Public Organizations

§ 306.85   Private corporations and unincorporated associations (including nominees).

Securities registered in the name of, or assigned to, an unincorporated association, or a private corporation in its own right or in a representative or fiduciary capacity, or as nominee, may be assigned in its behalf for any authorized transaction by any duly authorized officer or officers. Evidence, in the form of a resolution of the governing body, authorizing the assigning officer to assign, or to sell, or to otherwise dispose of the securities will ordinarily be required. Resolutions may relate to any or all registered securities owned by the organization or held by it in a representative or fiduciary capacity. (Form PD 1010, or any substantially similar form, may be used when the authority relates to specific securities; Form PD 1011, or any substantially similar form, may be used for securities generally.) If the officer derives his authority from a charter, constitution or bylaws, a copy, or a pertinent extract therefrom, properly certified, will be required in lieu of a resolution. If the resolution or other supporting document shows the title of an authorized officer, without his name, it must be supplemented by a certificate of incumbency. (Form PD 1014 may be used.)

§ 306.86   Change of name and succession of private organizations.

If a private corporation or unincorporated association changes its name or is lawfully succeeded by another corporation or unincorporated association, its securities may be assigned in behalf of the organization in its new name or that of its successor by an authorized officer in accordance with § 306.85. The assignment must be supported by evidence of the change of name or successorship.

§ 306.87   Partnerships (including nominee partnerships).

An assignment of a security registered in the name of or assigned to a partnership must be executed by a general partner. Upon dissolution of a partnership, assignment by all living partners and by the persons entitled to assign in behalf of any deceased partner's estate will be required unless the laws of the jurisdiction authorize a general partner to bind the partnership by any act appropriate for winding up partnership affairs. In those cases where assignments by or in behalf of all partners are required this fact must be shown in the assignment; otherwise, an affidavit by a former general partner must be furnished identifying all the persons who had been partners immediately prior to dissolution. Upon voluntary dissolution, for any jurisdiction where a general partner may not act in winding up partnership affairs, an assignment by a liquidating partner, as such, must be supported by a duly executed agreement among the partners appointing the liquidating partner.

§ 306.88   Political entities and public corporations.

Securities registered in the name of, or assigned to, a State, county, city, town, village, school district or other political entity, public body or corporation, may be assigned by a duly authorized officer, supported by evidence of his authority.

§ 306.89   Public officers.

Securities registered in the name of, or assigned to, a public officer designated by title may be assigned by such officer, supported by evidence of incumbency. Assignments for the officer's own apparent individual benefit will not be recognized.

§ 306.90   Nontransferable securities.

The provisions of this subpart apply to Treasury Bonds, Investment Series B–1975–80.

Subpart K—Attorneys in Fact

§ 306.95   Attorneys in fact.

(a) *General.* Assignments by an attorney in fact will be recognized if supported by an adequate power of attorney. Every power must be executed in the presence of an authorized certifying officer under the conditions set out in § 306.45 for certification of assignments. Powers need not be submitted to support redemption-exchanges or exchanges pursuant to advance refunding or prerefunding offers where the securities to be issued are to be registered in the same names and forms as appear in the inscriptions or assignments of the securities surrendered. In all other cases, the original power, or a photocopy showing the grantor's autograph signature, properly certified, must be submitted, together with the security assigned on the owner's behalf by the attorney in fact. An assignment by a substitute attorney in fact must be supported by an authorizing power of attorney and power of substitution. An assignment by an attorney in fact or a substitute attorney in fact for the apparent benefit of either will not be accepted unless expressly authorized. (Form PD 1001 or 1003, as appropriate, may be used to appoint an attorney in fact. An attorney in fact may use Form PD 1006 or 1008 to appoint a substitute. However, any form sufficient in substance may be used.) If there are two or more joint attorneys in fact or substitutes, all must unite in an assignment, unless the power authorizes less than all to act. A power of attorney or of substitution not coupled with an interest will be recognized until the Bureau receives proof of revocation or proof of the grantor's death or incompetency.

(b) *For legal representatives and fiduciaries.* Assignments by an attorney in fact or substitute attorney in fact for a legal representative or fiduciary, in addition to the power of attorney and of substitution, must be supported by evidence, if any, as required by §§ 306.57 (d), 306.66(b), 306.75, and 306.76. Powers must specifically designate the securities to be assigned.

(c) *For corporations or unincorporated associations.* Assignments by an attorney in fact or a substitute attorney in fact in behalf of a corporation or unincorporated association, in addition to the power of attorney and power of substitution, must be supported by one of the following documents certified under seal of the organization, or, if it has no seal, sworn to by an officer who has access to the records:

(1) A copy of the resolution of the governing body authorizing an officer to appoint an attorney in fact, with power of substitution, if pertinent, to assign, or to sell, or to otherwise dispose of, the securities, or

(2) A copy of the charter, constitution, or bylaws, or a pertinent extract therefrom, showing the authority of an officer to appoint an attorney in fact, or

(3) A copy of the resolution of the governing body directly appointing an attorney in fact.

If the resolution or other supporting document shows only the title of the authorized officer, without his name, a certificate of incumbency must also be furnished. (Form PD 1014 may be used.) The power may not be broader than the resolution or other authority.

(d) *For public corporations.* A general power of attorney in behalf of a public corporation will be recognized only if it is authorized by statute.

§ 306.96   Nontransferable securities.

The provisions of this subpart shall apply to nontransferable securities, subject only to the limitations imposed by the terms of the particular issues.

Subpart L—Transfer Through Judicial Proceedings

§ 306.100   Transferable securities.

The Department will recognize valid judicial proceedings affecting the ownership of or interest in transferable securities, upon presentation of the securities together with evidence of the proceedings. In the case of securities registered in the names of two or more persons, the extent of their respective interests in the securities must be determined by the court in proceedings to which they are parties or must otherwise be validly established.[10]

§ 306.101   Evidence required.

Copies of a final judgment, decree, or order of court and of any necessary supplementary proceedings must be submitted. Assignments by a trustee in bankruptcy or a receiver of an insolvent's estate must be supported by evidence of his qualification. Assignments by a receiver in equity or a similar court officer must be supported by a copy of an order authorizing him to assign, or to sell, or to otherwise dispose of, the securities. Where the documents are dated more than 6 months prior to presentation of the securities, there must also be submitted a certificate dated within 6 months of presentation of the securities, showing the judgment, decree, or order, or evidence of qualification, is in full force. Any such evidence must be certified under court seal.

§ 306.102   Nontransferable securities.

The provisions of this subpart shall apply to Treasury Bonds, Investment Series B–1975–80, except that prior to maturity any reference to assignments shall be deemed to refer to assignments of the bonds for exchange for the current series of 1½ percent 5-year EA or EO Treasury notes.

Subpart M—Requests for Suspension of Transactions

§ 306.105   Requests for suspension of transactions in registered securities.

(a) *Timely notice.* If prior to the time a registered security bearing an apparently valid assignment has been functioned, a claim is received from the owner or his authorized representative showing that (1) the security was lost, stolen, or destroyed and that it was unassigned, or

not so assigned as to have become in effect payable to bearer, or (2) the assignment was affected by fraud, the transaction for which the security was received will be suspended. The interested parties will be given a reasonable period of time in which to effect settlement of their interests by agreement, or to institute judicial proceedings.

(b) *Late notice.* If, after a registered security has been transferred, exchanged, or redeemed in reliance on an apparently valid assignment, an owner notifies the Bureau that the assignment was affected by fraud or that the security had been lost or stolen, the Department will undertake only to furnish available information.

(c) *Forged assignments.* A claim that an assignment of a registered security is a forgery will be investigated. If it is established that the assignment was in fact forged and that the owner did not authorize or ratify it, or receive any benefit therefrom, the Department will recognize his ownership and grant appropriate relief.

§ 306.106   Requests for suspension of transactions in bearer securities.

(a) *Securities not overdue.* Neither the Department nor any of its agents will accept notice of any claim or of pending judicial proceedings by any person for the purpose of suspending transactions in bearer securities, or registered securities so assigned as to become in effect payable to bearer which are not overdue as defined in § 306.25.[11] However, if the securities are received and retired, the department will undertake to notify persons who appear to be entitled to any available information concerning the source from which the securities were received.

(b) *Overdue securities.* Reports that bearer securities, or registered securities so assigned as to become in effect payable to bearer, were lost, stolen, or possibly destroyed after they became overdue as defined in § 306.25 will be accepted by the Bureau for the purpose of sus-

---

[10] Title in a finder claiming ownership of a registered security will not be recognized. A finder claiming ownership of a bearer security or a registered security assigned in blank or so assigned as to become in effect payable to bearer must perfect his title in accordance with the provisions of State law. If there are no such provisions, the Department will not recognize his title to the security.

[11] It has been the longstanding policy of the Department to assume no responsibility for the protection of bearer securities not in the possession of persons claiming rights therein and to give no effect to any notice of such claims. This policy was formalized on April 27, 1867, when the Secretary of the Treasury issued the following statement:

"In consequence of the increasing trouble, wholly without practical benefit, arising from notices which are constantly received at the Department respecting the loss of coupon bonds, which are payable to bearer, and of Treasury notes issued and remaining in blank at the time of loss, it becomes necessary to give this public notice, that the Government cannot protect and will not undertake to protect the owners of such bonds and notes against the consequences of their own fault or misfortune.

"Hereafter all bonds, notes, and coupons, payable to bearer, and Treasury notes issued and remaining in blank, will be paid to the party presenting them in pursuance of the regulations of the Department, in the course of regular business; and no attention will be paid to caveats which may be filed for the purpose of preventing such payment."

pending redemption of the securities if the claimant establishes his interest. If the securities are presented, their redemption will be suspended and the presenter and the claimant will each be given an opportunity to establish ownership.

Subpart N—Relief for Loss, Theft, Destruction, Mutilation, or Defacement of Securities

§ 306.110 Statutory authority and requirements.

Relief is authorized, under certain conditions, for the loss, theft, destruction, mutilation or defacement of U.S. securities, whether before, at, or after maturity. A bond of indemnity, in such form and with such surety, sureties or security as may be required to protect the interests of the United States, is required as a condition of relief on account of any bearer security or any registered security assigned in blank or so assigned as to become in effect payable to bearer, and is ordinarily required in the case of unassigned registered securities.

§ 306.111 Procedure for applying for relief.

Prompt report of the loss, theft, destruction, mutilation or defacement of a security should be made to the Bureau. The report should include:

(a) The name and present address of the owner and his address at the time the security was issued, and, if the report is made by some other person, the capacity in which he represents the owner.

(b) The identity of the security by title of loan, issue date, interest rate, serial number and denomination, and in the case of a registered security, the exact form of inscription and a full description of any assignment, endorsement or other writing.

(c) A full statement of the circumstances.

All available portions of a mutilated, defaced or partially destroyed security must also be submitted.

§ 306.112 Type of relief granted.

(a) *Prior to call or maturity.* After a claim on account of the loss, theft, destruction, mutilation, or defacement of a security which has not matured or been called has been satisfactorily established and the conditions for granting relief have been met, a security of like description will be issued to replace the original security.

(b) *At or after call or maturity.* Payment will be made on account of the loss, theft, destruction, mutilation, or defacement of a called or matured security after the claim has been satisfactorily established and the conditions for granting relief have been met.

(c) *Interest coupons.* Where relief has been authorized on account of a destroyed, mutilated or defaced coupon security which has not matured or been called, the replacement security will have attached all unmatured interest coupons if it is established to the satisfaction of the Secretary of the Treasury that the coupons were attached to the original

security at the time of its destruction, mutilation or defacement. In every other case only those unmatured interest coupons for which the Department has received payment will be attached. The price of the coupons will be their value as determined by the Department at the time relief is authorized using interest rate factors based on then current market yields on Treasury securities of comparable maturities.

§ 306.113 Cases not requiring bonds of indemnity.

A bond of indemnity will not be required as a condition of relief for the loss, theft, destruction, mutilation, or defacement of registered securities in any of the following classes of cases unless the Secretary of the Treasury deems it essential in the public interest:

(a) If the loss, theft, destruction, mutilation, or defacement, as the case may be, occurred while the security was in the custody or control of the United States, or a duly authorized agent thereof (not including the Postal Service when acting solely in its capacity as public carrier of the mails), or while in the course of shipment effected under regulations issued pursuant to the Government Losses in Shipment Act (Parts 260, 261, and 262 of this chapter).

(b) If substantially the entire security is presented and surrendered and the Secretary of the Treasury is satisfied as to the identity of the security and that any missing portions are not sufficient to form the basis of a valid claim against the United States.

(c) If the security is one which by the provisions of law or by the terms of its issue is nontransferable or is transferable only by operation of law.

(d) If the owner or holder is the United States, a Federal Reserve bank, a Federal Government corporation, a State, the District of Columbia, a territory or possession of the United States, a municipal corporation, or, if applicable, a political subdivision of any of the foregoing, or a foreign government.

Subpart O—Book-Entry Procedure

§ 306.115 Definition of terms.

In this subpart, unless the context otherwise requires or indicates:

(a) "Reserve Bank" means a Federal Reserve bank and its branches acting as Fiscal Agent of the United States and when indicated acting in its individual capacity.

(b) "Treasury security" means a Treasury bond, note, certificate of indebtedness, or bill issued under the Second Liberty Bond Act, as amended, in the form of a definitive Treasury security or a book-entry Treasury security.

(c) "Definitive Treasury security" means a Treasury bond, note, certificate of indebtedness, or bill issued under the Second Liberty Bond Act, as amended, in engraved or printed form.

(d) "Book-entry Treasury security" means a Treasury bond, note, certificate of indebtedness, or bill issued under the Second Liberty Bond Act, as amended, in the form an entry made as prescribed in

this subpart on the records of a Reserve Bank.

(e) "Pledge" includes a pledge of, or any other security interest in, Treasury securities as collateral for loans or advances or to secure deposits of public monies or the performance of an obligation.

(f) "Date of call" (see § 306.2) is "the date fixed in the official notice of call published in the FEDERAL REGISTER * * * on which the obligor will make payment of the security before maturity in accordance with its terms."

(g) "Member bank" means any national bank, State bank or bank or trust company which is member of a Reserve Bank.

§ 306.116 Authority of Reserve Banks.

Each Reserve Bank is hereby authorized, in accordance with the provisions of this subpart, to (a) issue book-entry Treasury securities by means of entries on its records which shall include the name of the depositor, the amount, the loan title (or series) and maturity date; (b) effect conversions between book-entry Treasury securities and definitive Treasury securities; (c) otherwise service and maintain book-entry Treasury securities; and (d) issue a confirmation of transaction in the form of a written advice (serially numbered or otherwise) which specifies the amount and description of any securities, that is, loan title (or series) and maturity date, sold or transferred and the date of the transaction.

§ 306.117 Scope and effect of book-entry procedure.

(a) A Reserve bank as fiscal agent of the United States may apply the book-entry procedure provided for in this subpart to any Treasury securities which have been or are hereafter deposited for any purpose in accounts with it in its individual capacity under terms and conditions which indicate that the Reserve bank will continue to maintain such deposit accounts in its individual capacity, notwithstanding application of the book-entry procedure to such securities. This paragraph is applicable, but not limited to securities deposited:[13]

(1) As collateral pledged to a Reserve bank (in its individual capacity) for advances by it;

(2) By a member bank for its sole account;

(3) By a member bank held for the account of its customers;

(4) In connection with deposits in a member bank of funds of States, municipalities, or other political subdivisions; or

(5) In connection with the performance of an obligation or duty under Federal, State, municipal, or local law, or judgments or decrees of courts.

The application of the book-entry procedure under this paragraph shall not derogate from or adversely affect the

[13] The appendix to this subpart contains rules of identification of book-entry securities for Federal income tax purposes.

relationships that would otherwise exist between a Reserve bank in its individual capacity and its depositors concerning any deposits under this paragraph. Whenever the book-entry procedure is applied to such Treasury securities, the Reserve bank is authorized to take all action necessary in respect of the book-entry procedure to enable such Reserve bank in its individual capacity to perform its obligations as depositary with respect to such Treasury securities.

(b) A Reserve bank, as fiscal agent of the United States, shall apply the book-entry procedure to Treasury securities deposited as collateral pledged to the United States under current revisions of Department of the Treasury Circulars Nos. 92 and 176 (Parts 203 and 202 of this chapter), and may apply the book-entry procedure, with the approval of the Secretary of the Treasury, to any other Treasury securities deposited with a Reserve bank, as fiscal agent of the United States.

(c) Any person having an interest in Treasury securities which are deposited with a Reserve bank (in either its individual capacity or as fiscal agent) for any purpose shall be deemed to have consented to their conversion to book-entry Treasury securities pursuant to the provisions of this subpart, and in the manner and under the procedures prescribed by the Reserve bank.

(d) No deposits shall be accepted under this section on or after the date of maturity or call of the securities.

§ 306.118   Transfer or pledge.

(a) A transfer or a pledge of book-entry Treasury securities to a Reserve bank (in its individual capacity or as fiscal agent of the United States), or to the United States, or to any transferee or pledgee eligible to maintain an appropriate book-entry account in its name with a Reserve bank under this subpart, is effected and perfected, notwithstanding any provision of law to the contrary, by a Reserve bank making an appropriate entry in its records of the securities transferred or pledged. The making of such an entry in the records of a Reserve bank shall (1) have the effect of a delivery in bearer form of definitive Treasury securities; (2) have the effect of a taking of delivery by the transferee or pledgee; (3) constitute the transferee or pledgee a holder; and (4) if a pledge, effect a perfected security interest therein in favor of the pledgee. A transfer or pledge of book-entry Treasury securities effected under this paragraph shall have priority over any transfer, pledge, or other interest, theretofore or thereafter effected or perfected under paragraph (b) of this section or in any other manner.

(b) A transfer or a pledge of transferable Treasury securities, or any interest therein, which is maintained by a Reserve bank (in its individual capacity or as fiscal agent of the United States) in a book-entry account under this subpart, including securities in book-entry form under § 306.117(a) (3), is effected,

and a pledge is perfected, by any means that would be effective under applicable law to effect a transfer or to effect and perfect a pledge of the Treasury securities, or any interest therein, if the securities were maintained by the Reserve bank in bearer definitive form. For purposes of transfer or pledge hereunder, book-entry Treasury securities maintained by a Reserve bank shall, notwithstanding any provision of law to the contrary, be deemed to be maintained in bearer definitive form. A Reserve bank maintaining book-entry Treasury securities either in its individual capacity or as fiscal agent of the United States is not a bailee for purposes of notification of pledges of those securities under this subsection, or a third person in possession for purposes of acknowledgment of transfers thereof under this subsection. Where transferable Treasury securities are recorded on the books of a depositary (a bank, banking institution, financial firm, or similar party, which regularly accepts in the course of its business Treasury securities as a custodial service for customers, and maintains accounts in the names of such customers reflecting ownership of or interest in such securities) for account of the pledgor or transferor thereof and such securities are on deposit with a Reserve bank in a book-entry account hereunder, such depositary shall, for purposes of perfecting a pledge of such securities or effecting delivery of such securities to a purchaser under applicable provisions of law, be the bailee to which notification of the pledge of the securities may be given or the third person in possession from which acknowledgment of the holding of the securities for the purchaser may be obtained. A Reserve bank will not accept notice or advice of a transfer or pledge effected or perfected under this subsection, and any such notice or advice shall have no effect. A Reserve bank may continue to deal with its depositor in accordance with the provisions of this subpart, notwithstanding any transfer or pledge effected or perfected under this subsection.

(c) No filing or recording with a public recording office or officer shall be necessary or effective with respect to any transfer or pledge of book-entry Treasury securities or any interest therein.

(d) A Reserve bank shall, upon receipt of appropriate instructions, convert book-entry Treasury securities into definitive Treasury securities and deliver them in accordance with such instructions; no such conversion shall affect existing interests in such Treasury securities.

(e) A transfer of book-entry Treasury securities within a Reserve bank shall be made in accordance with procedures established by the bank not inconsistent with this subpart. The transfer of book-entry Treasury securities by a Reserve bank may be made through a telegraphic transfer procedure.

(f) All requests for transfer or withdrawal must be made prior to the maturity or date of call of the securities.

§ 306.119   Withdrawal of Treasury securities.

(a) A depositor of book-entry Treasury securities may withdraw them from a Reserve bank by requesting delivery of like definitive Treasury securities to itself or on its order to a transferee.

(b) Treasury securities which are actually to be delivered upon withdrawal may be issued either in registered or in bearer form, except that Treasury bills and EA and EO series of Treasury notes will be issued in bearer form only.

§ 306.120   Delivery of Treasury securities.

A Reserve bank which has received Treasury securities and effected pledges, made entries regarding them, or transferred or delivered them according to the instructions of its depositor is not liable for conversion or for participation in breach of fiduciary duty even though the depositor had no right to dispose of or take other action in respect of the securities. A Reserve bank shall be fully discharged of its obligations under this subpart by the delivery of Treasury securities in definitive form to its depositor or upon the order of such depositor. Customers of a member bank or other depositary (other than a Reserve bank) may obtain Treasury securities in definitive form only by causing the depositor of the Reserve bank to order the withdrawal thereof from the Reserve bank.

§ 306.121   Registered bonds and notes.

No formal assignment shall be required for the conversion to book-entry Treasury securities of registered Treasury securities held by a Reserve bank (in either its individual capacity or as fiscal agent) on the effective date of this subpart for any purpose specified in § 306.117(a). Registered Treasury securities deposited thereafter with a Reserve bank for any purpose specified in § 306.117 shall be assigned for conversion to book-entry Treasury securities. The assignment, which shall be executed in accordance with the provisions of Subpart F of this part, so far as applicable, shall be to "Federal Reserve Bank of _____ ____, as fiscal agent of the United States, for conversion to book-entry Treasury securities."

§ 306.122   Servicing book-entry Treasury securities; payment of interest, payment at maturity or upon call.

Interest becoming due on book-entry Treasury securities shall be charged in the Treasurer's account on the interest-due date and remitted or credited in accordance with the depositor's instructions. Such securities shall be redeemed and charged in the Treasurer's account on the date of maturity or call, and the redemption proceeds, principal and interest, shall be disposed of in accordance with the depositor's instructions.

Subpart F—Miscellaneous Provisions

§ 306.125   Additional requirements.

In any case or any class of cases arising under these regulations the Secretary of the Treasury may require such additional evidence and a bond of indemnity, with or without surety, as may in his judgment be necessary for the protection of the interests of the United States.

§ 306.126   Waiver of regulations.

The Secretary of the Treasury reserves the right, in his discretion, to waive or modify any provision or provisions of these regulations in any particular case or class of cases for the convenience of the United States or in order to relieve any person or persons of unnecessary hardship, if such action is not inconsistent with law, does not impair any existing rights, and he is satisfied that such action would not subject the United States to any substantial expense or liability.

§ 306.127   Preservation of existing rights.

Nothing contained in these regulations shall limit or restrict existing rights which holders of securities heretofore issued may have acquired under the circulars offering such securities for sale or under the regulations in force at the time of acquisition.

§ 306.128   Supplements, amendments or revisions.

The Secretary of the Treasury may at any time, or from time to time, prescribe additional supplemental, amendatory or revised regulations with respect to U.S. securities.

APPENDIX TO SUBPART E—INTEREST—COMPUTATION OF INTEREST ON TREASURY BONDS, TREASURY NOTES, AND TREASURY CERTIFICATES OF INDEBTEDNESS, AND COMPUTATION OF DISCOUNT ON TREASURY BILLS—INTEREST TABLES

COMPUTATION OF INTEREST ON ANNUAL BASIS

One Day's Interest is 1/365 or 1/366 of 1-Year's Interest

Computation of interest on Treasury bonds, notes, and certificates of indebtedness will be made on an annual basis in all cases where interest is payable in one amount for the full term of the security, unless such term is an exact half-year (6 months), and it is provided that interest shall be computed on a semiannual basis.

If the term of the securities is exactly 1 year, the interest is computed for the full period at the specified rate regardless of the number of days in such period.

If the term of the securities is less than 1 full year, the annual interest period for purposes of computation is considered to be the full year from but not including the date of issue to and including the anniversary of such date.

If the term of the securities is more than 1 full year, computation is made on the basis of one full annual interest period, ending with the maturity date, and a fractional part of the preceding full annual interest period.

The computation of interest for any fractional part of an annual interest period. is made on the basis of 365 actual days in such period, or 366 days if February 29 falls within such annual period.

COMPUTATION OF INTEREST ON SEMIANNUAL BASIS

One Day's Interest is 1/181, 1/182, 1/183 or 1/184 of 1/2 Year's Interest

Computation of interest on Treasury bonds, notes, and certificates of indebtedness will be made on a semiannual basis in all cases where interest is payable for one or more full half-year (6 months) periods, or for one or more full half-year periods and a fractional part of a half-year period. A semiannual interest period is an exact half-year or 6 months, for computation purposes, and may comprise 181, 182, 183 or 184 actual days.

An exact half-year's interest at the specified rate is computed for each full period of exactly 6 months, irrespective of the actual number of days in the half-year.

If the initial interest covers a fractional part of a half-year, computation is made on the basis of the actual number of days in the half-year (exactly 6 months) ending on the day such initial interest becomes due. If the initial interest covers a period in excess of 6 months, computation is made on the basis of one full half-year period, ending with the interest due date, and a fractional part of the preceding full half-year period.

Interest for any fractional part of a full half-year period is computed on the basis of the exact number of days in the full period, including February 29 whenever it falls within such a period.

The number of days in any half-year period is shown in the following table:

For The Half-Year

Interest period	Beginning and ending days are 1st or 15th of months listed under interest period (number of days)		Beginning and ending days are last days of months listed under interest period (number of days)	
	Regular year	Leap year	Regular year	Leap year
January to July	181	182	181	182
February to August	181	182	184	184
March to September	184	184	183	183
April to October	183	183	184	184
May to November	184	184	183	183
June to December	183	183	184	184
July to January	184	184	184	184
August to February	184	184	181	182
September to March	181	182	182	183
October to April	182	183	181	182
November to May	181	182	182	183
December to June	182	183	181	182
1 year (any 2 consecutive half-years)	365	366	365	366

The following are dates for end-of-the-month interest computations.

When interest period ends on—	Interest-computation period will be from but will not include—
Jan. 31	July 31.
Feb. 28 in 365-day year.	Aug. 31.
Feb. 29	Do.
Mar. 30, 31	Sept. 30.
Apr. 30	Oct. 31.
May 30, 31	Nov. 30.
June 30	Dec. 31.
July 31	Jan. 31.
Aug. 29, 30 or 31	Feb. 28 in 365-day year. Feb. 29 in leap year.
Sept. 30	Mar. 31.
Oct. 30, 31	Apr. 30.
Nov. 30	May 31.
Dec. 30, 31	June 30.

USE OF INTEREST TABLES

In the appended tables decimals are set forth for use in computing interest for fractional parts of interest periods. The decimals cover interest on $1,000 for 1 day in each possible semiannual (Table I), and annual (Table II) interest period, at all rates of interest, in steps of 1/8 percent, from 1/8 to 9 percent. The amount of interest accruing on any date (for a fractional part of an interest period) on $1,000 face amount of any issue of Treasury bonds, Treasury notes, or Treasury certificates of indebtedness may be ascertained in the following way:

(1) The date of issue, the dates for the payment of interest, the basis (semiannual or annual) upon which interest is computed, and the rate of interest (percent per annum) may be determined from the text of the security, or from the official circular governing the issue.

(2) Determine the interest period of which the fraction is a part, and calculate the number of days in the full period to determine the proper column to be used in selecting the decimal for 1 day's interest.

(3) Calculate the actual number of days in the fractional period from but not including the date of issue or the day on which the last preceding interest payment was made, to and including the day on which the next succeeding interest payment is due or the day as of which the transaction which terminates the accrual of additional interest is effected.

(4) Multiply the appropriate decimal (1 day's interest on $1,000) by the number of days in the fractional part of the interest period. The appropriate decimal will be found in the appended table for interest payable semiannually or annually, as the case may be, opposite the rate borne by the security, and in the column showing the full interest period of which the fractional period is a part. (For interest on any other amount, multiply the amount of interest on $1,000 by the other amount expressed as a decimal of $1,000.)

TREASURY BILLS

The methods of computing discount rates on U.S. Treasury bills are given below:

Computation will be made on an annual basis in all cases. The annual period for bank discount is a year of 360 days, and all computations of such discount will be made on that basis. The annual period for true discount is 1 full year from but not including the date of issue to and including the anniversary of such date. Computation of true discount for a fractional part of a year will be made on the basis of 365 days in the year, or 366 days if February 29 falls within the year.

BANK DISCOUNT

The bank discount rate on a Treasury bill may be ascertained by (1) subtracting the sale price of the bill from its face value to obtain the amount of discount; (2) dividing the amount of discount by the number of days the bill is to run to obtain the amount of discount per day; (3) multiplying the amount of discount per day by 360 (the number of days in a commercial year of 12 months of 30 days each) to obtain the amount of discount per year; and (4) dividing the amount of discount per year by the face value of the bill to obtain the bank discount rate.

For example:

91-day bill:

Principal amount—maturity value _____ $100.00
Price at issue—amount received__ 99.50

Amount of discount_____ .50

$0.50 ÷ 91 × 360 ÷ $100 = .01978 or 1.978 percent

TRUE DISCOUNT

The true discount rate on a Treasury bill of not more than one-half year in length may be ascertained by (1 and 2) obtaining the amount of discount per day by following the first two steps described under "Bank Discount"; (3) multiplying the amount of discount per day by the actual number of days in the year from date of issue (365 ordinarily, but 366 if February 29 falls within the year from date of issue) to obtain the amount of discount per year; and (4) dividing the amount of discount per year by the sale price of the bill to obtain the true discount rate.

For example:

91-day bill:

Principal amount—maturity value _____ $100.00
Price at issue—amount received_ 99.50

Amount of discount_____ .50

$0.50 ÷ 91 × 365 ÷ $99.50 = .02016 or 2.016 percent

TABLE I—DECIMAL FOR 1 DAY'S INTEREST ON $1,000 AT VARIOUS RATES OF INTEREST, PAYABLE SEMIANNUALLY OR ON A SEMIANNUAL BASIS, IN REGULAR YEARS OF 365 DAYS AND IN LEAP YEARS OF 366 DAYS (TO DETERMINE APPLICABLE NUMBER OF DAYS, SEE "COMPUTATION OF INTEREST ON SEMIANNUAL BASIS")

Rate per annum (percent)	Half-year of 184 days	Half-year of 183 days	Half-year of 182 days	Half-year of 181 days
⅛	$0.003 396 739	$0.003 415 301	$0.003 434 066	$0.003 453 039
¼	.006 793 478	.006 830 601	.006 868 132	.006 906 077
⅜	.010 190 217	.010 245 902	.010 302 198	.010 359 116
½	.013 586 957	.013 661 202	.013 736 264	.013 812 155
⅝	.016 983 696	.017 076 503	.017 170 330	.017 265 193
¾	.020 380 435	.020 491 803	.020 604 396	.020 718 232
⅞	.023 777 174	.023 907 104	.024 038 462	.024 171 271
1	.027 173 913	.027 322 404	.027 472 527	.027 624 309
1⅛	.030 570 652	.030 737 705	.030 906 593	.031 077 348
1¼	.033 967 391	.034 153 005	.034 340 659	.034 530 387
1⅜	.037 364 130	.037 568 306	.037 774 725	.037 983 425
1½	.040 760 870	.040 983 607	.041 208 791	.041 436 464
1⅝	.044 157 609	.044 398 907	.044 642 857	.044 889 503
1¾	.047 554 348	.047 814 208	.048 076 923	.048 342 541
1⅞	.050 951 087	.051 229 508	.051 510 989	.051 795 580
2	.054 347 826	.054 644 809	.054 945 055	.055 248 619
2⅛	.057 744 565	.058 060 109	.058 379 121	.058 701 657
2¼	.061 141 304	.061 475 410	.061 813 187	.062 154 696
2⅜	.064 538 043	.064 890 710	.065 247 253	.065 607 735
2½	.067 934 783	.068 306 011	.068 681 319	.069 060 773
2⅝	.071 331 522	.071 721 311	.072 115 385	.072 513 812
2¾	.074 728 261	.075 136 612	.075 549 451	.075 966 851
2⅞	.078 125 000	.078 551 913	.078 983 516	.079 419 890
3	.081 521 739	.081 967 213	.082 417 582	.082 872 928
3⅛	.084 918 478	.085 382 514	.085 851 648	.086 325 967
3¼	.088 315 217	.088 797 814	.089 285 714	.089 779 006
3⅜	.091 711 957	.092 213 115	.092 719 780	.093 232 044
3½	.095 108 696	.095 628 415	.096 153 846	.096 685 083
3⅝	.098 505 435	.099 043 716	.099 587 912	.100 138 122
3¾	.101 902 174	.102 459 016	.103 021 978	.103 591 160
3⅞	.105 298 913	.105 874 317	.106 456 044	.107 044 199
4	.108 695 652	.109 289 617	.109 890 110	.110 497 238
4⅛	.112 092 391	.112 704 918	.113 324 176	.113 950 276
4¼	.115 489 130	.116 120 219	.116 758 242	.117 403 315
4⅜	.118 885 870	.119 535 519	.120 192 308	.120 856 354
4½	.122 282 609	.122 950 820	.123 626 374	.124 309 392
4⅝	.125 679 348	.126 366 120	.127 060 440	.127 762 431
4¾	.129 076 087	.129 781 421	.130 494 505	.131 215 470
4⅞	.132 472 826	.133 196 721	.133 928 571	.134 668 508
5	.135 869 565	.136 612 022	.137 362 637	.138 121 547
5⅛	.139 266 304	.140 027 322	.140 796 703	.141 574 586
5¼	.142 663 043	.143 442 623	.144 230 769	.145 027 624
5⅜	.146 059 783	.146 857 923	.147 664 835	.148 480 663
5½	.149 456 522	.150 273 224	.151 098 901	.151 933 702
5⅝	.152 853 261	.153 688 525	.154 532 967	.155 386 740
5¾	.156 250 000	.157 103 825	.157 967 033	.158 839 779
5⅞	.159 646 739	.160 519 126	.161 401 099	.162 292 818
6	.163 043 478	.163 934 426	.164 835 165	.165 745 856

TABLE II—DECIMAL FOR 1 DAY'S INTEREST ON $1,000 AT VARIOUS RATES OF INTEREST, PAYABLE ANNUALLY OR ON AN ANNUAL BASIS, IN REGULAR YEARS OF 365 DAYS AND IN LEAP YEARS OF 366 DAYS

Rate per annum (percent)	Regular year, 365 days	Leap year, 366 days
⅛	$0.003 424 658	$0.003 415 301
¼	.006 849 315	.006 830 601
⅜	.010 273 973	.010 245 902
½	.013 698 630	.013 661 202
⅝	.017 123 288	.017 076 503
¾	.020 547 945	.020 491 803
⅞	.023 972 603	.023 907 104
1	.027 397 260	.027 322 404
1⅛	.030 821 918	.030 737 705
1¼	.034 246 575	.034 153 005
1⅜	.037 671 233	.037 568 306
1½	.041 095 890	.040 983 607
1⅝	.044 520 548	.044 398 907
1¾	.047 945 205	.047 814 208
1⅞	.051 369 863	.051 229 508
2	.054 794 521	.054 644 809
2⅛	.058 219 178	.058 060 109
2¼	.061 643 836	.061 475 410
2⅜	.065 068 493	.064 890 710
2½	.068 493 151	.068 306 011
2⅝	.071 917 808	.071 721 311
2¾	.075 342 466	.075 136 612
2⅞	.078 767 123	.078 551 913
3	.082 191 781	.081 967 213
3⅛	.085 616 438	.085 382 514
3¼	.089 041 096	.088 797 814
3⅜	.092 465 753	.092 213 115
3½	.095 890 411	.095 628 415
3⅝	.099 315 068	.099 043 716
3¾	.102 739 726	.102 459 016
3⅞	.106 164 384	.105 874 317
4	.109 589 041	.109 289 617
4⅛	.113 013 699	.112 704 918
4¼	.116 438 356	.116 120 219
4⅜	.119 863 014	.119 535 519
4½	.123 287 671	.122 950 820
4⅝	.126 712 329	.126 366 120
4¾	.130 136 986	.129 781 421
4⅞	.133 561 644	.133 196 721
5	.136 986 301	.136 612 022
5⅛	.140 410 959	.140 027 322
5¼	.143 835 616	.143 442 623
5⅜	.147 260 274	.146 857 923
5½	.150 684 932	.150 273 224
5⅝	.154 109 589	.153 688 525
5¾	.157 534 247	.157 103 825
5⅞	.160 958 904	.160 519 126
6	.164 383 562	.163 934 426

APPENDIX TO SUBPART O—BOOK-ENTRY PROCEDURE

RECORDS FOR FEDERAL INCOME TAX PURPOSES

There are attached three documents in connection with the book-entry procedure which simplify recordkeeping for Federal income tax purposes. They apply to transferable Treasury bonds, notes, certificates of indebtedness, or bills issued under the Second Liberty Bond Act, as amended, and to "any other security of the United States." The quoted term is defined to include a bond, note, certificate of indebtedness, bill, debenture, or similar obligation which is subject to the provisions of 31 CFR Part 306, or other comparable Federal regulations and which is issued by any department or agency of the Government of the United States, or the Federal National Mortgage Association, the Federal Home Loan Banks, the Federal Land Banks, the Federal Intermediate Credit Banks, the Banks for Cooperatives, or the Tennessee Valley Authority.

The three documents are:

(1) The substance of Treasury Department Decision 7081, published in the FEDERAL REGISTER on December 31, 1970; [1]

(2) Revenue Ruling 71–21, published in Internal Revenue Bulletin 1971–3, dated January 18, 1971; and

(3) Revenue Ruling 71–15, published in Internal Revenue Bulletin 1971–3, dated January 18, 1971.

The first document modifies the tax identification rules regarding the determination of basis and holding period of securities held as investments. It applies to the sale or transfer of book-entry securities pursuant to a written instruction by a taxpayer. It permits the taxpayer in its written instruction to its bank or to the person through whom the taxpayer makes the sale or transfer to identify the securities being sold or transferred by specifying the unique lot number which he has assigned to the lot containing them.

The taxpayer may make the specification either—(a) in the written instruction, or (b) in the case of a taxpayer having a book-entry account at a Reserve bank, in a list of lot numbers with respect to all book-entry securities on the books of the Reserve bank sold or transferred by him on that date: *Provided*, The list is mailed to or received by the Reserve bank on or before the latter's next business day.

These provisions apply only if the taxpayer assigns lot numbers in numerical sequence to successive purchases of securities in the same loan title (series) and maturity date, except that securities of the same loan title (series) and maturity date which are purchased at the same price on the same date may be included within the same lot.

The written advice of transaction furnished to the taxpayer by the Reserve bank, or by his bank or any other person through whom the taxpayer makes the sale or transfer, which specifies the amount and the description of the securities sold or transferred and the date of the transaction is sufficient confirmation. The Reserve bank need not use or refer to the lot number.

The second document concerns an owner of securities who has assigned sequential numbers to his successive purchases. The owner retains full interest in the securities but transfers them to a bank which has a book-entry account with a Reserve bank, or

[1] Filed as part of the original document. See 26 CFR 1.1012–1(c) (7).

to another party which transfers them to a bank which has a book-entry account with a Reserve bank.

When at a later date the bank instructs the Reserve bank to sell or transfer securities held in book entry for its customer, the bank need not refer to the sequential number which had been assigned on the owner's books.

The tax identification requirements are satisfied if the owner's written instruction to his bank or to the person through whom the taxpayer makes the sale or transfer sufficiently identifies the securities to be sold or transferred and refers to the lot number assigned to them in the owner's books. The bank's instruction to the Reserve bank will not refer to lot numbers; the Reserve bank will confirm the sale to the bank in the manner it deems appropriate. The member bank will confirm the sale or transfer to its customer by furnishing a written advice of transaction specifying the amount and description of the securities sold and the date of sale. The confirmation need not refer to lot number.

This document also permits substantially the same kind of identification and confirmation procedures when securities are purchased through the book-entry account for the bank's customers.

The third document provides that a dealer, who properly holds securities in inventory in accordance with § 1.471–5 of the Income Tax Regulations and proposes to transfer them to a book-entry system in a Reserve bank, will continue to maintain its books and records for Federal income tax purposes with respect to such securities in accordance with § 1.471–5 of the regulations and not § 1.1012–1 of the regulations.

Section 1012—Basis of Property—Cost

26 CFR 1.1012.1 *Basis of property. Rev. Rul. 71–21.*[1] A taxpayer owns as investments Treasury securities and certain other securities described in the new § 1.1012–1(c)(7)(iii)(a) of the Income Tax Regulations. The taxpayer owner will assign a lot number to

the securities in his books. The numbers will be assigned in numerical sequence to successive purchases of the same loan title (series) and maturity date, except that securities of the same loan title (series) and maturity date which are purchased at the same price on the same date may be included in the same lot.

The owner proposes to retain full interest in the securities but he will transfer possession of them to a bank. That bank will not keep records of the above-described lot numbers. The bank will also take possession of like securities for other taxpayers.

The bank will transfer all of these securities to a book-entry system of a Federal Reserve bank. The securities will be entries in the book-entry account of the bank and, as such, the securities will no longer exist in definitive form. That account will not reflect the fact that the bank holds securities for several taxpayers.

When the owner wishes to sell certain securities, he will so instruct the bank in writing. The owner's instruction will sufficiently identify the securities to be sold, and will also refer to the lot number assigned in the books of the owner to the securities to be sold. The bank will then instruct, in writing, the Federal Reserve bank to transfer the securities. The latter instruction will not refer to the pertinent lot number. The Federal Reserve bank will confirm the sale to the bank in the manner it deems appropriate. The bank will confirm the sale to the owner by furnishing a written advice of transaction specifying the amount and description of the securities sold and the date of the sale. The confirmation will not refer to lot numbers.

When the owner desires to buy additional securities as investments of the kind described in the new § 1.1012–1(c)(7)(iii)(a) of the regulations, he will order the bank to purchase them. The bank will instruct the Federal Reserve bank to obtain the securities and to put them in the bank's book-entry account. The confirmation of the purchase from the Federal Reserve bank to the bank and from the bank to the owner will be of the nature used for the sale of securities. The owner will assign lot numbers in the

manner described above to these purchased securities:

Held, the above procedure is consistent with the tax record requirements of new § 1.1012–1(c)(7) of the regulations. This procedure exemplifies the tax record requirements when securities are transferred by parties to a bank who has an account in the book-entry system of a Federal Reserve bank. The tax record requirements in the case of a bank who puts its own investment securities in the book-entry system are set forth in new § 1.1012–1(c)(7) of the regulations.

Section 471—General Rule for Inventories

26 CFR 1.471–5 *Inventories by dealers in Rev. Rul. 71–15*[1] *securities. (Also section 1012; 1.1012–1.)* A dealer, as defined in section 1.471–5 of the Income Tax Regulations, holds Treasury securities and other securities of the United States. "Other securities of the United States" means a transferable bond, note, certificate of indebtedness, bill, debenture, or similar obligation which is subject to the provisions of 31 CFR Part 306 or other comparable Federal regulations and which is issued by (1) any department or agency of the Government of the United States, or (2) the Federal National Mortgage Association, the Federal Home Loan Bank, the Federal Land Banks, the Federal Intermediate Credit Banks, the Banks for Cooperatives, or the Tennessee Valley Authority.

The dealer properly holds such securities in inventory in accordance with § 1.471–5 of the Income Tax Regulations. He proposes to transfer those securities to a book-entry system maintained by a Federal Reserve bank. The dealer will continue to maintain his books and records for Federal income tax purposes with respect to such securities in accordance with § 1.471–5 of the regulations.

Held, the dealer is not subject to the provisions of § 1.1012–1 of the regulations relating to identification of property with respect to such securities. Such a dealer must, however, comply with the provisions of § 1.471–5 of the regulations relating to inventory by dealers in securities.

[FR Doc.73–4897 Filed 3–14–73;8:45 am]

---

[1] Also released as Technical Information Release 1063, dated Dec. 30, 1970.

[1] Also released as Technical Information Release 1064, dated Jan. 14, 1971.

Appendix ***H***

***The Number of Each Day of
the Year***

Day of Month	Jan.	Feb.	Mar.	Apr.	May	Jun.	Jul.	Aug.	Sep.	Oct.	Nov.	Dec.
1	1	32	60	91	121	152	182	213	244	274	305	335
2	2	33	61	92	122	153	183	214	245	275	306	336
3	3	34	62	93	123	154	184	215	246	276	307	337
4	4	35	63	94	124	155	185	216	247	277	308	338
5	5	36	64	95	125	156	186	217	248	278	309	339
6	6	37	65	96	126	157	187	218	249	279	310	340
7	7	38	66	97	127	158	188	219	250	280	311	341
8	8	39	67	98	128	159	189	220	251	281	312	342
9	9	40	68	99	129	160	190	221	252	282	313	343
10	10	41	69	100	130	161	191	222	253	283	314	344
11	11	42	70	101	131	162	192	223	254	284	315	345
12	12	43	71	102	132	163	193	224	255	285	316	346
13	13	44	72	103	133	164	194	225	256	286	317	347
14	14	45	73	104	134	165	195	226	257	287	318	348
15	15	46	74	105	135	166	196	227	258	288	319	349
16	16	47	75	106	136	167	197	228	259	289	320	350
17	17	48	76	107	137	168	198	229	260	290	321	351
18	18	49	77	108	138	169	199	230	261	291	322	352
19	19	50	78	109	139	170	200	231	262	292	323	353
20	20	51	79	110	140	171	201	232	263	293	324	354
21	21	52	80	111	141	172	202	233	264	294	325	355
22	22	53	81	112	142	173	203	234	265	295	326	356
23	23	54	82	113	143	174	204	235	266	296	327	357
24	24	55	83	114	144	175	205	236	267	297	328	358
25	25	56	84	115	145	176	206	237	268	298	329	359
26	26	57	85	116	146	177	207	238	269	299	330	360
27	27	58	86	117	147	178	208	239	270	300	331	361
28	28	59	87	118	148	179	209	240	271	301	332	362
29	29		88	119	149	180	210	241	272	302	333	363
30	30		89	120	150	181	211	242	273	303	334	364
31	31		90		151		212	243		304		365

* For leap years, add one day to the number given in the table for those days after February 28.

Index